T0286026

Vajra Wisdom

Vajra Wisdom

Deity Practice in Tibetan Buddhism

Kunkyen Tenpe Nyima and
Shechen Gyaltsap IV

FOREWORD BY
Chökyi Nyima Rinpoche

Translated by the
Dharmachakra Translation
Committee

Snow Lion

Snow Lion
An imprint of Shambhala Publications, Inc.
2129 13th Street
Boulder, Colorado 80302
www.shambhala.com

This edition published 2022

Cover art: Saraswati by Pema Namdol Thaye
Cover design: Gopa & Ted2, Inc.
Interior design: Gopa & Ted2, Inc.

9 8 7 6 5 4 3 2 1

First paperback edition
Printed in the United States of America

Shambhala Publications makes every effort to print on acid-free, recycled paper.

Snow Lion is distributed worldwide by
Penguin Random House, Inc., and its subsidiaries.

The Library of Congress catalogues the hardcover edition of this book as follows:

Bstan-pa'i-ñi-ma, Kun-mkhyen, 19th century.
[Bskyed rim gyi zin bris cho ga spyi 'gros ltar bkod pa man ṅag kun btus. English]
Vajra wisdom: deity practice in Tibetan Buddhism / Kunkyen Tenpe Nyima
and Shechen Gyaltsap IV; foreword by Chökyi Nyima Rinpoche; translated
by the Dharmachakra Translation Committee.
pages cm
Includes bibliographical references.
ISBN 978-1-55939-397-3 (hardcover) | ISBN 978-1-55939-440-6 (paperback)
1. Meditation—Rñiṅ-ma-pa (Sect) 2. Rñiṅ-ma-pa (Sect)—Rituals.
I. Źe-chen Rgyal-tshab Padma-'gyur-med-rnam-rgyal, 1871–1926. Bskyed rim
spyi'i rnam par bźag pa ñuṅ gsal go bder brjod pa rab gsal nor bu'i me loṅ. English.
II. Dharmachakra Translation Committee, translator. III. Title.
BQ7662.6.B7813 2012
294.3'923—dc23
2012016843

Contents

FOREWORD BY
CHÖKYI NYIMA RINPOCHE

OUR COMPASSIONATE TEACHER, the perfectly enlightened Buddha, offered those in need of guidance an inconceivable number of Dharma teachings. These can all be condensed into the categories of sūtra and tantra. The latter of these two, in turn, contains the ocean of tantras, statements, and oral instructions.

In India and Tibet the practice of this vajra vehicle of Secret Mantra flourished and the number of practitioners who gained liberation through these practices is truly beyond count. Today the legacy of these great beings is still with us in the form of an uninterrupted lineage of realized masters who uphold the teachings and practices of the vajra vehicle. In this way it is still in our hands to connect with this tradition and make enlightenment a living experience for us as well.

To accomplish this we must rely on living lineage masters and key scriptures that outline the practice and theory of tantra. I am therefore pleased to present translations of two important guidance manuals concerned with the practice of tantra. Both Kunkyen Tenpe Nyima and Shechen Gyaltsap were extraordinary teachers, and today their works are among the most cherished scriptures on the practice of the development stage. In fact, although both texts focus predominantly on the development stage, the key points of the whole of tantric practice are all contained in these pithy instructions. I am therefore confident that sincere practitioners will find great inspiration and guidance in these precious texts.

Even though the message laid out in these translations is generally clear and ready to be applied, it is of utmost importance to first receive the guidance of a realized master of the lineage. Only by connecting with such a master and receiving empowerment, reading transmission, and oral instructions are we fully able to benefit from the tantric path. In fact, it is said that, without the blessing of a realized master, the practice of tantra is likely to do more harm than good. Still, if practiced correctly, these teachings have the potential to transform your being into the state of complete awakening in a short time span and through only little hardship. Such is the power of the tantric path. I therefore sincerely request all readers to study these texts under the guidance of a genuine master of the lineage.

May the precious wisdom of the practice lineage spread and flourish throughout the world and may this publication be a positive circumstance for that. In this way, may all sentient beings quickly traverse the path of the four knowledge holders and awaken to the full and complete enlightenment of the four bodies and five wisdoms.

Translators' Introduction

Over the last forty years Buddhism has spread to all corners of the world. In this process, Tibetan Buddhism has often been represented in ways that play into our need to re-enchant an increasingly materialistic world with the magic, drama, and supernatural elements of a lost wisdom nurtured in isolation on the roof of the world. For this approach to Buddhism, the development stage, with its attention to colorful deities, magical mantras, and exotic rituals, has become a popular form of practice. Deity practice is ripe with evocative and inspiring imagery that seems a perfect cure for our weariness and disenchantment with the ordinary world. And these practices, which today are performed at numerous Dharma centers around the world, do undeniably help build communities and provide devotees with a ritual register and a sense of belonging. Still, in recent years, it has become clear to many Western practitioners of Tibetan Buddhism that the development stage is a much richer practice than what first meets the eye.

To fully appreciate the depth of development stage practice it is important to study the works of the lineage masters, in particular the texts that apply the often detailed and complicated tantric theory directly to practical experience in clear, concise, and practical statements. Recently we have been fortunate that an increasing number of such texts have been made available in translation. As these texts now become available to the Western world, one may hope that they will provide a foundation through which the practice of the development stage in the West can develop and grow in a way that is suited to the Western mind, yet remain faithful to its Indian and Tibetan origins. If we are able to appreciate the richness and depth of the tradition beyond simply a superficial fascination with a curious cultural phenomenon, we may be better suited to assimilate the crucial aspects of the tradition rather than latching on to the mere outer characteristics of such practices. Perhaps this could be one way to challenge our fondness for spiritual materialism that Chögyam Trungpa so kindly pointed out?

The translations found in this volume are of texts written in Tibet during the nineteenth and twentieth centuries. The authors, Kunkyen Tenpe Nyima and Shechen Gyaltsap, were masters who shined with their life examples on the very eve of a millennium of Buddhist practice in Tibet. Both masters inherited the full tradition of Tantric Buddhism through the lineages of the famed wisdom teachers Jigme Lingpa, Jamyang Khyentse Wangpo, and Jamgön Kongtrul. As such, both texts represent a summary of more than a thousand years of tantric practice that present the highest insights of the tradition in a simple yet inspiring format that is excellently suited for the beginner as well as the advanced practitioner when traveling the path to the peak of human achievement.

At this point in time, when the vast majority of this incredibly precious Tibetan Buddhist culture is threatened with extinction, it seems that texts such as these are important to study. While we still have the precious fortune of sharing this world with genuine wisdom masters, who embody the very pinnacle of the Buddhist path, we must therefore strive to receive their blessings and guidance. Only then can we assimilate the wisdom they brought with them as their gift to the world when they fled the Chinese occupation. We therefore hope that this publication may be able to, in a small way, assist this process.

Kunkyen Tenpe Nyima and *The Compendium of Oral Instructions*

The colophon of *The Compendium of Oral Instructions*[1] informs us that, at the request of some of his devoted students, the author, Kunkyen Tenpe

1. Kun mkhyen bstan pa'i nyi ma, *bsKyed rim gyi zin bris cho ga spyi 'gros ltar bkod pa man ngag kun btus*. Delhi: Chos Spyod Publications, 2000.

Nyima, gathered the instructions from the recitation manuals of various accomplished masters and from his own guru.

Although *The Compendium* is a practice manual on development stage widely used by followers of the Nyingma School, authorial attribution of this text has turned out to be a complex matter with several options and opinions. Several masters by the name Tenpe Nyima flourished in nineteenth-century East Tibet and we have been unable to settle the matter definitively. However, based on advice by the late Gene Smith and colophonic information in one of the manuscripts, we have attributed this text to a certain Khartrul Kunkyen Tenpe Nyima (Mkhar sprul kun mkhyan bstan pa'i nyi ma, nineteenth cent.).

His brief biography is found in a collection of hagiographies of tantric practitioners from the far eastern province of Rebkong.[2] The biography is concise and very little is said about the actual life of Tenpe Nyima. What we can glean from his hagiography is that he was a master from Rebkong who was regarded as the reincarnation of the eighth-century Indian scholar Śāntarakṣita. Tenpe Nyima belonged to the Longchen Nyingthig tradition that his father had transmitted to him. His father, Chöying Thobden Dorje, was a close student of the first Dodrubchen, Jigme Trinley Öser, the heart son of Jigme Lingpa, and his association with this lineage was therefore obvious. Institutionally, Tenpe Nyima was associated with Dzogchen Namgyal Ling, the monastery founded by his father. His date of birth is not mentioned, but his hagiography states that he was born shortly after his father founded Dzogchen Namgyal Ling in 1818.

From his father he received empowerments and instructions on the general sūtras and tantras and, in particular, on the Longchen Nyingthig He also received in full the transmission of the volumes of scriptures composed by his father, such as the *Treasury of Sūtras and Tantras*, and put them into practice. Eventually he attained realization, perfected his training, and was empowered as a Great Lord of the Dharma. Then, we are told, in accordance with their individual potential, he established

2. *Reb kong sngags mang gi lo rgyus phyogs bsgrigs* (Ye shes 'od zer sgrol ma, 2004).

countless disciples on the path of ripening and liberation through offering them mind training, advice, empowerments, guidance, and pointing-out instructions. In this way, he engaged in activities of inconceivable kindness.

The Compendium is a guidance manual that describes the different types of ritual activities associated with the practice of the development stage, pertaining particularly to the Treasure lineage of the Nyingma School.

This text explains the general structure of deity practice in the mahāyoga tradition, without focusing on any particular sādhana. It belongs to a class of Tibetan literature called "notes" (*zin bris*), consisting of a series of annotations, written down by the author for his own purpose based on the oral instructions of his guru and later compiled for the benefit of others. These texts are usually very practical in their intent. This is clearly the case for *The Compendium of Oral Instructions*, and in fact one recension of our text contains additional notes apparently added by a later unidentified author, but we have not translated those here. Tenpe Nyima's text explains extensively the different stages—preliminaries, visualization, recitation of the mantra, meditative absorption, and subsequent practices—that must be covered in deity yoga, emphasizing always their concrete application within the context of retreat practice.

The ritual activities explained in *The Compendium* follow a uniform structure that can be applied to any particular Nyingma sādhana. The unique features of this text are the detailed technical explanations and advice given by the author for each particular step of the practice. The structure of the text follows the usual sequence found in other revealed mahāyoga sādhanas.

Each stage of deity practice, with its liturgies, visualizations, practice articles, and so forth, is thus described in exhaustive detail and is always accompanied by precise and useful practical advice. The clarity of its explanations, its abundance of technical advice, and its emphasis resolutely placed on practical application make *The Compendium of Oral Instructions* an ideal companion for the practitioners of deity yoga, particularly in the context of a retreat.

SHECHEN GYALTSAP AND *Illuminating Jewel Mirror*

Shechen Gyaltsap Pema Namgyal (1871–1926) was born in the middle of the exciting renaissance in Tibetan spiritual culture that took place during the latter half of the nineteenth century. At that time Jamyang Khyentse Wangpo (1820–1892) and Jamgön Kongtrul Lodrö Thaye (1813–1899) had begun promoting the nonsectarian movement through their extensive activities and oeuvres, while Patrul Chökyi Wangpo (1808–1887) and Ju Mipham (1846–1912) were spearheading a revival of practice and study within the Nyingma School. Each of these masters was, in turn, to act as a mentor to the young child who was prophetically identified as the reincarnation of Orgyen Rangjung Dorje (nineteenth cent.), the third regent of Shechen Monastery in eastern Tibet.

Educated in his early years largely by his uncle, Lama Kyiyang, and later by Troshul Khenpo Tsultrim Gyamtso, he eventually took monastic ordination under the famous preceptor of Dzogchen Monastery, Khenpo Pema Benza, who gave him the name Gyurme Pema Namgyal. His two primary teachers, though, were, above all, Khyentse and Kongtrul. Based on their instructions and empowerments, and by transmitting their major works to him, they fostered him as a torchbearer of their spiritual insight. Moreover, they played a critical role in guiding him during a major turning point that occurred in his life at the age of twenty. At that time, during a pilgrimage throughout all Tibet, he underwent a spiritual transformation whereby, to use Dilgo Khyentse's words, the "knot of hope and fear snapped all by itself." This led him to lose interest in worldly affairs, even institutional monasticism. Under the counsel of his two teachers, he then stepped aside from the everyday management of Shechen Monastery to live the life of a carefree vagabond.

Traveling to meet the great visionaries of his day, it seems he was a perpetual student. From Patrul he received teachings on *The Way of the Bodhisattva* during the course of which Patrul is said to have spontaneously waved his hand through a solid pillar. Journeying to Karmo Taktsang, he received from Mipham transmission and instruction on several of his major works, in particular his famous Abhidharma compendium,

Gateway to Knowledge, and his commentary on the Eight Sādhana Teachings. He also is said to have sought guidance, again and again, from Mipham on his inner realization until their minds became inseparable.

At the same time, however, it seems he lived his entire life in seclusion, engrossed in contemplation and meditation. His main personal deity was apparently a form of Vajrakīlaya known as "Innermost Razor of Kīlaya," which he practiced for at least three months each year. In the biography that Dilgo Khyentse composed about his teacher,[3] he recounts how miraculous signs appeared even the first time Shechen Gyaltsap practiced the Innermost Razor of Kīlaya in retreat. The story goes that, while carrying out the recitation, one day a pack of "iron wolves" gathered around Shechen Gyaltsap's retreat house, even on its roof, howling and trying to find a way in. Despite this terrifying turn of events, Shechen Gyaltsap simply supplicated his master and performed the practice of "mingling their minds into one," thereby pacifying the frightening development, although this subjugation took several days! Through the power of this he displayed the signs of accomplishment in the practice after only one hundred days, although it was predicted to take three years. At this time he is also said to have left a footprint in solid rock, which another lama (named Barchung) insistently prodded him to finally admit.

While living mostly as a hermit spending his time in meditation practice, he nonetheless somehow also found time to author an immense thirteen-volume corpus of texts spanning topics from grammar, astrology, and poetics to a wide range of treatises on Buddhist philosophy, ritual, and practice. Last, but not the least, he nurtured the next generation of budding luminaries, acting as teacher to the remarkable reincarnations of his own teachers—Dzongsar Khyentse Chökyi Lodrö (1893–1959), Shechen Kongtrul (1901–1960), and Dilgo Khyentse (1910–1991)—as well as many other highly regarded scholar-practitioners, such as Khenpo Kunpal (1872–1943) and Khenpo Nuden (nineteenth/twentieth cent.).

3. Dil mgo mkhyen brtse 'gyur med theg mchog bstan pa'i rgyal mtshan, "Mkhas shing dngos grub brnyes pa'i rdo rje'i rig pa 'dzin dbang 'gyur 'gyur med padma rnam rgyal dpal bzang po slob brgyud dang bcas pa'i rnam thar nyung ngur brjod pa ngo mtshar zla ba bdud rtsi'i 'dzum phreng," in *The Collected Works of skyabs rje dil mgo mkhyen brtse rin po che,* vol. 1 (ka). New Delhi: Shechen Publications, 1994.

All of this he accomplished despite passing away at the young age of fifty-five. In the last year of his life, 1926, perhaps in foresight of his passing, he pitched a tent on the hillside above Shechen where he proceeded to grant audiences to all of his students, monks, and patrons. There he stayed while performing ceremonies and giving his last counsel until one day, just before his passing, he was visited by the heir to Shechen, a weeping young Rabjam Tulku, to whom he bestowed an unspoken, symbolic final teaching by simply pointing to his heart.

Composed in the latter part of his life, it seems that Shechen Gyaltsap intended *Illuminating Jewel Mirror*[4] to be a general guidebook for development stage practitioners of any particular yidam deity. In that way it serves the purpose of tying together the features of all sādhanas, thus highlighting their universal functions and meaning.

Structurally, after enumerating in detail the prerequisites for engaging in sādhana practice, the text follows the standard framework of most sādhana manuals. Shechen Gyaltsap weaves in, however, another thread in the introductory discussions that he uses to string together all the manifold elements of this complex practice. This is the fourfold scheme of the "basis, object, process, and result of purification." In the introductory section he characterizes the first—the ground for the development stage transformations—as "true reality, suchness, or the essence of the bliss-gone." The latter three aspects then serve as a refrain that repeats at every step as the basis for Shechen Gyaltsap's commentary, presenting a rich portrait of the way in which the elaborate development stage visualizations transform the various stages of birth, death, and rebirth into a set of corresponding events in the process of spiritual awakening. In part, these descriptions inform the student about how the seemingly esoteric images and themes of Tantric Buddhism have a deep foundation in Great Vehicle Buddhism. They also, however, highlight the unique, paradoxical vision of the Vajra Vehicle, which states that we are actually already divine, enlightened beings. In this vision, the lavish and colorful

4. Zhe chen rgyal tshab 'gyur med padma rnam rgyal, *bsKyed rim spyi'i rnam par bzhag pa nyung gsal go bder brjod pa rab gsal nor bu'i me long*. New Delhi: Shechen Publications, 2004.

worlds the practitioner "imagines" are actually more real than his or her ordinary experience, and serve as methods to lead him or her closer to the way things actually are.

About the Translations

It was Chökyi Nyima Rinpoche who first suggested that we translate these precious texts, as he found them to be particularly relevant and helpful for practitioners of Tibetan Buddhism today.

A group consisting of Benjamin Collet-Cassart, Cortland Dahl, Catherine Dalton, Andreas Doctor, and James Gentry translated *The Compendium*. The individual manuscripts were then compiled, compared against the Tibetan, and edited by Cortland Dahl. Zachary Beer translated *Illuminating Jewel Mirror*, while Andreas Doctor compared the translation against the Tibetan and edited the text. Graham Sunstein and Shenpen Lhamo also looked through the manuscript and offered helpful advice.

Along the way we received much help and guidance from a number of learned and realized masters. Chökyi Nyima Rinpoche guided our translation work by giving instruction on the "enlightened mind" section of *Illuminating Jewel Mirror* and offering numerous teachings on the general themes of the development stage and the importance of bringing the teachings into direct daily experience. Dzigar Kongtrul Rinpoche kindly took the time to clarify the meaning of the more complex development stage passages of *Illuminating Jewel Mirror*.

Khenpo Tashi Palden, or Kyabje Khenpo as he is also known by his students, gave the full reading transmission of *The Compendium* together with a brief commentary on the full text and elucidated some of the more vexing passages. Kyabje Khenpo himself received the transmission in his youth from the renowned master Jamyang Khyentse Chökyi Lodrö (1893–1959), and later from both Dilgo Khyentse Rinpoche (1910–1991) and Tulku Urgyen Rinpoche (1920–1996).

Beyond these, many other teachers from Ka-Nying Shedrub Ling Monastery offered their wisdom and patience in helping to unravel the profound and often mysterious world of development stage practice for us. In particular, we would like to thank Lama Tenzin Sangpo, Tulku Jampal Dorje, Lama Tsultrim Sangpo, Khenpo Sherab Dorje, Trokpa Tulku, Tulku Pasang Tsering, and Lama Kunga Sangpo for assisting with guidance on numerous complicated passages. We are therefore indebted to these kind teachers, without whom it would have been impossible to translate these texts.

We are also grateful to the Tsadra Foundation for generously sponsoring the translation of this book. The vision of Tsadra is truly remarkable and the foundation's impact on the survival of Tibetan Buddhism is a source of continual joy for us. We also wish to thank Snow Lion for publishing this book and for their hard work in bringing the Buddhist classics to the West.

We sincerely apologize for any mistakes these translations may contain. They are exclusively our own due to our limited understanding of the profound nature of tantra. Lastly, we dedicate whatever goodness may result from this publication to the benefit of all sentient beings and to the long life of Chökyi Nyima Rinpoche and all other wisdom teachers.

The Compendium of Oral Instructions

General Notes on the Rituals of the Development Stage

Kunkyen Tenpe Nyima

Magical dance of the wisdom, love, and ability of all victorious ones,
As the lord of the maṇḍala and the universal master of the hundred buddha families,
You are a powerful wish-fulfilling jewel that bestows supreme happiness upon others—
I pay homage to you, my peerless and benevolent master.

For countless disciples who fill the furthest reaches of space
You make the nectar of the definitive secret shower down like a rain of Dharma
From the cloud banks of your tremendous compassion—
I bow down to you, omniscient father and son, and the masters of your lineage.

By unfolding the wings of the two stages—
The union of means and knowledge of the swift path, the vajra essence of the supreme vehicle—
I will now set forth a banquet for those fortunate ones
Who wish to swiftly arrive at the kingdom of the four bodies.

Utilizing the profound practice of the two stages on the direct path of the vajra vehicle of Secret Mantra allows you to actualize the level of a vajra holder in this very lifetime. Those suitable individuals who wish to reach this level should begin their practice by earnestly arousing renunciation through the mind training of the common preliminary practices and engendering the precious mind of awakening. Next, they should receive the four empowerments in full from a qualified master, cultivate faith, and abide by the samaya vows. Those who have done so may enter this path.

This discussion consists of three main topics: (1) the preparation, (2) the main practice, and (3) the concluding activities.

THE PREPARATION

The Bright Effulgence states:

> First, find the right place and time,
> And gather supportive conditions and the articles for your practice.
> Then, in the interim, practice secretly.

Concerning the appropriate location for practice, beginners must stay far away from places that are filled with diversions, busyness, and distraction, as well as those that elicit attachment and aversion. *The Questions of Adhyasaya Sūtra* instructs:

> It is best to travel one hundred leagues
> From places where you have responsibilities or find disputes.
> Do not stay a single instant in places
> Where afflictive emotions are present.

It is said that in monastic centers where the saṅgha quarrels past virtue will decline and not develop in the future, and the earth will be scorched down to seven layers so that every good thing pertaining to the environment and its inhabitants will decline. In particular, neither signs of fruition nor positive qualities will manifest from practice in such places. You should therefore abandon these places.

The Ornament of the Sūtras states that a place of practice should have five qualities:

> The place where a wise person practices
> Should have readily available goods
> And be in a wholesome environment and healthy location
> With good companions and positive qualities.

It is taught in *The Wheel of Time Root Tantra*:

> A yogi should practice well in a place
> Where the ruler is faithful to the Dharma,
> Where all beings live in constant harmony
> And without dispute.

As stated here, in general you should practice in a place where there is a monarch devout to the Dharma, where the local lay people engage in wholesome, virtuous actions, and where there are no enemies, thieves, or disputes. More specifically, *The Tantra of the Layered Lotus Stems* explains:

> It is extremely important
> For any general or specific places—
> Sacred locations, countries, or places where the Victorious One came—
> To be auspicious and agreeable to the mind.

Sacred locations and lands imbued with blessings, as well as places where the Great Master of Uḍḍiyāna and other accomplished masters of the past practiced, are highly praised. *The Condensed Realization* states:

> It is easier to gain accomplishment by practicing one day
> In such places than by practicing for a year in ordinary places.

More specifically, it is also said that places for practice should have certain geomantic features, such as particular shapes and colors of the sky and the earth that are in accord with each of the four activities. If you cannot arrange such locations, *Resting in Meditation* explains:

> In summary, a place that is delightful at first but later becomes unpleasant is a place of less spiritual accomplishment. A place that is initially frightening and unpleasant yet later becomes

> delightful is a place filled with great blessings, where you will attain spiritual accomplishments quickly and without obstacles. Apart from those, all others are neutral, without particular benefit or harm.

This passage explains that you should practice in a place that you find delightful, once you have gotten used to it, and which has no impediments to meditative concentration. It is important to stay in secluded and delightful places that agree with your mind. *The Condensed Realization* states:

> If it agrees with your mind, even a city is a suitable place.

The Condensed Tantra also mentions:

> You should practice wherever your mind is content, O Lord of Men. Sitting on your soft bedding and cushion, observe your mantra recitation.

Concerning the appropriate time to practice, *The Tantra of the Layered Lotus Stems* states:

> The waxing period of the first month of each of the four seasons
> Causes auspiciousness and excellence to manifest.
> On a full moon, new moon, and on the eighth day of the lunar month
> Practice flourishes, together with good omens.

These days are propitious times for great accomplishment. Moreover, it states:

> During the king of constellations and so forth your wishes are fulfilled.
> The waxing period of the planets and the moon . . .

A tantra explains:

> Undertake activities on the eighth day of the waxing period of the moon.
> Engage in the vast conduct of enlightenment during the great king of constellations.
> In order to attain the secret and supreme spiritual accomplishments swiftly,
> Practice when the planets and stars are in an auspicious configuration.

Although those with confidence in nonconceptuality do not make distinctions in terms of place and time, it is said that for beginners it will generate extraordinary results to practice when the dates and positions of the planets and stars form an auspicious connection that accords with the four activities. *The Awesome Flash of Lightning* comments:

> Excellent conditions and time are indeed conceptual thoughts,
> But due to them the signs and marks
> Of spiritual accomplishments occur.

Whatever the case, gradually gather as much virtuous supportive strength as you can by ransoming the lives of animals, freeing fish, restoring dangerous paths, making figurines and tormas, performing the four hundred offerings and making other offerings, or reading the words of the Buddha, such as the Five Sūtra Collections or a condensed version of them. In particular, engage in wrathful fire offerings and other such rituals. You should also bring together all that you need, including practice companions, provisions, and practice articles. You can learn more details on how to perform these activities from scriptures such as *The Treasury of Oral Instructions.*

Next, clean your place and display representations of enlightened body, speech, and mind if you have them. Place the offerings in the correct order, arranging them beautifully and in an attractive way. When you look at them, you should feel at ease and sense their blessings. If the place is new to you, you need a ritual to consecrate the land, which includes self-visualization in its preliminaries. If it is an old place, this is not necessary. Outside, in an unsheltered area, visualize the spirits of the eight classes in general, and the earth lords of the ground and other such spirits in particular, and give them whatever elaborate or simplified offering you can, such as the Great Offering of All Saṃsāra and Nirvāṇa, the Three-Part Torma Offering, the Offering to the Eight Classes of Spirits, smoke offerings, and so forth. Doing so, urge them to act as allies in your practice. At this point, you can also expel obstructing forces, establish a boundary, and set up the guardian kings' poles.

Facing the maṇḍala, draw clockwise-swastikas with white grains or white chalk beneath your seat. If you want to take a more elaborate approach, spread kusha or durva grass on the ground, with the roots turned outward and the tips turned inward, and place your cushion on top of them. It is also explained that it is good to have the back of your seat slightly elevated.

In this context, the importance of making tormas and other offerings with pure materials and substances and arranging them beautifully is taught. The tormas should be made from select portions of excellent ingredients. These ingredients must not be obtained through wrong livelihood, or be of inferior quality, stale, and so forth; they must be ritually pure. With these ingredients, begin by mixing a small amount of the three white substances and make small offering tormas for the deities. For the torma dough, mix nectarlike medicinal powder, made by someone free from samaya breaches, together with beer, the three white substances, and the three types of sweets. Corresponding to the amount of food you have, make the torma with the quality of sādhana tormas stipulated by the text you are using. You may then paint it either maroon or white, whichever is appropriate.

Whatever the torma's shape, its corners should not point toward you and it should be adorned with various types of butter adornments and foodstuffs. A parasol of a matching color should also cover it, and to its right and left there should be nectar and rakta, along with their respective substances. When you find the right occasion, you may also include any appropriate tormas, such as those for oath-bound protectors, Dharma protectors, treasure guardians, and local deities, as well as the articles for feast offerings and so forth.

If you are inclined to include dhāraṇīs in the tormas, draw the root mantra of the main deity and its retinue on Chinese paper with saffron or vermilion ink, followed by the sky treasury mantra. Next, write a supplication to the assembly of the noble deities and their retinue to grant you the supreme and mundane spiritual accomplishments. Finally, draw the *Ye-dharma* dhāraṇī one time. Starting at the beginning of the mantra, roll the paper such that the letters are turned inward. Wrap it in brocade of the same color as the deity and, without turning the mantra upside down, insert it into a bamboo shaft or copper container and then into the torma itself.

If you want to take a more elaborate approach, visualize the shrine torma as the deity and maintain the visualization for as long as you render offerings to it. The perpetual torma is kept for a specific duration of months or years. The sādhana torma, also called the offering torma, is offered and received by the deities as a gift. As a means to delight them, mending tormas serve as an offering substance symbolizing sense pleasures and enjoyments. The captured torma is kept until an activity is accomplished, after which it is to be offered. The purpose of this torma is to ensure that an activity is accomplished swiftly and without delay. The session torma, also called the daily torma, is given occasionally in order to enjoin certain temporary activities. A simple renunciant practitioner may also make these tormas using simply the best portions of his or her own food and drink.

You should also know that tormas can be viewed in a threefold or fourfold manner, depending on the context in which they are used. *The Condensed Realization* states:

> A torma can represent four things:
> At the time of receiving the blessings and empowerments,
> It is visualized as the guru, yidam, ḍākinī, and so forth.
> Those who desire the spiritual accomplishments
> View it as the nectar from which every desired manifestation appears.

> When destroying the activities of the obstructing spirits,
> It is visualized as sharp weapons.
> During the supreme and mundane mending rituals,
> It is visualized as the individual mending substances—
> The offering clouds of sense pleasures and enjoyments.
> Know that a torma can perform these different functions.

The same applies in the context of sādhana practice. *The Key of the Crucial Instructions of the Eight Sādhanas* teaches:

> In terms of practice, torma can be understood in four different ways:
> The great balimṃta torma can be understood
> As an offering, as the deity,
> As armies, and as magical weapons.

While practicing a ritual text, the torma can be viewed as an offering. During exorcising rituals, the torma can be viewed as the deity. During covenant rituals, the torma can be viewed as an army. During the throwing ritual, imagine the wisdom being of the torma dissolving into yourself. Viewing the samaya being of the torma as weapons, fireballs, poisonous vapor, molten bronze, and other such things, you then visualize all demons, together with their dwelling places and strongholds, dwelling within the fire and throw the torma into it.

You should also know that, for those of superior faculties, on the outer level everything is an inexhaustible adornment torma. The world is the torma vessel and the beings are the torma ingredients. On the inner level the aggregates are the torma vessel and the flesh and bones are the torma ingredients. On the secret level, the emptiness of inherent nature is the torma vessel and appearances are the torma itself.

In terms of presentation, in front of the representations and on the upper level of a two-tiered covered stand, set out medicine, nectar, torma, and the practice articles on top of grain heaps, following the instructions of the text you are using. On the lower level, arrange the five sense enjoyments in a row, preceded by the two types of water offering. For the practice of approach these offerings will suffice. The outer offerings are transformed by chanting "*argham* . . ." These are referred to as "circumstantial offerings" in the detailed commentary of *The Clear Realization.*

To the north of the land of Uḍḍiyāna, on the slopes of the Glorious Mountain, water possessing eight special qualities is found. It is clean and free from any impurity, clear and unsullied, cool and aromatic, smooth and free from defect, sweet smelling and fragrant, delicious and of supreme flavor, fulfilling and rejuvenating, and delightful and healthy. It is taught that this water resembles that which is diligently prepared as an offering at the time of great Dharma festivals.

Jigme Lingpa elaborates:

> The offering substances represent the aspect of skillful means, appearances, and bliss. They are not of the highest type. The recipients of the offering, the victorious ones and their heirs, represent the aspect of knowledge and complete liberation. It is advisable to start presenting the offerings from the left side, the side of knowledge.

Jamyang Khyentse Rinpoche explains further:

> Whether during self- or frontal visualization, the female deities have their face turned towards the recipients of the offerings. Therefore, start the offerings from the left side of these offering recipients.

And Lingtrul teaches that:

> For peaceful offerings made during self-visualization, you should begin offerings from the left side of the offering torma.

Nevertheless, followers of the New Schools and the majority of those in our own tradition also teach that offerings must begin from the right to left for both self- and frontal visualizations since the head of the row occupies that side. During frontal visualization, when approach and accomplishment are practiced together, you can place a real or painted maṇḍala, or else just heaps of grains, in front or behind the offerings of the self-visualization, whichever is the most convenient.

First, arrange the practice materials according to the instructions found in the text you are using and then begin the peaceful offerings with flowers in the northeast. This serves to prevent the influence of obstructing forces. Next, place drinking water in the east, bathing water in the southeast, and the remaining offerings clockwise in a circular manner.

When wrathful offerings are called for, place the following wrathful offerings in a counterclockwise circle. From the west, set out blood as drinking water in the southwest—the cannibal island—followed by poisonous water for bathing, sense faculties as flowers, human flesh as incense, human fat as a butter lamp, bile as scented water, and flesh and bones as food offerings. It is also said that peaceful offerings should be arranged in rows and wrathful offerings in a circle. Surround these offerings with all the individual ornaments you have, place them on a tigerskin and so forth. As a convenient alternative, place the peaceful offerings in a row starting from the right side of the frontal visualization and the wrathful offerings in a row starting from the left side. Between these rows place the daily tormas.

Do not carelessly mix the outer with inner offerings, such as nectar and rakta. The Great Master of Uḍḍiyāna said:

> In short, you should understand that no fault entails if the light rays of lower offerings strike the higher offerings, but if the light rays of the higher offerings strike the lower offerings, those who like common offerings, such as water, will not receive them.

It is also said that obstructing spirits will enter the tormas and offerings if they are not consecrated as soon as they are displayed. Therefore, perform a brief consecration by sprinkling them with pure water.

The Common Preliminaries

Next, according to how much free time you have, train in the preliminaries for an appropriate number of days. The path of liberation is rooted in the genuine attitude of renunciation, while the four mind-changings are the method that engenders this attitude. The path of the Great Vehicle is rooted in the precious mind of awakening, while the four immeasurables are the method that engenders this mindset. When these trainings have transformed your mind and conviction has arisen within you, focus on the practices of going for refuge, generating the mind of awakening, and reciting the seven-branch prayer. In particular, concentrate on the meditation and recitation of Vajrasattva to purify the obscurations, on the maṇḍala offering to gather the accumulations, and on guru yoga to receive the guru's blessings.

Before you begin your practice in the afternoon and evening sessions, cleanse your mouth with water from the vase and sit in this purified state. Next, exhale the stale breath, rest your body and mind in their natural state, and refresh your motivation. Imagine a blue HŪṂ syllable in your heart as the essence of the innate awakened mind. Light radiates out from this syllable, invoking from the natural abode the essence of your root guru in the form of the deity of any class of tantra: the principal figures, the three jewels, the gurus of the lineage, ḍākinīs, and Dharma protectors surrounded by all the objects of refuge without exception. Visualize them all gathered in the space before you, like cloud banks in the sky.

Imagine yourself going for refuge, over and over, together with all sentient beings. Doing so with your body, speech, and mind is the relative act of going for refuge. The ultimate act of going for refuge is to take refuge in the dharma body, the inconceivable true nature of reality in which the objects of refuge are inseparable from your own mind. This is the wisdom of the empty essence. The enjoyment body is the luminous nature, while the emanation body is unified compassion. Directing your attention to the inherent presence of the three bodies is the ultimate act of going for refuge.

The relative mind of awakening involves thinking, "I will practice this profound path to establish all sentient beings in the state of complete enlightenment." The ultimate mind of awakening involves resting evenly in the true nature wherein nothing ultimately exists. Relatively speaking, however, the true nature can manifest as anything. This is the state in which emptiness and dependent arising are inseparable. Apply yourself earnestly as prescribed here. Further details about these practices, including the acts of going for refuge and generating the mind of awakening, may be learned from other sources.

Since the entire range of the methods for accumulating, purifying, and increasing is contained in the seven-branch prayer, train in gathering the accumulations. To conclude, dissolve the field of accumulation into yourself and then rest for a moment in the state wherein your minds mingle inseparably. More elaborately, you can consecrate the vajra, bell, purifying water, and other articles at this point, following the instructions of other texts.

The Unique Preliminaries

Expelling Obstructors

Next, go outside and, while visualizing yourself as a deity, present a white torma and request supportive activity. In front of your doorway, place the torma for the obstructing forces adorned with flesh, blood, garlic, onions, and so forth.

With the pride and overwhelming, radiant confidence that comes from visualizing yourself as a wrathful protector deity, such as the heruka Hayagrīva, focus on the torma and utter the three syllables. The syllable OṂ cleanses and purifies all impure defilements. The syllable ĀḤ multiplies the substance such that it increases and expands infinitely. The syllable HŪṂ transforms it into sublime sense pleasures that manifest as precisely whatever one desires. Finally, the syllable HOḤ consecrates the torma by transforming it into the nectar of undefiled wisdom.

Next, imagine countless wrathful Ṭakkirājas emanating from your heart center. They are pink in color and have one face and two arms. Brandishing hammers in their right hands and hooks in their left, they summon into your presence all the mischievous spirits, obstructing forces, and elemental spirits, all of whom are powerless to disobey you. Issue your command to these beings, then offer them a torma and send them off to their respective dwellings. Visualize that all those who ignore your command and set out to make obstacles are, in a single instant, threatened, chased away, and crushed by wrathful weapons and powerful flaming rays. As you imagine all this, recite the verses for expelling obstructing forces from your sādhana, burn some resin incense, throw wrathful mantras and charmed substances, and seal your practice by remaining free of reference point.

Drawing the Boundary

Following this, write down the name mantras of the Four Great Kings along with requests addressed to them. Place these on a small altar composed of piled-up white stones, which can be situated either seventy steps away from the place where you are practicing or beside your door. Once this is done, visualize that the Great Kings are mobilized and dissolve into the altar, then present offerings, praise, and request their protective activity. Imagine that the Four Kings oversee the periphery with delight, and that the entire surroundings become completely covered by a protective dome. This is the establishment of the outer boundary. In the context of approach, practices such as subjugating samaya demons and sealing your door are not necessary; these elements are necessary only in the context of the great accomplishment.

Next, come back inside, close your door, and abandon distractions and wanderings. For the inner boundary, visualize the entire base of the protection dome as a ground composed of vajras and the entire upper part as a vajra dome and canopy. Completely surrounding this, in both the cardinal and intermediate directions, is a vast, spacious, and elevated circular vajra fence. The fence is devoid of gaps; instead, every opening is patched by small conjoined vajras that seem melded together. The exterior is covered by a lattice which is completely bound by crossed-vajra cords. The top of the dome is covered by half-vajra tips and the midsection braced by strings of vajras. The whole dome is blue and is shaped like a helmet. Wisdom fire of five colors radiates out from this dome, spreading in all directions. Some systems describe the shape of the dome as either oval or spherical, but they all come down to the same essential meaning: the fact that there are no open spaces anywhere within the vast and spacious protection dome. The dome is surrounded by various kinds of small wrathful emanations and weapons, which amass like rainclouds. These, in turn, are themselves surrounded by three successive domes of fire, water, and wind.[5]

Alternatively, in the limitless expanse of space and amid a blazing mass of fire, visualize a ten-spoked wheel with a rim and hub emanating out from the syllable BHRŪṂ. Its center is vast and spacious, while its spokes are as far-reaching as the basic space of phenomena. Between the ten inner spokes, on seats made of lotus, moon, and sun discs, visualize ten wrathful emanations emerging from ten HŪṂ syllables.

Other visualizations may also be taught at this point, such as visualizing the deity Uṣṇīṣacakravartin as the vast and spacious belly of Vairocana in the inner empty part of the protective dome, but it suffices to follow the instructions that are mentioned in each sādhana ritual.

Thus, having established a boundary with the protective dome, imagine that all demons and treacherous spirits are prevented from approaching, while you and all those in need of protection are safe inside. As you imagine all this, chant the verses for establishing the boundary. This comprises the inner boundary.

Concerning the secret boundary, *Commentary on the Secret Essence* states:

> Subdue the king of demons, discursive thoughts,
> With the king of boundaries, nonconceptual wisdom.

Within the state of innate luminosity, which has never been tainted by the dualistic delusion of a perceiver and perceived, seal your practice by seeing the lack of inherent nature of all the demons, obstructing forces,

5. Author's note: These three are the fire dome made of blazing masses of fire, the dome of vajra rivers made of wild, stormy waves, and the violent black vajra tempest dome that cuts anything it touches like a razor.

and adventitious conceptual imputations. This constitutes the extraordinary protective dome. Sealing the practice nonconceptually, in this way, establishes the secret boundary.

If you will need to meet someone during your retreat, visualize that person included within the protective dome. Do not come into contact with anyone else, and stop engaging in any material exchange with the outside world. Do not dissolve this protective dome until the last session at the end of the retreat, and visualize it at the beginning of each practice session. There are also practice traditions whereby other activities may be performed at this point, such as arranging offerings, accumulating merit, and purifying the obscurations.

To summarize, from the establishment of the inner boundary onwards you must maintain the physical retreat of not seeing other people, the verbal retreat of refraining from ordinary communication, and the mental retreat of not getting caught up in negative thought patterns associated with the afflictions, such as attachment and aversion. At the same time, you must also maintain mindfulness, introspection, and attention. For your virtuous endeavors to be effective, you should practice in four sessions: at dawn, in the morning, in the afternoon, and in the evening.

Shower of Blessings

For the shower of blessings to take place, with fervent devotion visualize yourself as the deity and imagine rays of light emanating from your heart center. Accompany this with specially prepared incense, melodious chanting, and music. In this way, invoke the assembly of deities of the three roots. From the natural expanse imagine all their blessings of wisdom, love, and ability, as well as their spiritual accomplishments, in the form of rays of light, rainbow-hued clouds, flowers, spheres of light, and so forth. Their enlightened bodies appear as divine forms, their enlightened speech as seed syllables, and their enlightened minds as symbolic implements. Imagine that all of these dissolve into you, your dwelling place, and all the ritual articles, endowing you with the nourishing power of glorious, great wisdom.

For those of superior faculties, whenever any perception of the six collections of consciousness arises, the knot of perceiver and perceived vanishes—self-liberated from the moment it manifests. Through this, whatever appears arises as the outer, inner, and secret offering clouds. This is the descent of blessings of the great wisdom of infinite purity.

Consecrating the Offering Articles

According to the sūtras, the vehicle of characteristics, the actual offerings are consecrated and emanated through the recitation of dhāraṇī mantras, knowledge mantras, the power of devotion, and the power of truth. In the mantra vehicle, however, they are consecrated by five practices: going for refuge, deity, mantra, meditative absorption, and mudrā. With this in mind, visualize yourself as the deity and imagine the syllables RAṂ, YAṂ, and KHAṂ emanating from your heart center.

Transforming respectively into wisdom fire, wind, and water, they incinerate, scatter, and wash away all the impure stains, faults, and defects of believing that the offering articles are real, until nothing remains. From the state of emptiness the syllable BHRŪṂ then appears and transforms into a vast, open jewel vessel. Within this vessel the syllable OṂ gives rise to the flowers of divine substances and the rest of the five common outer offerings, to the unique inner offerings, including the self-arisen flowers of the five sense faculties, to the wrathful offerings of the charnel grounds, and so forth. Every desirable thing throughout saṃsāra and nirvāṇa is present, without anything missing. Imagine that clouds of countless offering goddesses, each carrying her own individual offering, radiate out from each of these offerings and fill the entirety of space.

The Inner Offerings of Medicine, Rakta, and Torma

For the inner offering of medicine, visualize wind, fire, and a tripod made from a human skull arising from the syllables YAṂ, RAṂ, and KHAṂ. On top of the tripod a vast open skull cup, containing the five meats and the five nectars, emerges from the syllable ĀḤ or the syllable BHRŪṂ. Human flesh and excrement are in the middle of this skull cup, cow meat and semen in the east, dog meat and brain in the south, horse meat and menses in the west, and elephant meat and urine in the north. Next, visualize the syllables HRĪḤ and BAṂ, TRĀṂ and MAṂ, OṂ and MUṂ, and ĀḤ and TĀṂ above each of their respective offering substances. These syllables then transform into the male and female buddhas of the five families.[6] A stream of red and white bodhicitta then flows from the place where the male and female deities unite and fills the skull cup. At the conclusion of this process, the deities melt into light and dissolve into the offering substances. Imagine that this becomes a swirling ocean of wisdom nectar, and that sense pleasure goddesses emanate from each of its droplets. *The Condensed Realization* states:

> The skull cup is heated by blazing fire stirred by the wind from below.
> Rays of light, from the vapor of the boiling articles, spread in the ten directions.
> They summon the wisdom nectar, which dissolves in the skull cup.
> The deities, sacred substances, and wisdom nectar
> Mingle indivisibly, swirling white and red.
> For deities the nectar becomes pleasing and appeasing articles.
> For spiritual companions the nectar is an elixir of spiritual accomplishments.
> For enemies it becomes a dangerous weapon.
> For obstructing forces it becomes a charmed substance that pulverizes them.
> Envision it as nectar that meets the needs of whomever it comes into contact with.

For the inner offering of rakta, atop the wind, fire, and skull stand described above, visualize a vast, open vessel made from a fresh skull with

6. Author's note: HRĪḤ and BAṂ transform into Amitāba in union with his consort; HŪṂ and LAṂ transform into Vajrasattva in union with his consort; TRĀṂ and MAṂ transform into Ratnasaṃbhava in union with his consort; OṂ and MUṂ transform into Vairocana in union with his consort; and ĀḤ and TĀṂ transform into Amoghasiddhi in union with his consort.

the hairs still on it. Next, imagine that all the concepts of craving and attachment related to the three realms coalesce within it in the form of blood. In the middle of this swirling blood visualize the rakta goddess Gitima. Red and naked, she holds a knife and a skull cup. From her bhaga, a stream of rakta flows down, mingling inseparably with the substances of the skull cup and filling it completely. Finally, the goddess melts into light and dissolves into the articles. This creates surging waves within the ocean of rakta, which is essentially detached great bliss, and causes clouds of sense pleasures to emanate forth.

For the inner offering of torma, visualize a vast, open skull cup or jewel vessel. Within this vessel is a torma made of various foods, a divine nectar endowed with a hundred flavors and an inexhaustible treasure made of a mass of desirable things. Imagine that countless clouds of offering goddesses emanate from the torma, each carrying delightful and appeasing offering articles for all the outer, inner, and secret guests.

Everything up to this point concerns the stages of the common and unique preliminaries.

THE MAIN PRACTICE

This section consists of (1) an abridged teaching on the general meaning and (2) an elaborate explanation of the meaning of the scripture.

An Abridged Teaching on the General Meaning

This section covers (1) the intent of the individual classes of tantra, (2) the deity meditation as applied to the purification of habitual tendencies of the four types of birth, and (3) how deity meditation can be practiced in relation to the varying capacities of individuals.

The Intent of the Individual Classes of Tantra

A tantra explains:

> All skillful practitioners
> Who aspire to the completion stage
> Should practice the development stage, starting with the foundation.

The Instructions of the Lord of Secrets states:

> In short, the development stage involves transforming all impure appearances into pure appearances and meditating on the maṇḍala circle. The completion stage involves meditating conceptually on the channels, winds, and essences in order to realize the wisdom of empty bliss and meditating nonconceptually on the absorption of the true nature.

The first of these two, the development stage, can be divided into three types: (1) the illusory development stage, in which you realize that objective appearances are not real, (2) the profound development stage, in which these manifest spontaneously as empty appearances, and (3) the emanated development stage, which refers to the divine form with faces, hands, etc. Here I shall discuss the development stage from the perspective of the last of these three approaches.

The defining characteristic of the development stage is to give rise to the divine form of empty appearance using concepts and fabrications concomitant with blissful melting. Furthermore, the development stage has four unique qualities, as described by the saint Kunga Nyingpo in the following passage:

> Its unique rituals are the complete development stage rituals taught in the tantras. Its unique result is the capacity to develop the power of mantra. Its unique essence is the nature of emptiness and blissful melting. Its unique function is the completion of purification, perfection, and maturation.

In *Resting in the Nature of Mind* Longchenpa explains the three outer classes of tantra in the following way:

In action tantra the practitioner is seen as inferior and the deity as supreme;
You receive the spiritual accomplishments of practice
In the manner of a master and a servant.

In performance tantra the practitioner and the deity are seen as equals;
With the wisdom deity before you as the samaya being,
You receive spiritual accomplishments as though from a friend.

In practice tantra the two are indivisible during the main practice,
Yet in the preparatory and concluding stages they are two, as the deity is invoked and later departs.
The spiritual accomplishments are received nondually, like water poured into water.

As outlined here, in action tantra generally the practitioner does not imagine himself as the deity. However, in particular instances, the deity, or the wisdom being, is regarded as a king and you, the samaya being, regard yourself as his subject. With this approach you emphasize acts of ritual purity and other outer actions through which you receive the spiritual accomplishments. *The Tantra of Receiving the Spiritual Accomplishments of All Buddha Families* explains as follows:

Looking at the body of the king, your master,
And thinking of yourself as a servant,
Accomplish the mantra and receive the most supreme—
The essence of spiritual accomplishment.

In performance tantra the view is the same as in practice tantra while the conduct is the same as in action tantra. Here you receive the spiritual accomplishments as though you and the deity are siblings or friends. This occurs through a state of equality between you as the practitioner, visualized as the samaya being, and the wisdom deity that you have visualized in front of yourself. *The General Tantra of the Three Families* mentions this:

The sacred spiritual accomplishments should be received
As though from a sibling or a friend.

In practice tantra you meditate on yourself as the deity and, by invoking and dissolving the wisdom deity, you and the wisdom deity become indivisible. At the conclusion of performing offerings, praise, and recitations, you receive the spiritual accomplishments and the deity is requested to depart. *The Vajra Element* states:

The nondual expanse of reality
And receipt of the highest, sacred spiritual accomplishment . . .

The meditations of the three inner tantras are also described in *Resting in the Nature of Mind*:

Mahā stresses the energies, the development stage, and skillful means.
Anu emphasizes the elements, the completion stage, and knowledge.
Ati highlights that everything is nondual wisdom.
All three practice with the knowledge
That all phenomena are primordial equality.

In mahāyoga the emphasis is on gradually developing the maṇḍala based on the three samādhis, whereby you meditate on the indivisibility of the deity and concept. In anuyoga it is held that all phenomena are, by their very nature, indivisible from the three maṇḍalas, and that the root maṇḍala of the awakened mind is primordially enlightened. As such, the form of the deity emerges as an expression of the unceasing play of Samantabhadra. *The Magical Key to the Treasury* explains:

The anuyoga of completion holds that
The aggregates, elements, and sense sources
Are not developed, but perfect
As the maṇḍala of male and female deities.

And also:

In the vehicle of anuyoga,
By merely expressing the essence,
You meditate on the deity, which is perfected without being
developed.

The Compendium teaches:

Within the primordial openness of the great perfection,
Samantabhadra,
The outer, inner, and secret maṇḍalas are arranged.

According to atiyoga the spontaneously present appearances of the Direct Crossing manifest from the primordial pure basic space of the Thorough Cut as the gathering of divine forms. These forms are the expression of awareness, the natural manifestation of unceasing dependent arising. In this way the mind focuses on the vivid appearance of the thoroughly established deity of great purity and equality. This accords with the approach of most of the practice manuals in the tradition of the key instructions of the heart essence.

The difference between the outer and inner tantras is also described in *The Condensed Realization*:

In the outer tantras the deities are either male or female
And the completion stage relates to syllables or essences.
In the inner tantras the deities are joined in union
And the completion stage is the Great Seal.

In terms of ornaments, deities of the outer tantras have jewel
crowns,
While in the inner tantras they wear bone ornaments and other
such things.
In the outer tantras you offer the three white substances,
Whereas in the inner tantras the five meats and five nectars
are offered.

> In the outer tantras you use a jewel vessel,
> While a kapāla is used in the inner tantras.
> Tormas, fire offerings, consecration, clay statues, and vase rituals
> Are common to the outer and inner tantras alike.

Deity Meditation and the Four Types of Birth

The appearances of the various phenomena of saṃsāra manifest in dependence upon our having taken birth within existence. For this reason, the primary elements of saṃsāra are the four types of birth. To purify the habitual tendencies associated with these four types of birth, four corresponding styles of development stage meditation are taught. A tantra explains:

> To purify the four types of birth
> There are four types of development:
> The very elaborate, the elaborate,
> The simple, and the completely simple.

The Very Elaborate Development Stage

First we will examine the very extensive development stage that purifies egg birth. The following accords with the process of being born from an egg, which takes place in two stages. Begin by taking refuge and giving rise to the awakened mind. Next, visualize yourself instantly as the primary male and female consorts and invite the deities of the maṇḍala into the space before you. After presenting offerings, praise, supplications, daily confessions, and so on, gradually dissolve the visualization and rest evenly in emptiness for a moment.

The unique feature of this approach is to first visualize in a concise manner and then in an extensive manner according to the systems of your own children and another's child. *The Eight Great Sādhana Teachings* mention this process:

> There are five steps involved in making others your child:
> (1) the primary male and female consorts are generated from

> the seed syllable; (2) the buddhas of the ten directions are invoked and dissolve into the space of the female consort; (3) sentient beings are summoned and their obscurations purified; (4) the greatness of nonduality is developed; and (5) the deities are evoked from space and established upon their seats.
>
> Making yourself the child of another has eight parts: (1) the primary male and female consorts dissolve into light and transform into the seed syllable; (2) the male and female consorts develop fully from this seed syllable; (3) the male consort's conceptuality transforms into syllables; (4) light emanates from the female consort and supplicates the deity; (5) all maṇḍalas dissolve into you, arousing divine pride; (6) the male and female consorts join and the maṇḍala is generated in space; (7) your forty-two concepts are visualized as deities and projected externally; and (8) the deities are bound and sealed with the four seals.

As outlined here, since you yourself are a thus-gone one at the time of the ground, the thus-gone ones are transformed into your children. And to ensure that the potential of the thus-gone ones does not decline, you become the child of others. This is how the great Rongzom explained it. He also taught that when you meditate on these practices there is no fixed progression.

The Elaborate Development Stage

Next we will examine the intermediate development stage that purifies womb birth. This stage involves three approaches. First, the condensed approach, the ritual of the three vajras, which accords with father tantra. Its objects of purification are (1) the intermediate existence, (2) the fetus, and (3) birth. The process of purification involves meditating on the features of the symbolic implements, such as the five-spoked vajra. This, in turn, purifies the mind (the object of purification), transforming it into vajra mind. The symbolic implements are then transformed into, or visualized as being marked by, a HŪṂ or another such syllable. This perfects your speech into enlightened speech. Next, light radiates out from this seed syllable and is then reabsorbed, performing the twofold benefit. Finally, the symbolic implement undergoes a fundamental transformation into the complete form of the deity, along with its ornaments and apparel. This ripens the ordinary body into the enlightened body.

Next is the medium-length ritual, the four manifestations of enlightenment, which corresponds to mother tantra. *The Galpo Tantra* describes this as follows:

> First, emptiness and the mind of awakening.
> Second, the occurrence of the seed.
> Third, the complete form.
> Fourth, setting out the syllable.

Here the corresponding objects of purification are (1) the death state and the intermediate stage, (2) a disembodied consciousness coalescing with the semen and ovum, (3) the gradual formation of the body through the ten winds, and (4) the faculties engaging with objects subsequent to birth.

Lastly, the extensive ritual, the five manifestations of enlightenment. Here the respective objects of purification are (1) the intermediate state consciousness, (2) the moment before consciousness enters the womb, (3) entry into the womb, (4) the ten months of physical development in the womb, and (5) birth.

These five can be applied to the five paths. The process of purification for the first three is the three samādhis. The process of purification for the fourth is the five manifestations of enlightenment. *The Hevajra Tantra* explains:

> The moon is mirrorlike wisdom,
> The seven of seven, equality.
> Discernment is said to be the deity's
> Seed syllable and symbolic implements.
> All becoming one is perseverance itself,
> And perfection, the pure expanse of reality.

The process of purification for the fifth element begins with visualizing divine appearance (the support and the supported of the Great Seal) and extends throughout the four aspects of approach and accomplishment that contain the instructions on the "four stakes that bind the life force" all the way up to the ritual's dissolution stage.

The Simple Development Stage

The condensed development stage ritual purifies the habitual tendencies connected with birth from heat and moisture. In this approach the object of purification is the completion of a body that emerges from heat and moisture. The process of purification involves visualizing the transformation of the seed syllable, which rests upon layered sun and moon discs, into the complete form of the deity.

The Completely Simple Development Stage

The extremely concise development stage ritual purifies the habitual tendencies associated with miraculous birth. Here the deity is instantaneously visualized merely by uttering the essential syllable. On this topic *The Tantra of the Natural Arising of Awareness* states:

> What is instantaneous practice?
> The deity is not developed, but perfected by recalling its essence.

In this way an individual of the highest caliber can visualize the primordial deity, the essence of mind, recalling it perfectly in a single moment, just as though he or she were seeing a reflection in a mirror.

Of these four types of birth, womb birth and egg birth are purified using the mahāyoga approach, while birth from heat and moisture is purified with the anuyoga approach and miraculous birth is purified using the atiyoga approach.

When practicing these approaches, the existence that resembles cyclic existence is cleansed and purified, while the fruition that resembles passing beyond suffering is perfected in the ground. Both of these features will mature you for the completion stage. This is the general understanding.

Generally speaking, for those who begin these practices, these four approaches, with their varying levels of complexity, are primarily taught as specific ways to purify each of the four types of birth. In reality, however, there is no difference in terms of the degree of purification achieved by these four approaches.

Deity Meditation and the Various Types of Practitioner

The Condensed Realization explains:

> Practitioners of superior capacity understand that utterly pure simplicity—which is unfabricated, naturally occurring, spontaneously present, and primordially clear—is the essence of the deity. Practitioners of moderate capacity understand that the self-existing expression of unfabricated and nonconceptual compassion is the brilliant deity of the pure channels. Practitioners of the lowest capacity practice within the nonconceptual state where all forms are male and female deities. In this way the deities manifest like fish jumping from a lake. With pure faith and samaya vows intact, the deity is clearly visualized through the five manifestations of enlightenment and the three samādhis.

According to *The Tantra of the Layered Lotus Stems*, each of these three categories can be divided into three subcategories, for a total of nine divisions. Such variations may be learned from their respective sources.

The Elaborate Explanation of the Scripture's Meaning

This section consists of (1) the practice of equipoise and (2) the practice of the ensuing attainment.

The Practice of Equipoise

The practice of equipoise has three divisions: (1) the visualization practice of enlightened body, (2) the recitation practice of enlightened speech, and (3) the luminosity practice of enlightened mind.

Enlightened Body

There are five subdivisions in this section: (1) the framework of the three samādhis, (2) visualizing the maṇḍalas of the support and the supported, (3) invoking the wisdom beings and requesting them to remain, (4) the activities of homage, offering, and praise, and (5) focusing on the deity's appearance, the primary focal point.

The Framework of the Three Samādhis

The system of developing the visualization by means of the three samādhis is something that is found in mahāyoga and the other inner tantras.

The Samādhi of Suchness

First, relax your mind and do not chase after any confused thoughts. Then let go for a moment, and rest in the simplicity of reality—the state of empty awareness that transcends words and concepts. This is the samādhi of suchness, also known as "the practice of great emptiness," "the vajralike absorption," and "the absorption of emptiness." This samādhi eliminates the extreme of permanence and purifies the habitual tendencies associated with the formless realm. It also purifies the death state into the dharma body. Hence, this is classified as the essence of awareness, the inconceivable aspect. In this context, you rest without visualizing the protection dome and the other elements outlined above. However, you must understand that they are not entirely absent either.

The Samādhi of Total Illumination

Out of this state of emptiness, meditate for a brief moment with non-referential illusory compassion towards all sentient beings who do not realize their own in-dwelling wisdom. This is the samādhi of total illumination. The practice of illusory compassion is also known as "the absorption of the heroic gait" and "the absorption of wishlessness." It eliminates the extreme of nihilism and purifies the habitual tendencies connected to the form realm. It also transforms existence in the intermediate state and perfects it into the enjoyment body. Hence, this samādhi is classified as the radiance of awareness, the aspect of the unobstructed nature of compassion.

The Causal Samādhi

Once compassion has stirred the mind out of this nonconceptual state, the essence of your mind assumes the form of a seed syllable, such as a HŪṂ or a HRĪḤ, which manifests brilliantly in the unsupported, empty expanse of space. Focusing on such a seed syllable is the causal samādhi, the training in the subtle syllable that is one aspect of the single mudrā. The causal samādhi is also known as "the illusory absorption" and "the absorption of no characteristics." It purifies the view of a self and the stains of apprehending characteristics. It also purifies the habitual tendencies connected to the desire realm, thereby ripening birth into the emanation body. It is therefore classified as the expression of awareness, the aspect that manifests as objects.

Here meditating on the assembly of deities connected with the support and the supported constitutes the training in the coarse divine form, while meditating in a more elaborate way with companions, faces, hands, etc. constitutes the training in the elaborate mudrā. These are the four practices of the path of accumulation. The states of the four knowledge holders are then gradually attained in reliance on the proximate cause of the group practice that takes place on the path of joining.

In this context you will find the mantra OṂ SVABHĀVA ŚUDDHAḤ SARVADHARMĀḤ SVABHĀVA ŚUDDHO 'HAṂ. In reciting this mantra, you are saying, "Just as all phenomena are naturally pure, so too am I pure by nature," which captures the meaning of the samādhi of suchness. The meaning of the mantra OṂ MAHĀ ŚŪNYATĀ JÑĀNA VAJRA SVABHĀVĀTMAKO 'HAṂ is "I am the very embodiment of the nature of vajra wisdom and great emptiness." In this mantra the phrase "great emptiness" refers to the samādhi of suchness, while the remainder refers to the samādhi of total illumination and the causal samādhi.

The Maṇḍalas of the Support and the Supported

Next you visualize the supportive celestial palace and the supported deities.

The Supportive Celestial Palace

As explained in the *Appendix to the Recitation Manual of the Embodiment of the Sugatas*, begin by imagining that the syllables E, YAṂ, RAṂ, BAṂ, LAṂ, SUṂ, and BHRŪṂ emerge, one by one, within the space of a vast protective dome. They emerge from the previously visualized seed syllable of the causal samādhi. The letter E completely purifies all clinging to reality and then transforms into a blue triangle of limitless size whose nature is the empty expanse of space. Above the upward-facing wide opening of this triangle is the syllable YAṂ, which transforms into a wind maṇḍala shaped like a dark-green cross rimmed with dark-green light. Above this cross the syllable RAṂ transforms into a fire maṇḍala shaped like a red triangle rimmed with red light. Above this, the syllable BAṂ transforms into a white spherical water maṇḍala rimmed with white light. Further up, the syllable LAṂ becomes a golden ground shaped like a yellow square rimmed with yellow light. On top of the golden ground, the syllable SUṂ transforms into Mount Meru composed of four types of jewels and with four terraces. Upon Mount Meru is a multicolored crossed-vajra in the center of which is BHRŪṂ, the seed syllable of Uṣṇīṣacakravartin.

This syllable then transforms into a square celestial palace of precious wisdom. To indicate that reality itself is free from elaborations, its center is spherical. Its four walls represent the four truths, and it is surrounded by a gallery that represents the unity of the two truths. As a sign that each of the wisdoms is endowed with the four superior wisdoms through which the wishes of those to be tamed are fulfilled, beautiful bejeweled ledges with the colors of the four families jut out from the four walls.

The four entryways, representing the four complete liberations, are accompanied by beautiful porticos. To indicate traversing the eight vehicles, there are four steps inside and outside of the doorways respectively—these are the eight causal architraves. As a sign that the qualities of the tenet systems of the vehicles are perfected thereby, above the vestibules are ornaments called *toraṇa*. The eight resultant architraves consist of the horse ankle, the lotus, the casket, the lattice, the cluster ornament, the garland, and the rainspout ledge, layered one upon the other forming a sort of projected molding, the top of which is ornamented with garuḍa heads.

On top of each vestibule there is a Dharma wheel resting on a lotus and surmounted by a parasol. Two deer sit beautifully next to each Dharma wheel, one to each side. At the top of the five layers of the wall, which represent the display of nondual wisdom, are jeweled hangings—pearl lattices and tassels suspended from lion heads. Above these are jewel lattices and tasseled streamers of the top border. Facing outward from these are jewel rainspouts suspended from the eaves, above which is a parapet that ornaments the palace. Banners, parasols, victory banners, and so forth are displayed all around.

Symbolizing that the sense pleasures are not abandoned, but arise as ornaments of realization, many offering goddesses bearing aloft offering substances are gathered like clouds on the platform of delights that protrudes from the palace. Envision all of this as completely transparent and open. As a sign that the wisdom of the basic space of phenomena is limitless, the pinnacle of a heap of jewels at the center of the roof is adorned with a jewel vajra top-ornament that one never tires of beholding. Door ornaments, bells, silk streamers, trees, and every other adornment also beautify the area. Encircling the outer enclosure are lotuses, along with charnel grounds encircled by vajra fences and blazing fires.[7]

The specific characteristics of wrathful maṇḍalas are as follows. There is an ocean of rakta, a ground of human skin, and Mount Meru, which is composed of skeletons. On its summit is a multicolored crossed-vajra resting within a great mass of wisdom fire. At the center of this crossed-vajra is a square celestial palace with four doors. Its gallery is composed

7. Author's note: This does not mean the outer protective dome.

of either gold or blood, whichever is appropriate, and its walls are made of fresh, dry, and shriveled skulls that are nailed together with nails of meteoric iron and glued together with blood. On top of the walls is a border of various types of skulls with garlands of intestines and hearts. On the streamers of the top border are lattices and tassels made of snakes and garlands of skulls. The rainspouts are made of hands and feet; the ledge is made of backbones and ribs; and the lower part of each door is made of turtles, with upper parts made of crocodiles. There are poisonous male vipers that constitute the planks on either side of the door, while the planks of the door itself are made of human skin. To the right and left of the Dharma wheel are baby crocodiles resting atop the architraves. Above them are parasols made of human skin. The ceiling is also made of human skin. The central chamber has a skylight for the sun and the moon and is made of the overturned skull of Mahādeva, which is surmounted with a top-ornament of a heart, and so forth.

In the center, cardinal, and intermediate directions of the palace are the seats for the deities. As a sign of fulfilling the wishes of those to be tamed, these thrones are made of precious jewels and are supported by fearless lions, mighty elephants, and so on. They are surmounted by jeweled lotuses, which symbolize being untainted by the flaws of saṃsāra. The anthers of the lotus are covered with the sun and moon discs of skillful means and knowledge. These and other elements are included, depending on the context. Wrathful deities may be seated on animals, Rudra, a corpse, lotus, sun and moon discs, and so forth. These aspects of the visualization should be spelled out in the text you are using.

The Supported Deities

The Condensed Realization states:

> Gradually generate the celestial palace from the outside.
> Gradually generate the deities from the inside.

As indicated here, to visualize the supported deities imagine that the previously visualized seed syllable descends onto the central seat. This syllable then either transforms into the complete main deity or into the symbolic implement, held in the deity's right hand, which is marked by the deity's life-force syllable. In the latter case, light radiates out from the implement and is then absorbed back into it, accomplishing the twofold benefit. When the light is absorbed back in, the implement transforms into the form of the deity, complete with all of its ornaments and attire. You may then gradually visualize the main deities and their retinue in their entirety, as spelled out in the particular ritual text you are using.

Next is the blessing of the three places. In the bone mansion at the crown of the main deity, as well as in those of all the deities of the retinue, imagine white OṂ syllables resting upon white discs. Red ĀḤ syllables rest upon red eight-petaled lotuses in the center of their throats. In their heart centers blue HŪṂ syllables rest upon sun discs in front of their hearts. Thus, the visualized deities are sealed by clearly visualizing these three syllables as the essence of vajra body, speech, and mind. In some contexts, you may imagine that they are sealed by visualizing that the three syllables emit and absorb light and then transform into Vairocana, Amitābha, and Akṣobhya, each of whom wears enjoyment-body ornaments. You then recite mantras, perform the gestures at each of your own three places, and generate the confidence of the three vajras.

Next, for the bestowal of empowerment, light radiates out from the seed syllable at your heart center, or from the heart center of the wisdom being, and invites all the sūgatas, in the form of male and female empowerment deities of the five families, to come from their natural abode. Joined in inseparable union, the fire of their passionate desire creates a stream of the five wisdoms, which melts and flows down onto the five places at your crown, conferring empowerment and purifying the stains of the five afflictions. The liquid that overflows from the top of your head transforms into a crown endowed with the adornments of the five emanation-body families, with your own family in the position of the lord. By purifying the five aggregates, give rise to the confidence of the buddhas of the five families. Make the empowerment mudrās of the five families at each of your five places and recite the mantras for receiving empowerment. In some cases, blessing your three places or receiving empowerment may be unnecessary. There may also be other variations. Hence, practice as stipulated in the text you are using.

Invoking the Wisdom Beings and Requesting Them to Remain

The Invocation

From the letter HŪṂ at your heart center countless red light rays shine forth. These light rays, which are bent slightly inwards at the tip like hooks, invoke the assembly of deities, the maṇḍala of the victorious ones of the three roots who abide in manifold buddhafields that pervade all of space. As the embodiment of the manifold aspect of the dharma body, the deities are invoked along with their retinues, which include the guardian deities and Dharma protectors.

While not moving from the dharma body, imagine that the power of their compassion arouses the display of the form bodies, which arrive immediately. In the same way that you must first send an invitation when requesting the presence of a king in a worldly context, here the samaya being must show reverence and respect to the wisdom maṇḍala as the object of veneration. In addition, if you practice the deity yoga of the development stage with unshakable devotion, it is the nature of things that the commitment of the host of deities of the three roots will naturally be invoked and they will immediately come to the place of devotion where they are being visualized. For this reason, generate intense devotion and recite the words of the invocation melodiously while playing music and offering incense. With these words imagine countless wisdom beings identical to the deities of the visualized maṇḍala—the supportive celestial palace together with its protective dome—along with whatever peaceful or wrathful deities are being invoked. Like snowflakes in a blizzard, they gather like clouds in the space above the samaya maṇḍala, all the way out to the mountains of flames. These wisdom beings represent a display of illusory wisdom and an overwhelming mass of wisdom, love, and capacity.

Alternatively, in some contexts it is taught that four mudrā goddesses are emanated from your heart as the samaya being. The Hook Goddess invokes the commitment of the wisdom beings, the Noose Goddess invites them, the Shackle Goddess arouses them from their dwelling places, and the Bell Goddess delights them and invites them into the space in front of you.

The Request to Remain

At this point you supplicate the entire wisdom maṇḍala to merge indivisibly with yourself as the samaya maṇḍala. Imagine that, with loving delight, the wisdom maṇḍala dissolves into you like snowflakes landing on a lake and merges indivisibly with the samaya maṇḍala. On this point *The Oral Instructions* state:

> The samaya being is the element of buddha nature itself, established as the primordially pure maṇḍala of the deity, while the wisdom being is the body of all buddhas. The primordial inseparability of these two is the meaning of the inseparability of the samaya and wisdom beings.

And Jigme Lingpa writes:

> You must understand that the invocation, and so on, enable you to recall the primordial indivisibility of the samaya and wisdom beings; it is not as though you are placing one into the other.

Moreover, Tsele Natsok Rangdrol explains:

> When making the invocation, it is not as though something "other" is invoked and then arrives from some other place. To purify impure deluded perception, we do indeed recite words that invoke particular deities by name, mention the places where they reside, and do other such things. Nevertheless, in fact there is nowhere in the world of appearance and existence that is not pervaded by the magical display of self-aware awakened mind. Since this is the case, the innate awareness that is the samaya being is indivisible from the wisdom being; these are not two different things. Thus, the wisdom being is invoked *as being indivisible* from the samaya being.

When you have not realized the primordial inseparability of the samaya being and the wisdom being, you may bring this to mind through the mere symbolic invocation and dissolution of the wisdom beings, which take place from the perspective of the way things appear in an unimpeded, illusory, and relative manner.

In this context we find the syllables DZAḤ HŪṂ BAṂ HOḤ. Imagine that the samaya being uses the syllable DZAḤ to summon the wisdom being. With HŪṂ the wisdom being dissolves indivisibly into the samaya being. The syllable BAṂ binds the wisdom being, compelling it to remain until your wishes are accomplished. Finally, with the syllable HOḤ the wisdom being joyfully remains. This stabilizes the indivisible blending of the samaya and wisdom beings.

Homage, Offering, and Praise

Homage

Ultimately, your mind and the deity are indivisible. Knowing this is the homage of meeting the view, and is the true homage. On a symbolic level, however, you still recall the qualities of the deities and respectfully pay homage, make offerings, and so forth in the following way. Just as the gods in the Realm of Enjoying Emanations amuse themselves and partake of the sense pleasures that they themselves have emanated, here you imagine that four knowledge goddesses emerge from your heart center as the main deity. From the four gates they exclaim, "ATIPŪ HOḤ," and the deities of the maṇḍala respond, "PRATĪCCHAHOḤ." The goddesses are then gathered back into your heart center.

Alternatively, with a frontal visualization, the four emanated goddesses emerge from the heart center of yourself (visualized as the deity) and then pay homage to the deity visualized in front of you. Meanwhile, four goddesses also emerge from that deity's heart center and offer homage back in response. To conclude, they are all gathered back into the heart centers from which they came. This is how Jigme Lingpa explained it. Patrul Rinpoche teaches that paying homage can simply mean showing humility and respect with your body, speech, and mind, and that it is not necessary for there to be a particular object to which homage is paid and one who pays homage, regarding these as two different things.

The Offerings

The Outer Offerings

First, to make the outer and inner general offerings imagine countless offering goddesses, in the form of the Vajra Lady and so forth, emanating from your heart center. Holding the seven enjoyments, the five sense pleasures, and other offering substances, they sing and dance. Each particle of the offering emanates inconceivable clouds of desirable objects that please and satisfy the deities. More specifically, the offering goddesses offer drinking water endowed with the eight qualities to the deities' mouths; clear, cool, and pleasing water to refresh their hands and feet; excellent garlands of divine flowers for their heads; the scent of natural and produced fragrant incense for their noses; jewels, butter lamps, and other lights for their eyes; medicinal waters scented with sandalwood and saffron for the deities' bodies; delicious and nutritious foods for their tongues; and the melodious sound of beautiful music that is blown, played, beaten, and so forth for their ears. To conclude, imagine that the goddesses dissolve into the very places to which they made offerings.

Jigme Lingpa explains further:

> In the context of offerings and praises, it is as if the deities are making offerings and praises to themselves. This, however, is indeed suitable, as it purifies impure worlds and beings into pure worlds and beings. When transformed into the development stage of emanated pure realms and pure beings, where would you find someone ordinary to make offerings, anyway?

Alternatively, Patrul Rinpoche teaches that the offering goddesses who dwell on the external foundation make the offerings. Either is acceptable, but it is good to practice these approaches simultaneously.

In the context of frontal visualizations, imagine that the goddesses dissolve into all of the individual deities and then emerge from them as though being born. They then dissolve into your own places, bringing about the attainment of spiritual accomplishments. This is taught in the tantras.

Additionally, there are also beautifully arrayed offering substances; the offerings of absorption whereby the arrayed offerings are visualized and offered as the offering clouds of Samantabhadra; the offering of melody whereby you recite the verses of offering in a melodious manner; the offering of symbolic mudrā, meaning gestures that are respectfully offered by means of the "revolving lotus"; and the offering of mantra, meaning ARGHAM and the other mantras of the offering verses. Tingtrul Rinpoche teaches that those of superior faculties can emanate whatever they experience as great clouds of the treasury of space and offer it as such.

The Inner Offerings

Medicine

The inner offering of medicine is a samaya substance that is composed of eight primary and one thousand subsidiary substances. It is derived from the realization that all phenomena are equal and are not to be accepted or rejected. As such, it is an elixir that dispels the demon of dualistic concepts. This unsurpassed great medicine has the nature of the four accomplishments and three ways of being.

With the sun and moon sphere of your thumb and ring finger, respectively, scoop up the nectar and scatter it. Envision the droplets of nectar dissolving into the mouths of the deities and satisfying them with the taste of great bliss. You should know the general and specific ways of rendering offerings. To conclude, once the nectar touches your own tongue and dissolves into the three places, imagine that you have received the accomplishments of enlightened body, speech, and mind.

Torma

Visualize a vast and open jewel vessel. Inside is a torma made of various types of food and drink. Although it is made of all kinds of desirable objects, in essence this torma is wisdom nectar. Imagine that the deities imbibe and partake of the torma with tongues that are hollow, made of light, and have the form of three-pronged vajras. This delights them. Next, imagine that countless torma goddesses of the sense pleasures, having aroused delight in the deities, dissolve into you. In actuality, here the food of the five objects and the drink of the five consciousnesses are enjoyed within the expanse of luminosity.

Rakta

Here you imagine the negative emotions, the root of the suffering of existence, coalescing in the form of blood. This is offered within the expanse of great bliss, free from attachment, to liberate intractable beings through compassion. To this end, imagine that this blood is completely consumed and saṃsāra is liberated into unborn basic space.

The Secret Offerings

The Offering of Union

First is the offering of union. Subjective appearances correspond to the masculine principle of skillful means. In contrast, the object—emptiness—corresponds to knowledge, the feminine principle. The indivisible unity of these two is the great primordial union of everything.

In the present context, the taste of great bliss that appears from this union satisfies the entire maṇḍala. This is symbolized by the male and female consorts being joined together as individual couples in union. Single female deities are also joined in union with the symbolic form of the lord of the family, the concealed masculine principle, which takes the form of a khaṭvāṅga. Through this union an extraordinary blissful melting occurs in which the descending flow and the ascending stabilization are gradually perfected. Once the mind settles on the wisdom of great bliss, all the deities give rise to the pride of being inseparable from this passion.

The Offering of Liberation

Second is the offering of liberation. That which is to be liberated here is the belief in a self—the concepts associated with apprehended phenomena and apprehending thoughts. Insofar as this belief propels you into saṃsāra and prevents the realization of nondual wisdom, it is the enemy. Liberation is performed with the weapon of wisdom devoid of dualistic thoughts. It liberates dualistic fixation and desirous thoughts into unborn space. This is the meaning of the great primordial universal liberation.

Generate great compassion from within that state so that you can free all sentient beings who are among the ten objects from the unbearable suffering that results from the negative karma they accumulate. In essence, just like a trick or an optical illusion, the self and that which is to be liberated do not truly exist. With this realization you will free them and purify all your thoughts into the basic space of phenomena. Imagine that you perform this offering within the state of the single flavor of saṃsāra and nirvāṇa.

The Offering of Reality

Since saṃsāra and nirvāṇa are primordially and spontaneously present as the infinite purity of the great maṇḍala of the victorious ones, without conceptualizing the three spheres bring to mind the nature of the Great Seal and rest within that.

Praises

Here praises are offerings of vajra songs. To offer praise, imagine that goddesses emanate from your heart center and devotedly call out melodious praises enumerating the ocean of qualities of the deities of the maṇḍala, including the inconceivable secrets of their complete liberation, enlightened body, speech, and mind; their spontaneously and effortlessly accomplished enlightened activity, endowed with the five wisdoms and three bodies; the signs of the manifestation of the form bodies; and the strengths and other qualities that embody their sublime abandonment and realization. These praises should be offered with the knowledge that the object of praise and the one praising are beyond meeting and parting.

Alternatively, you may also imagine that Brahmā, Indra, and other great gods offer praise from the courtyard surrounding the celestial palace. Jigme Lingpa teaches:

> Since the purpose of offering praise is to recall purity, you should be certain of the fact that the deity does not exist in and of itself.

In this and other contexts you will find many variations on the visualizations and their order, yet these different approaches do not contradict one another. As Gotsangpa explains:

> It is not the case that, having trained in one visualization, it is unacceptable to then train in another. All of this is the display of your mind. It is, however, unacceptable to be narrow-minded, thinking things like, "This and that do not fit together." This is the most important general point.

Jigme Lingpa also notes:

> Since this is the case, you will go astray if you harbor doubts about the deity being a solid entity that can be touched and felt, and think that this one and the other cannot fit together, or that having taken up one, you must give up another. All such doubts are unnecessary!

Training in the Appearance of the Main Deity

This topic is divided into three sections: (1) vivid appearance, (2) stable pride, and (3) recollecting purity. Of these three, Getse Tulku explains that you should understand the first as the main explanation of the development stage, and the second two as subsidiary topics that will help you avoid what is unfavorable and accomplish what is favorable for the practice.

Vivid Appearance

In general, the matured practitioner should begin by placing offerings in front of an authentic painting of the deity, crafted by a skilled artisan, and do the preliminary practices in either an extensive or abbreviated form, whichever is appropriate. Then, as is taught in the *Condensed Realization of the Gurus*, visualize Guru Vajradhara—the embodiment of all refuge objects—above your head, seated on a lion throne on a lotus and on sun and moon discs. Filled with devotion, offer your body and all your wealth and enjoyments to the guru. Then offer the following supplication with one-pointed concentration: "Essence of the buddhas of the three times, truly kind precious root guru, I supplicate you. Please bless my mind, especially so that the genuine absorption of the development stage will arise in my being right now!" The guru then smiles joyfully, melts into red light, and dissolves into your crown. Mingling your mind inseparably with the guru's, rest for a while in that state.

Next, look at the image of the deity in front of you. Sometimes close your eyes and check if you can visualize the image just as clearly as when you see it. Once you are able to visualize the deity, even with your eyes closed, transfer the visualization to your own body. Work at familiarizing yourself with the visualization by alternating between periods of meditating with your eyes open and closed. Having accustomed yourself to this practice, strengthen your training by visualizing the deity as being either large or small, single or multiple, by sometimes focusing on the main deity, then sometimes on the retinue, and so forth. Likewise, alternate between visualizing the entire body of the deity all at once and visualizing each individual aspect of the body and adornments one by one.

At first keep your mind focused on the main deity alone, visualizing each and every detail, from the top of the deity's crown down to the lotus seat upon which he or she sits. Clearly visualize the color of the body, the face, hands, ornaments, garments, the pupils and whites of the eyes, the signs on the hands and feet, the appearance of the major and minor marks, the projection and absorption of light, and so forth.

The deity should not be flat like a wall painting or slightly protruding like a relief. In other words, it is neither a material entity nor insentient like a rainbow. It should be clearly defined in every respect—its front and back, left and right sides, proportions, and so forth. Yet, at the same time, it should be devoid of internal organs or any sense of materiality. Train as though the deity were actually present in the form of a body of light endowed with wisdom, knowledge, love, and capacity.

Once you are able to focus your mind on the visualization, gradually bring forth the vivid appearance of the retinue, the palace, and the arrangement of the celestial realm, all the way up to the protective dome. At times focus on the visualization as a whole; at other times focus on specific details. Training in allowing the entire supportive and supported maṇḍala to arise clearly in your mind is called "vivid appearance." This is one of the primary functions of the development stage; it is a unique method that will allow you to practice calm abiding by focusing your mind on the deity. For this very reason it is important to meditate by assiduously keeping your awareness on the vivid appearance of the deity. As you grow accustomed to this, the five experiences will arise in turn.

In this context, the specific details of the deity, such as its color and symbolic implements, can be learned from the ritual text you are using. Here I will offer a few general observations. *The Awesome Flash of Lightning* states:

> Each of their supreme forms
> Possesses nine traits:
> They are soft, well-proportioned,
> Firm, supple, and youthful;
> Clear, radiant, attractive,
> And blazing with intense presence.

These are the nine traits of peaceful deities. Their bodies are soft because they have purified pride. Having purified anger, their bodies are well-proportioned. Having purified desire, their bodies are not loose, but firm. Having purified jealousy, their bodies are straight and supple. Having purified stupidity, their bodies are youthful. Having abandoned ignorance, their bodies are clean and clear. Due to the blossoming of wisdom, their bodies are bright and radiant. Having perfected the major and minor marks, their bodies are resplendent, appealing, and, therefore, attractive. Having subjugated everything through their great qualities, they are endowed with a great intense presence. The first five of these are the essential qualities, whereas the latter four are aspectual qualities.

The deity should be seated within the expanse of clear and pure multicolored light that radiates out in the ten directions. As a sign of purifying the suffering of the negative emotions of those to be tamed, the deity wears the five silk Dharma robes made of celestial silk. As a sign of fulfilling the wishes of beings by not abandoning the sense pleasures but perfecting them as an ornament, there are eight precious ornaments. Thus, the deity is adorned with thirteen ornaments.

The five silken Dharma robes consist of a white silk shawl with golden embroidery; a *dhoti*, which is a multicolored skirt; a yellow sash or Dharma robe; a green dancing blouse that resembles a short-sleeved vest; multicolored silken streamers that are worn under the crown of the five families, and blue silken ribbons that hang down from the back. In some cases the belt or Dharma robe is omitted and the streamers and ribbons are counted separately.

The eight ornaments are a jeweled crown, earrings, a short necklace, a belt, bracelets, anklets, a long necklace that reaches below the navel and is a garland composed of jewels, and a shorter necklace that reaches to the breast. Alternatively, symbolizing the seven branches of enlightenment, the deity wears the seven precious ornaments: a crown, a long necklace, bracelets, earrings, arm bands, a medium-length necklace, and a flower garland.

Wrathful deities display the nine expressions of the dance. *The Heruka Galpo* states:

> Captivating, heroic, and terrifying,
> Laughing, ferocious, and fearful,
> Compassionate, intimidating, and tranquil:
> Assume these nine expressions of dance.

On this topic it is taught:

> Their expression of desire should be *captivating*, their expression of anger *heroic*, and their expression of stupidity *terrifying*. These are their three physical expressions. They should be laughing out loud with expressions like "ha ha" and "hee hee." They should shout *ferocious* things like "Capture! Strike!" They should also be *fearsome*, with a voice like the roaring of

> a thousand rolls of thunder and a thousand bursts of lightning occurring in a single instant. These are their three verbal expressions. They should also be *compassionate*, taking ignorant beings and realms under their care; *intimidating*, as they subdue barbaric sentient beings with their wrath; and *peaceful* in the sense that they experience everything as having the same taste within reality. These are their three mental expressions. These are the nine expressions of the dance.

With respect to ornamentation, the body of the Great Glorious One is primordially and naturally adorned with the eight glorious ornaments. A tantra explains:

> His hair streaming upward is the ornament of reversing saṃsāra. His vajra garuḍa wings are the ornament of means and knowledge. His violet vest is the ornament of having overwhelmed permanence and nihilism. The half-vajra on the crown of his head is the ornament of the family. His powerful rhinoceros-hide armor is the ornament of blazing and increasing magnificence. Being joined in indivisible union is the ornament of the wisdom consort. Being a hero, who turns back all harmful forces, he is ornamented with iron. Burning up the negative emotions, he is ornamented with the vajra fire.

Otherwise, alternatively:

> This can be presented in a slightly different manner:
> Because Hayagrīva revels in the three realms,
> His tiger skin shows his expansive heroic absorption.
> A crossed iron vajra shows that he repels all harsh negative forces.
> An entrusted vajra indicates his knowledge absorption.
> His powerful red armor shows his majestic presence.
> A black viper symbolizes his elegant heroic majesty.
> His fangs of absorption show that he is the devourer of Īśvara.

His vajra robe indicates violet.
The skin of the fierce leopard shows his magnetizing strength.

Thus, the ornaments are explained as the eight liberations.

The eight charnel-ground ornaments are as follows. The three garments consist of an upper garment of elephant skin that symbolizes having conquered stupidity by means of the ten strengths, a belt of human skin that symbolizes having conquered desire through the awakened mind, and a tiger-skin skirt that symbolizes having conquered anger through heroic, fierce, and wrathful activities. He is thus liberated. The two fastened ornaments are as follows. The snake ornaments are the white hair-ribbon of the caste of nāga kings, the yellow earrings of the caste of nobles, the red short necklace and medium-length necklace of the priestly caste, the green belt and long necklace of the commoner caste, and the black bracelet of the outcaste. The skull ornaments include a crown of five dry skulls, a long necklace of fifty fresh dripping heads, and the armbands made of skull fragments. The three smeared substances are a mass of human ashes smeared on the forehead, and drops of rakta on each cheek and on the tip of the nose. Alternatively, it is sometimes explained that there are drops of rakta on the cheeks and forehead, a drop between the eyes, and grease smeared across the throat. Adding the mass of wisdom fire and two vajra wings to these eight, there are ten glorious ornaments in all.

The light of the sun and moon, radiating from his left and right earrings, are the two ornaments of clarity. The six bone-ornaments are a necklace, representing generosity; bracelets, representing discipline; earrings, representing patience; a wheel on the crown of the head, representing diligence (this is a thousand-spoked wheel at the center of which his hair is piled in a topknot); a belt, representing meditative concentration; and a long garland called "held aloft to make offerings," representing wisdom.

The five bone-mudrās are these six, minus the long necklace. These represent the five wisdoms.

In the past, when Heruka liberated Rudra, he claimed Rudra's wrathful ornaments and wore them as a sign of his heroism. These have come to be known as the eight wrathful ornaments.

It is generally taught that wrathful ornaments are not suitable for peaceful deities, whereas peaceful ornaments are not disallowed for wrathful deities. However, although there may be slight variations in the color of the body and the ornamentation of the deity in different ritual manuals, it is, in fact, suitable for the deity to appear in whatever way accords with the wishes of those to be tamed, as the compassion and activity of the deity know no limitations. Therefore, though there is no contradiction here, it is important to follow along with the context of whatever ritual text you are using.

Also, here in the context of generating the deity, according to the *Magical Web* the deity of each single mudrā has a wisdom being similar to itself, but without any ornamentation, at its heart, the deities of the five buddha families as a crown, and the blessing deities in its three places wearing the ornaments of the enjoyment body. When these nine subsidiary deities are added to the main deity itself, this makes ten deities in all. Alternatively, because the single lord of the family on the crown embodies them all, they are counted as one. In this case the term "the body of the deity endowed with the five branches of mantra" is used.

Looking at rituals from a general perspective, the presence of the five forms of suchness is referred to as "being endowed with the five branches of mantra." These five are the suchness of the self (the self-visualization), the suchness of the deity (the form of the deity visualized in front of oneself who is invited, requested to remain, and so forth), the suchness of Secret Mantra, the suchness of recitation, and the suchness of projection and absorption. Moreover, principally the vivid arising of the deity's form is the radiance of the unfabricated basic nature. This apparent aspect is explained to be genuine vivid appearance. That being the case, the celestial palace and its deities arise solely from the great magical display of bliss, clarity, and emptiness—the magical display of the unimpeded wisdom of the main deity itself. Indeed, they are not different from it. Like a rainbow arising in a clear sky or like the planets and stars reflected in a limpid pond, your visualization appears but is not truly established. Rest while keeping in mind the dependent arising of this intrinsic nature, which can arise as any form whatsoever. This is taught to be an important point.

Stable Pride

The deities, who are the objects of meditation, are not simply supports for mental visualization; the appearance of the deity you meditate upon and you the meditator are not different. When you train without losing touch with the thought that you are the deity, this confident outlook will serve the unique function of destroying self-grasping and preventing obstacles from taking hold. On this point *The Condensed Realization* explains:

> There is no imputation
> In equipoise or subsequent attainment.
> To have stable pride is a vitally important point,
> Though your visualization may be clear or unclear.
> Think, "I am the deity,"
> And do not hold on to your ordinary perceptions.

While Tsele notes:

> It is indispensable to know how the world and its contents
> Are the primordially pure deity and mantra.

And *Resting in the Nature of Mind* explains:

> Your mind has been the nature of the deity from the start.
> Your body is the maṇḍala; and sounds and words, Secret Mantra.
> Within this great wisdom, where everything is spontaneously perfected,
> The samaya and wisdom beings are indivisible.
> There is no one to invite or who remains, nor is there any need to request someone to leave.
> Not good or bad, beyond accepting and rejecting, it has been the maṇḍala from the very start.
> In the visualization where you know this is its identity
> You are not creating something that is not already there.

As stated here, that which is to be purified is birth, death, and the intermediate state, as well as the subtle body, speech, and mind. The results of purification are the three bodies of the victorious ones. Once you have come to definitively understand that the objects of purification have the nature of the three vajras, and that they have been so from the very beginning, the temporary stains will be purified. The process of purification consists of the three samādhis and stable pride, which involves sealing appearance, sound, and awareness with the play of deity, mantra, and wisdom, while never failing to bring the three aspects of clarity onto the path.

Recollecting Purity

Such visualizations should not be clung to as true, as entities with their own characteristics. In actuality they are the self-appearances of the wisdom maṇḍala. As such they are devoid of the conceptual constructs of color, shape, face, hands, and the rest, yet the various attributes of the support and supported do manifest as signs that symbolize the qualities of self-appearing buddhahood to those who are to be tamed.

The purity of the supportive celestial mansion was briefly described above. What follows concerns the purity of the supported deity. As a symbol of all phenomena being one taste in suchness, deities have one face. Three faces symbolize the three liberations, or the three bodies. Two hands symbolize means and knowledge, while four hands symbolize the four immeasurables. Six hands can symbolize the six wisdoms (five wisdoms along with self-arisen wisdom) or the six perfections. Four legs symbolize the four means of magnetizing and two legs symbolize ethical discipline and meditative absorption. The cross-legged position symbolizes the equality of existence and peace, while the standing position symbolizes being unflagging in the service of beings. Three eyes symbolize seeing throughout the three times and four fangs symbolize uprooting the four types of birth. Male and female consorts symbolize the union of means and knowledge.

The nakedness of the female consort symbolizes the freedom from the overlay of the concepts connected with phenomenal characteristics. The consort being sixteen years of age symbolizes her being endowed with the sixteen joys pertaining to immutable great bliss. Her flowing hair symbolizes the boundless expansion of wisdom from basic space. Union with her secret space represents the fusion of calm abiding and insight.

In terms of the consort's complexions, white symbolizes being unstained by blemishes, yellow represents the development of qualities, red symbolizes the welling up of compassion, green indicates unobstructed activity, and black symbolizes the immutability of reality.

The consort's implements have symbolic values as well. The five-pronged vajra represents the five wisdoms. The wheel symbolizes cutting through the afflictive emotions. The gem represents the source of desired qualities. The lotus symbolizes remaining untainted by shortcomings. The crossed-vajra represents manifold unobstructed activities. The curved blade symbolizes severing all concepts. The skull cup represents nourishing the bliss of nonconceptual wisdom while the blood it contains symbolizes destroying the four demons. The sword represents uprooting birth and death. The khaṭvāṅga staff symbolizes uprooting the three poisons, and so forth.

The purity of their adornments was described briefly above.

The purity of appearance and existence as the individual divine maṇḍalas, in accordance with the meanings of the symbols praised above and elsewhere, is called "the phenomenal purity of gods and goddesses."

When visualizing the sporting of male and female deities in union, or when meditating upon the union of the development and completion stages, a mere semblance of great bliss may manifest by penetrating the vital points of the body during the completion stage, thereby sealing the development stage. Whatever the case, suffusing the development stage with the passion of great bliss is the purity of self-aware great bliss.

Sealing the illusionlike apparent aspect with the view of the freedom from conceptual constructs is to meditate on the unity of appearance and emptiness. This is the purity of the suchness of reality itself.

Jamyang Khyentse taught, "You are trained and habituated when the perception of each aspect of purity and its real meaning emerges naturally whenever the form of the deity is seen." Beginners, however, are not able to do this. They adhere to a belief whereby they set up the visualization of the deity and then think, "These elements are the play of great wisdom, the enlightened mind of buddhahood, manifesting as symbols that represent the qualities of enlightenment." Adhering to this belief brings about an approximation of the recollection of purity and invites the pitfall of clinging to the deity as existing in its own right.

In summary, developing your training in the illusory play of empty appearance, wherein you do not veer from the nature of the dharma body even while appearing as the form bodies, is called "recollecting purity."

In all those contexts the development stage purifies clinging to ordinary appearances and is the very goal of meditation while on the path. Thus, since the features of form, sound, smell, taste, and texture, manifesting as objects of the five sense faculties, and the features of phenomena, manifesting as mental objects, constitute "appearances," then visualizing such features as pure is taught to be what purifies them. Once the universe and its inhabitants are visualized as a celestial mansion and deities, and sounds are naturally perceived as mantra, the mind will no longer gravitate toward objects.

"Clinging" is twofold: clinging to the self and clinging to things. The first of these, clinging to self, is the self-grasping that has occurred since beginningless time, whereby you think, "I." Stable pride is taught to be the antidote to this form of clinging. With stable pride you cast off the clinging to the "I" or to the ordinary and stabilize a certainty whereby you think, "I am the yidam deity." Of clear visualization and stable pride, stable pride is more important, for without the complete conviction that you are the deity your mind will remain ordinary despite your clear visualization. This will render the practice pointless. On the other hand, when you have the pride of thoroughly believing that you are the deity, self-grasping collapses and the vivid appearance manifests automatically.

In clinging to things you cling to the universe and its inhabitants, rigidly believing they are real and permanent. This is termed the "self of phenomena." The recollection of purity is taught to be the antidote to this form of clinging. Since celestial mansions, deities, and their faces and hands are only symbolic images for the nature of the thirty-seven factors of enlightenment and the like, which are the qualities present in the enlightened mind-streams of buddhas, the recollection of purity purifies the clinging that grasps things as being truly existent.

Consequently, because this triad is crucial, train the mind by alternating between them. These are not like the dialectical vehicle, whereby you behave as though the object to be relinquished and its antidote are contradictory, as when you dissect objects into extremely subtle particles as the antidote to appearances or meditate on selflessness as the antidote to the self. On the contrary, due to the superiority of the skillful means of Secret Mantra, just as water stuck in the ear canal is flushed out by pouring in more water, and the pain from being burned by fire is treated with fire, the skillful means of mantra recitation brings about the eradication of impure concepts by meditating conceptually as the antidote to concepts—for example, developing divine appearances to remedy deluded appearances and developing divine pride to remedy selfish pride. This is why the development stage is called "skillful means." While it is said that concepts and afflictive emotions need not be relinquished, this is the intended meaning. It must be understood that such statements do not mean that concepts and afflictive emotions of an ordinary nature are not to be relinquished.

When meditating in this manner, your awareness may become unclear, or you may become lethargic and cloudy or lose your enthusiasm for meditation. If any of these occur, invigorate your awareness and expand the scope of your mind. Without confining your awareness to aspects such as the deity's form, complexion, or symbolic implements, make the universe and its inhabitants, by nature, shine and shimmer as the deities, celestial palace, and light rays. Let sounds hum in the nature of mantra and thoughts settle in the nature of suchness. Sing a song of HŪṂ. Expand and elevate your awareness, slashing to pieces the tangle of concepts. Meditate expansively and freely, relinquishing the constrictions of worrying about whether the mind is resting or not, or whether it is clear enough or not.

Should your awareness become agitated and scattered, take a short break from reciting approach mantras and the like. Expel the stale air, relax your awareness, and gaze nakedly into your own nature. Within that state, yoke your attention to the seed syllable, the life force of enlightened mind, and meditate with your mind directed there. Do not be constricted by excessive expectation and worry about whether or not the visualization is clear enough, and the like. Yet do not be lax, just paying lip service without any real regard for whether the visualization is clear or not. Rather, find a balance between being too tight and too loose. From time to time turn inward and look into the face of the very one who is engaged in deity meditation and who is concerned about the clarity of the visualization. Completely let go of any subtle concepts about there being an object to look at, a looker, and so on, and maintain a state of bare awareness, free of questioning or identifying.

In that way, train in the stake of the unchanging realization of reality and the stake of absorption in the deity, alternating between the two or integrating them according to whatever works best. In all of these contexts recite the basic approach mantra—the stake of mantra recitation—unceasingly. Whenever you are about to end a session or end an approach mantra recitation retreat, perform the projection and absorption of light rays—the stake of the enlightened activity of projection and absorption— according to the approach mantra manuals. These "four stakes that bind the life force" are the Dharma terminology of the Old School of the Early Translations. Patrul Rinpoche said that since this is a unique pith instruction from the Second Buddha of Uḍḍiyāna, it is of the utmost importance.

Likewise, it is said in a tantra:

> A practitioner who possesses this stake can practice
> An evil demon in a charnel ground, and still,
> Whichever results he seeks, supreme or mundane,
> Will automatically, spontaneously emerge.
> Without realizing this stake, he will mistake the deity
> as concrete.
> In that mindset he may practice a wisdom being,
> And perhaps reach some temporary, trifling result,
> But an authentic fruition will be nearly impossible.

According to the Early Translation School this involves seven topics. There are the five preliminary topics that elicit the five experiences. These are (1) focusing the mind on the deity; (2) correcting flaws that involve changes; (3) parting from the deity; (4) bringing the deity onto the path; and (5) merging your mind with the deity. There is also one topic that comprises the main practice: (6) connecting the deity with reality (where you train on the path of the four linked divisions of approach and accomplishment as induced by meditative absorption) and another that is the concluding topic: (7) integrating the deity onto the path (which consists of the ten things to understand, the six samaya vows, and so on).

For the first stage you meditate on a complete visualization of the deity's form, including its complexion, face, hands, adornments, and apparel, with the five sensory gates withdrawn and without letting the mind become distracted elsewhere. When meditating in this manner it may seem as though the movement of your thoughts has become even more turbulent than before. This is the experience of movement, which can be likened to how the movement of fish, otters, and other such creatures cannot be seen below a rushing waterfall, although even the tiniest pebble is visible below a gentle current. This marks the beginning of the mind becoming somewhat settled.

Subsequently, as thoughts gradually still, the deity will manifest with brilliant clarity. This is the experience of attainment.

The second stage of meditation involves explicitly targeting whatever remains unclear in one's visualization, whether it is the deity's body, complexion, face, hands, or otherwise, while at the same time not falling under the sway of the general or specific flaws. The general flaws are taught as follows:

> The seven faults are (1) forgetting the focal point, (2) laziness, (3) doubting your ability to succeed, (4) dullness, (5) agitation, (6) overexertion (being dissatisfied, even though one's visualization appears clear), (7) underexertion (leaving the visualization unclear), and so forth.
>
> There are also twelve flaws that involve fluctuations in the visualization: (1) haziness, (2) vagueness, (3) shadowy darkness, (4) changes in size, (5) changes in apparel, (6) changes in shape, (7) changes in number, (8) changes in position, (9) appearing only as colors, (10) appearing only as shapes, (11) gradual disappearance, and (12) incomplete appearance.

The third stage involves alternating between sessions whereby you meditate diligently and without distraction by focusing the mind on the deity and sessions whereby you sustain the nature of things by looking into the very nature of the one who is meditating.

The fourth stage involves the continuous manifestation of the deity's appearance through meditating while altering the size, expressions, and other aspects of the deity. This is the riverlike experience of familiarity.

The fifth stage involves not separating from the vivid appearance of the deity, whereby one settles into a state of meditative equipoise in which the deity that one is meditating upon and the one who is meditating are nondual. This is the mountainlike experience of stability. In this context there are four measures of clarity. The deity should be clear, insofar as the apparent aspect of its enlightened body is visualized in precise detail, down to the pupils of its eyes. The deity should appear lucidly present, rather than clouded by one's experience of dullness devoid of the crisp clarity of awareness. It should possess the vitality of awareness, which is clear, empty, and vividly awake. It should be vibrant, since deities are not rainbowlike forms of lifeless matter, but are suffused with the wisdom of omniscience down to the very pores of their bodies and the strands of hair on their heads. This, in turn, causes them to manifest with brilliant presence, with hundreds of qualities, in conjunction with the sensory cognitions. Moreover, the deity should manifest vividly since the intellect cannot infer that such deities exist in a certain way. Rather, they manifest vividly as though they are directly present before the mind.

There are also four measures of stability. Rather than being subject to our forgetfulness, laziness, and so on, the visualization should remain unswayed by the general flaws. It should also be unchanged by specific faults, like haziness, vagueness, and the like. Moreover, once the visualization is clear, without even subtle concepts stirring, and not for just a short period, but when you rest in meditative equipoise day and night, it is totally unchanging. Complete malleability refers to one having gained mastery over each element of the meditation, be it the form of the deity's body, its complexion, face, hands, or movements, the projection and absorption of light rays, and so on. By unflaggingly meditating on these eight measures of clarity and stability, whatever appears dawns as the maṇḍala of the deity. This is the measure of attaining complete stability, the experience of perfection, which is referred to as "the wheel of divine appearance."

The sixth stage involves training on the path linked with the "four divisions of approach and accomplishment" by means of the pith instructions of the "four stakes that bind the life force" and in connection with the three meditative absorptions. The division of approach is the stake of absorption. The division of close approach is the stake of the essence mantra. The division of accomplishment is the stake of unchanging realization. The division of great accomplishment is the stake of the activity of projection and absorption. The four stakes that bind the life force are referred to as such because they are like stakes that bind all dualistic pairs into the singularity of nondual wisdom.

The "stake of meditative absorption in the deity" involves fully performing all facets of conferring empowerments, sealing, and the like while meditating, by means of the three meditative absorptions, on the universe and its inhabitants as the illusionlike empty appearance of the divine maṇḍala. In terms of saṃsāra, this purifies and refines away the habitual patterns of the body as they relate to the four modes of birth. In terms of buddhahood, the fruition will be perfected in the ground. Here the fruition refers to the secret of enlightened body, which is beyond conceptual constructs yet appears as manifestations of whatever is needed to tame beings. In terms of the path, the pure element of the channels will be refined into the deity. This, in turn, will mature you for the completion stage wherein the vital points of the vajra body are penetrated.

The "stake of the essence mantra" is to perform recitation with the mind focused on the absorption being, the life force of enlightened mind present in the form of a seed syllable in the heart of the wisdom being which is surrounded by the mantra garland. In terms of saṃsāra, this purifies the habitual patterns of deluded speech. In terms of buddhahood, the fruition will be perfected in the ground. Here the fruition is the secret of enlightened speech, which transcends sound and expression yet manifests as the inconceivable number of vehicles. In terms of the path, this stake refines the nature of verbal winds into the essence mantra. This, in turn, will mature you for the completion stage based on the winds, as is taught in the father tantras.

When meditating on any deity or mantra, the "stake of unchanging realization" refers to abiding in the dimension of suchness that transcends the intellect—all divisive, dualistic clinging is primordially purified and perfected in the vajra maṇḍala of the basic space of purity and equality. In terms of saṃsāra, this purifies negative mindsets, along with their habitual patterns. In terms of buddhahood, this perfects the fruition in ground. Here the fruition is the secret vajra of enlightened mind, which transcends conception and expression yet is the inconceivable wisdom of omniscience. From the perspective of the path, you will gain familiarity with the reality of nondual appearance and emptiness. This, in turn, will mature you for meditation on the completion stage of bliss, clarity, and emptiness.

The "stake of projection and absorption" involves achieving the twofold benefit by projecting infinite multicolored light rays from the deity's body and mantra garland, while the entire universe and its inhabitants remain unwavered from their nature of deity, mantra, and wisdom. Through this you will attain the supreme accomplishment; provisionally, you will attain the four activities—pacifying through white light rays, enriching through yellow light rays, and so forth—as well as the eight mundane accomplishments.

From the perspective of saṃsāra, this cleanses away and purifies saṃsāric activities associated with body, speech, and mind. From the perspective of buddhahood, the activities of all aspects of enlightened body, speech, and mind are perfected within the ground. From the perspective of the path, this will mature you for the common path with reference points and the realization of wisdom without reference points, which purifies all that appears and exists into a body of light.

Here the stake of unchanging realization is the view and, hence, the ground. The stake of absorption in the deity is meditation, as is the stake of the essence mantra. Indirectly, those two are also conduct and, hence, the path. The stake of projection and absorption is the enactment of buddha activity beginning from the present. Hence, it is the fruition. Thus, since here you train on a path in which view, meditation, conduct, and fruition (or ground, path, and fruition) are an undifferentiated and indivisible union, this is referred to as "the fruitional vehicle."

To elaborate, through the view of the ground, the circle of wisdom, you realize saṃsāra and nirvāṇa to be equality and thereby gain mastery over the life force of both peace and existence. Meditating on the path, the circle of deity and mantra, confers mastery over the life force of both development and completion stages. Spontaneously accomplishing the twofold benefit confers mastery over the life force of inconceivable great skillful means. Each one of these, moreover, possesses multiple crucial features and includes all of the essential points found in the path of the vajra vehicle of Secret Mantra.

In particular, Patrul Rinpoche has said that, since the stake of unchanging realization binds within it the life forces of the other three, it is especially important. It is also stated in a tantra:

> If the four stakes that bind the life force are not planted,
> Practice will never be fruitful, like running in place.

Here "running in place" stands for stationary feet. It is taught as an example for the futility of being without the crucial points of the four stakes, such that you are only exhausted no matter how frantically you move.

The seventh topic will be explained below [see p. 96].

Generally, in terms of the four divisions of approach and accomplishment, there are four divisions of approach and accomplishment in the context of accomplishment, four divisions of approach and accomplishment that are explained to provide a structure that subsumes the development stage, four divisions of approach and accomplishment that are explained as a structure that subsumes the completion stage, and four divisions of approach and accomplishment explained as a structure that subsumes both the development and completion stages.

From among these, here I shall discuss the four divisions of approach and accomplishment that relate to the context of accomplishment. Since that, too, is divided into the pair of approach and accomplishment, there are four divisions of approach. Thus, Khenpo Pema Dorje has said, "You should understand that there are four divisions of approach and accomplishment that pertain to the context of practice: the approach of approach, the close approach of approach, the accomplishment of approach, and the great accomplishment of approach." Alternatively, it is said in a tantric commentary:

> There are four divisions of approach and accomplishment in the context of the path: the absorptions of suchness and total illumination are the approach, the single and complex seals are the close approach, and group assembly practice is the accomplishment. From this point on, until you reach the levels of the four knowledge holders that result from the practice, is the great accomplishment.

There are also four divisions of approach and accomplishment in the context of union. Seeking a consort and adorning her with the accoutrements is the approach. Conferring blessing on her is the close approach. Causing seminal fluid to flow downward and retaining it based on sexual play is the accomplishment. Reversing its flow and evenly dispersing it is great accomplishment.

In the context of practice, these four divisions of approach and accomplishment are as follows. From gathering the causes and conditions up until commencing the accomplishment practice is called the "approach." The first fortnight of practice is called the "close approach." The latter half of the retreat, excluding the final day, is called the "accomplishment." Receiving the spiritual accomplishments on the final night is called the "great accomplishment."

Alternatively, in the context of great accomplishment practice, the approach involves preparing the accomplishment substances and so forth on the first day through the point where you perform the ritual once. The close approach is to perform the visualization of purifying misdeeds and obscurations by projecting and absorbing white rays of light. This phase lasts for half the total number of days in which the practice is to be performed. Accomplishment is to visualize the absorption of the supreme and mundane spiritual accomplishments into you by means of the projection and absorption of red light. This lasts for the remainder of the time in which the accomplishment is to be performed. Great accomplishment involves receiving the spiritual accomplishments on the final day.

One can also connect these four with a single session of a ritual. Here the approach involves the stages up through the point where you meditate on the three samādhis. Close approach involves meditating on you as the central deity. Accomplishment involves meditating on the entire assembly of retinue deities. Great accomplishment involves conferring empowerment, sealing, inviting, and so on up to recitation, presenting offerings, praise, and so forth.

Alternatively, it is also said that the approach involves focusing the mind on the central deity. Close approach involves focusing the mind on the central deity with its entire retinue. Accomplishment involves applying yourself to uttering recitations. Great accomplishment involves projecting and absorbing light rays. Since these presentations do contain slight differences, here I have presented them merely as a supplementary discussion.

To summarize, as stated by Jigme Lingpa, these four are illustrated by the example of gaining familiarity with a powerful object. He states:

> Approach is when your being gets closer to the wisdom that you want to reach. Close approach involves mingling the deity's enlightened mind and your own ordinary mind. Accomplishment involves gaining mastery over the wisdom that you have approached. Great accomplishment, which is primarily for the benefit of others, involves accomplishing the fourfold activities.

Moreover, when gathering the accumulations in conjunction with a reparation ritual, or when performing accomplishment and great accomplishment practices, you must visualize the deity in front of you. When conferring empowerment, guiding the deceased, and performing other elements for the welfare of others, you must also develop the vase as the deity. Thus, performing the self-, frontal, and vase visualizations together within the context of a single ritual is a feature unique to the highest yoga tantras of the Nyingma School of mantra.

To elaborate, in the context of ritual practice, with the same sweeping movement you develop yourself as the deity and visualize the deity in front of yourself without viewing these two as different. Next, at the conclusion of the praise, you say, "BHRŪṂ VIŚVA . . . ," up to "PHAṬ

JA." Here, with the syllable PHAṬ, the maṇḍala of the wisdom deity separates from the circle of yourself as the samaya being and is projected out in front of you. JA stabilizes the flaming mountains that surround the two maṇḍalas such that they touch. On this point, Minling Terchen taught:

> For example, just as the reflection of a single face can appear in two separate mirrors, everything is, in essence, identical yet appears like a mirror and its multitude of reflections due to the play of wisdom. Thus, within one protective dome, together with the elements layered one atop the other, you should simultaneously visualize yourself as the deity and also project it in front of you. The flaming mountains that surround both of their celestial mansions should touch one another.

While doing so, develop the vase deity in the empty space of the foyer to the east of the deity projected in the foreground. Whenever the ritual vase is needed for a particular circumstance, it should be visualized in front of you.

Alternatively, Karma Chagme taught that the deity in the foreground is developed within the charnel ground that surrounds the self-visualization. The protective dome, vajra enclosure, and fiery mountains that surround the self-visualization are spherical like a tent. Within that, you meditate on the vajra enclosure and fiery mountains like an iron fence encircling the front visualization.

Alternatively, in the New Schools the self- and front visualizations are developed separately, in succession, using different rituals.

It is said that, in the context of developing just yourself as the deity, this central deity, who is the support of the practice, is generally made up of your own aggregates, elements, and sense faculties. Even while developing the deity, the form aggregate is itself visualized as the celestial mansion. It is not as though you must newly transform your shape and meditate upon it as a celestial mansion.

In this manner, whether you are practicing self- or front visualization, during the main part of the development stage, the deity should be brought forth from within the practice of the samādhi of suchness by the compassion of the samādhi of total illumination. Without disconnecting these two, you should elicit the vivid appearance of the development-stage deity as much as possible. It does not suffice to only meditate on the samādhis of suchness and total illumination first, and then cast them aside.

The inseparability of the samādhi of suchness and the vivid appearance of the deity is the unity of clarity and emptiness, the indivisibility of profundity and clarity, or the unity of development and completion. That unity, inseparable from the momentum of compassion, constitutes the main practice of the path of the Great Vehicle. This is what we refer to as "emptiness with a core of compassion."

Thus, there is nothing more important than the two samādhis of suchness and total illumination, in that the unity of the two bodies, the two accumulations, the two truths, and means and knowledge should be understood as a unique feature of the profound and swift path of mantra.

Without understanding this point you may believe that the development stage, in and of itself, is an actual entity with its own characteristics. When this is the case, no matter how clear the appearance or how stable the divine pride, it will not become the path to enlightenment. On top of that, it will become a formidable obstacle that will bind you to saṃsāra. Even vicious demons have trained their minds in deity meditation yet failed to conjoin their training with the mind of awakening. Meditating with the belief that peaceful deities exist, in their own right, will cause you to be reborn as a god in the form realm, while meditating on wrathful ones with this belief will cause you to end up like the yogi in India who, after practicing Vajrabhairava, grew fangs and developed a layer of nine boils in the form of nine heads. Similarly, it is said in *The Root Tantra of Mañjuśrī* that this belief will cause you to be reborn as a demon or the lord of death in the guise of whichever deity you have meditated upon. You should have conviction that if your anger or passion increases by meditating on deities with wrathful or passionate expressions, then your practice has not become an authentic path.

Therefore, it is said to be very important to connect the deity to the meaning of the statement:

Best is the powerful deity of the view.
Mediocre is the strong deity of the remedy.
And least is the subjugating wisdom deity.

Likewise, it is necessary to connect all enlightened activities to the four gates of Secret Mantra scripture, which are taught as follows:

Reminding yourself of the ultimate meaning is the gate of expressive words.
Invoking the essence of the yidam is the gate of Secret Mantra.
Single-pointed visualization is the gate of mental meditative absorption.
Symbolic signs are the gate of mudrā and dance.

Thus, when reciting the words of the development stage visualization ritual step-by-step, do not be distracted elsewhere. Rather, recite slowly and, with each and every word, do not separate the visualization from the recitation. If you happen to get temporarily distracted, go back and do it again from the beginning. It is said that doing so will help you to avoid getting distracted from that point on.

When you have become exhausted with meditating one-pointedly on the clarity, purity, and stability of the development stage, you should engage in recitation. *The Thunder of the Precious Tantra of Enlightened Speech* states:

If practitioners with devotion and samaya vows
Wish for the supreme accomplishment,
And want to mingle indivisibly with the wisdom deity,
They should exert themselves in mantra.

Enlightened Speech

The second main point concerns the recitation practice of enlightened speech. The general understanding of this practice is as follows. The object of purification is our ordinary impure and confused speech, expressions, and meanings, along with all our habitual tendencies to ascribe reality to them. The process of purification, emphasizing mantra recitation, is the mantra that you continuously repeat and recite. This, in turn, establishes an interdependent connection with the result of purification, working for the welfare of others via the enlightened activity of vajra speech.

The specific purpose of this practice is to call out to the wisdom deities, just as a person will naturally come closer if you call out his or her name. *The Condensed Realization* states:

> The deity is like a companion that you search for in order to accomplish a given task. The mantra is like calling out to someone, saying, "Hey, my friend . . ."

A vajra song explains:

> The buddhas, bodhisattvas,
> Ḍākinīs, and your own queen—
> To bring them right before you
> Invoke them with mantra.

In essence, knowledge mantras have the nature of wisdom, and are the vajra speech of the buddhas. You meditate on the form of the ordinary syllables that resemble these knowledge mantras with the conviction that they are wisdom knowledge mantras. Doing so, they are recited continuously. In Sanskrit this is referred to as *jap*; this is the essence of recitation.

Moreover, as you develop the vivid appearance of the deity, picture yourself as the samaya being. In the jewel *citta* of your heart visualize a sphere of light that resembles a crystal dome. It is luminous, clear, and without any obscuring overlay. In the middle of this sphere is a seat made of layered sun and moon discs. This is where the wisdom being sits. The wisdom being resembles the samaya being, yet is bereft of ornaments and symbolic implements. In its heart center is a symbolic implement, which has within it a seat made of either a single sun disc or moon disc. Alternatively, the seat may be layered with both. In either case, the seat should be the size of a split pea. Upon it sits the absorption being, the root life force of enlightened mind, such as a HRĪḤ or HŪṂ syllable. The same color as the deity, this syllable should be as fine as though it were drawn with a single hair and as bright and dazzling as a candle flame. It should also be standing upright and face the same direction as the deity.

Although the three beings are tiered, it is said that you should not harbor distorted thoughts about them resembling containers stacked within one another. Moreover, the texts vary on this point—sometimes there are three beings in tiers and sometimes not, so you should follow the scripture of the ritual that you are performing.

The Tantra of Enlightened Body states:

> Since you and whatever appears from you
> Abide within a single samaya vow,
> The apparition is known as the samaya being.

As stated here, the term "samaya" is used since you visualize your body, speech, and mind as the deity's body, speech, and mind and subsequently do not break that visualization. The term "being" is used since you visualize the deity and abandon ordinary wrong views. Again, *The Tantra of Enlightened Body* explains:

> Since it appears as the king of awareness, primordial wisdom,
> It is the wisdom being.

While *The Garland of Light* says:

> It is called "wisdom" because it unmistakenly knows the primordial nature.

Moreover, according to Padma Mati, "wisdom" refers to knowing that the three bodies are primordially in-dwelling, while "being" indicates that you are free from the wrong view of dualism. Similarly, "absorption" connotes the method, or basis, for resting the mind one-pointedly and without distraction, while "being" refers to not being oppressed by dullness, agitation, and other such faults.

According to Karma Chagme, the syllable of the life force of enlightened mind faces forward. However, the intent of the Lord Guru is what I have just explained.

Styles of Recitation

For mantras that spin in a clockwise direction, the syllables begin in front of the life force of enlightened mind and face outward. They should be arranged from left to right, as though you could read them from the outside, with the letters standing upright and circling to the right like a chain. The first syllable, such as OṂ, should be connected to HŪṂ, HRĪḤ, or whatever the last syllable happens to be. As a skillful way to deal with long mantras, the first syllable of the mantra must be visualized right in front of the life force of enlightened mind with the other syllables following neatly after it in two or three outer rings, like a coiled snake.

When reciting mantras, the mantra chain should spin clockwise as though it were being read from the outside. Other mantra chains spin in a counterclockwise direction. With these, the syllables are visualized standing upright, beginning in front of the life force of enlightened mind as was the case above. The syllables should face inwards and be arranged from right to left, as if read from the inside. Long mantras circle from the inside out, just as above, but when chanted they spin in a counterclockwise direction. This is how it is explained in *Husks of Unity*.

Generally speaking, for male deities the mantra spins clockwise and for female deities counterclockwise. This is not always the case, however, so you should follow the approach of your own practice text. There are also other key points concerning visualizations that are meant to protect or repel, but these should be studied in their own contexts. It is also said that the more finely you can visualize the syllables of the life force of enlightened mind and the mantra chain, the better it will be for your concentration.

The considerations related to the intent of recitation are threefold: (1) silent recitation, (2) mental recitation, and (3) verbal recitation.

Silent recitation involves concentrating one-pointedly on the spinning of the mantra chain around the life force of enlightened mind while arresting the movement of the breath. In this way, you merely keep the intermediate breath smooth and balanced, without harming your health. Once the breath is exhaled, the life force of enlightened mind and the mantra chain emit five-colored light in the shape of a long braided string that emerges from the two nostrils, purifying all that appears and exists into a pure realm. As you inhale, all animate and inanimate objects—the world and its inhabitants—melt completely into five-colored light that enters the two nostrils and dissolves back into the mantra chain and the life force of enlightened mind. As the breath rests within, the intermediate breath is held and your awareness mingles indivisibly with the mantra chain. Such is the training in silent recitation.

Next, concentrate on the self-resounding tune emitted by the mantra chain and perform an exclusively mental recitation of the root mantra without any omissions or additions.

Finally, perform the verbal recitation. *The Awesome Flash of Lightning* states:

> The voice should be neither loud nor quiet,
> Not fast and not slow, nor rough or weak.
> Enunciate the syllables in their entirety.
> There should be no distraction or idle talk,
> Nor interruptions by yawning and the like.

Those are the ten faults of recitation that you must avoid. *The Condensed Realization* speaks in similar terms:

> When performing verbal mantra recitation, you should avoid an overly drawn-out pronunciation, which will strain your breath and interrupt your speech. Your recitation should also not be overly rushed as your breath will then lose its vigor, which, in turn, leads to a shortened lifespan or a dull complexion. If you recite too intensely, your health will be damaged. If your recitation is rough, you may harm nonhuman beings or cause them to faint, so avoid this fault as well. If your recitation is too weak, the mantra will lose its strength and delay

> its effectiveness, so avoid that. You should not take too much time with the recitation either, as the number of repetitions will be too few. If you rush the recitation, the words will not be pronounced properly and you will end up missing or adding words.

Hence, give up these six faults while you recite. *The Tantra of the Precious Thunder Roar* mentions:

> Consuming garlic is a nine-day setback.
> Consuming rasana is a twenty-one-day setback.
> Eating ginger is a three-day setback.
> Meat and alcohol that are not consecrated set you back by five days.
> Lies, gossip, and other
> Negative verbal acts
> Will permanently destroy the mantra's potency
> Or greatly delay the goal.
> Blessing worldly ones with your breath
> Must be avoided as it destroys the mantra's potency.

Avoid these general and specific faults, and recite clearly, correctly, and in a pleasant tone.

As you recite the mantra, focus your mind on the seed syllable surrounded by the mantra chain that rests in your heart center, and then recite the mantra as though you are reading. This is known as "the arranged recitation" or "the recitation that resembles a moon with a garland of stars." This style of recitation refers to the branch of approach. Sometimes it is taught that the recitation that resembles a moon with a garland of stars refers to focusing on the syllable and mantra chain while it is raised above the seat and spinning while resounding with its own sound. However, the intent of the tantras and the masters is as I have mentioned here.

The recitation of close approach is similar to a spinning firebrand. Here you visualize a second mantra chain being projected from the mantra chain in the heart center. The syllables stand upright and are stacked on top of each other, one above the other, like a chain. They touch one another to form a continuous chain, but are not joined. Resounding with its own sound, the mantra first emerges from the mouth of the wisdom being and then from the mouth of the samaya being before entering the mouth of the consort. It travels through the interior of the consort's body to the secret space where it reenters the samaya being through the passage of his jewel. Finally, as the essence of great bliss of the mind of awakening, it is reabsorbed into the life force of enlightened mind, bringing you all the supreme and common spiritual accomplishments without exception. Then maintain the recitation while visualizing that the mantra continues to spin as just described.

Alternatively, when the samaya and wisdom beings are separated, you should use the following visualization. First, the mantra chain emerges from your mouth and enters the mouth of the wisdom being in front of you. It then emerges from the navel of the wisdom being and enters your own navel. It is sometimes said that only the mantra's light spins, not the actual mantra chain. For all practices that involve a front visualization, the recitation should be applied in this manner. It should only be the mantra's light that is projected and absorbed in this exchange between yourself and the front visualization.

For accomplishment, we have the recitation that is intended to be like a king's messenger. Here light is projected from the seed syllable in the heart center. Gradually it reaches the retinue and invokes their wisdom minds. Light is then projected again from the mantra chain such that it pervades all of space. The light brings pleasing offerings to all the buddhas, thereby perfecting the two accumulations. All their blessings and spiritual accomplishments then take the form of light and dissolve into you. In this way you obtain the four empowerments, purify the four obscurations, and actualize the four bodies. This is known as "the recitation that gathers blessings for your own benefit." Light then projects out again, this time touching all six types of sentient beings throughout space. Imagine that this light purifies all their karmic actions and disturbing emotions, along with their latent tendencies, so that their body, speech, and mind are enlightened as the essence of the three vajras. This is referred to as "the activity recitation that benefits others."

The recitation of great accomplishment is likened to a broken beehive. Here limitless light rays stream forth from the deity and the mantra chain, cleansing and purifying the obscurations of the six types of beings. This transforms the world into a celestial palace and all beings into deities, forming the maṇḍala of the yidam deity. All sounds become the natural sound of mantra, humming like a broken beehive. All of the mind's thoughts and memories become the play of the dharma body, the wisdom of bliss, clarity, and nonconceptuality. Reciting within this nondual state is known as "the recitation beyond self and other."

In general, visualizing the projection and absorption of light takes place in the following way. First, light streams forth from the mantra chain in the heart center and emerges from the crown protuberance, the hair between the eyebrows, the tongue, the endless knot at the heart center, the pores of the skin, and other such places. The light pervades all the realms in the ten directions, such as our present billionfold world system. At the tip of the light rays are an inconceivable number of male and female bodhisattvas who bring forth offering clouds, songs of praise, showers of flowers, and streams of perfume. They make these offerings to all the buddhas and bodhisattvas and sing their praises, entreating them to accomplish the welfare of sentient beings. They all then assume the form of yidam deities of various sizes and appearances, arising as a display that guides those in need. Then all the deities project divine bodies and light from their navels, secret places, hips, knees, soles of their feet with thousand-spoked wheels, and other such places. This display utterly fills the entire world, which resounds with the sound of mantra. In this way, the karmic actions, disturbing emotions, and deluded perceptions, along with all habitual tendencies, of all six types of beings in the three realms are purified, like frost melted by sunlight. Everyone transforms into the form of the yidam deity and the mantra resounds on its own, humming like bees from a broken hive.

Once again the light rays gather back, bringing with them all the qualities of the knowledge, love, and ability of the victorious ones and their offspring. The entire visualization of the world and its beings as the pure circle gathers in the form of buddhas, syllables, symbolic implements, and light. It enters the root maṇḍala and the central deity through the pores in the skin and dissolves into the life force of enlightened mind. As that happens, all concepts of saṃsāra and nirvāṇa and self and other mingle indivisibly as one taste within the state of awareness wisdom. In this way the deity, appearances, and reality become one. This is an important point to observe, as taught by Khenpo Pema Dorje. The specific visualizations for each of the four activities should be performed as described in each individual scripture.

In short, you must possess the absorption of clearly visualizing the deity (the seal of the enlightened body), the genuine recitation of the Secret Mantra (the Dharma seal of enlightened speech), and the realization of everything as being unborn (the samaya seal of enlightened mind).

As there is no fixed rule that you must incorporate these four styles of recitation in a single ritual, it will suffice to link this description with the actual description of the visualization for the recitation as it is found in your individual practice text. In any case, according to Patrul Rinpoche, when you chant the mantra it is very beneficial and effective to imagine that the syllables of the mantra naturally hum their particular sounds, that the hosts of deities chant the mantra, and that all the worlds and their inhabitants, including all fauna and flora, become the nature of the deity and hum with the sound of the mantra.

As a beginner you should begin by focusing on the mantra chain as you chant the mantra. Develop the confidence that you are the deity and, as you recite, for each spin of the mantra chain refresh the visualization of the deity. Once you have gotten used to that, you can gradually train in the other aspects, such as the projection and absorption of light. Having completed the approach in this manner, you can practice the visualization and recitation of accomplishment. *The Key Instructions of the Single Sphere of Purity* explain:

> In one session, focus your mind on the deity.
> In one session, recite the secret mantra.
> In one session, follow the movement of the breath.
> In one session, apply the key point of direct perception—
> Uncontrived awareness, the Ever-excellent One.

The Great One from Uḍḍiyāna says:

> Recite with undistracted concentration.
> Should you become distracted elsewhere,
> Even reciting for an eon will bring no result.

The Secret Tantra says:

> Recitation that is corrupted by drowsiness and dullness
> Will cause the obstacle of malevolent spirits to enter.
> Recitation that is based on a misguided intention
> Will never become a path to enlightenment.

The Tantra of the Layered Lotus Stems states:

> The vitality of absorption, mantra, and recitation
> Mutually give rise to one another.
> So to have immaculate clarity, purity, and expression is important,
> As it results in the accomplishment of all that you wish.

As these verses mention, it is very important to maintain mindfulness and introspection during all deity meditations and mantra recitations. *The Condensed Realization* says:

> Good actions mixed with negativity
> Are like water running under hay—
> You risk not noticing your own confusion.
> Thus, at times reflect on the way you are,
> And consider the paths that result from good and bad.
> Short sessions, repeated often, agree with both the outer
> and the inner.
> Rest in the genuine natural state.

Moreover, the way to recite is described in *The Gradual Path*:

> Abandon the ten faults and, based on the three ways,
> Complete the number of recitations.

The ten faults were described above. The three ways refer to the recitation styles of (1) the threefold visualization, (2) the outer, inner, and secret ways, and (3) the three subtle ones.

The "recitation of threefold visualization" refers to imagining (1) you as the one who projects and reabsorbs, (2) the front visualization as that which receives the projection, and (3) light as the projection that passes in between. This is mentioned in *The Gradual Path*:

> Reciting to the wisdom being elevated before you
> Takes place with the threefold visualization.

With PHAṬ JAḤ you open up the maṇḍala of the wisdom being in the space before you, complete as the support and the supported. Light projects out from the heart center of yourself (visualized as the samaya being) and then returns, going back and forth like a spinning firebrand. As it revolves, the sound of the mantra resounds like the roar of a thousand thunderclaps. As you visualize this, perform the recitation within the state of the indivisibility of sound and emptiness.

Next are the outer, inner, and secret recitation styles. The outer recitation begins by opening the wisdom and samaya maṇḍalas. Next you recite the mantra while the projection and absorption of light take place, circling out from the mouths of the central deities and back through the pathway of the secret vajra. Alternatively, as the light is projected out, it initiates the purification of obscurations and, as it returns, makes you a suitable recipient for the spiritual accomplishments since the obscurations have been purified.

The inner recitation can be performed regardless of whether the maṇḍala of the wisdom being has been opened or not. Here light is projected out, thereby invoking the spiritual accomplishments. As it returns, you imagine that the spiritual accomplishments are attained.

In the secret recitation light is not projected out and only the spiritual accomplishments are absorbed. Alternatively, you can also visualize that the light circles out through the male deity's mouth and into the female deity's mouth before returning back through her secret space.

The recitation of the three subtle ones is as follows. When performing the projection and absorption, you project and absorb minute syllables, symbolic implements, and divine bodies. Alternatively, you may also perform the vajra recitation.

Moreover, there are also the recitation styles of (1) the voice, (2) the form, (3) the practice, and (4) the vajra. "Voice" refers to the various verbal recitation styles, such as the spinning firebrand, which were covered above. It may also involve the recitations of projection and absorption or those of the samaya being, the wrathful style, and that of the palanquin. "Form recitation" refers to recollecting the appearance of the deity. Practice recitation takes place by directing your mind to suchness. Vajra recitation is fourfold, as expressed in *The Prophecy of Realization*:

> Expressions, with focal point,
> Symbolic, and ultimate.

First, the "vajra recitation with expression" refers to verbally reciting the three syllables. Next, the vajra recitation with a focal point refers to meditating on the shape and color of the three letters. The "symbolic vajra recitation" refers to imagining the exhalation, inhalation, and resting of the breath as the melodies of the three syllables, and to thereby recite with the knowledge that the breath and mantra are indivisible. Finally, the "ultimate vajra recitation" refers to the realization that all names, words, and expressions are illusory by their very nature. This realization occurs by recognizing that the exhalation, inhalation, and resting of the breath, as well as your body, speech, and mind, are inseparable from the Great Seal.

The Rosary

At this point, the rosary for counting the mantras should be mentioned. The Great Master explains:

For a rosary the best substances are jewels.
Seeds that come from trees are second-best.
The lowest are clay, stones,
And the nine types of medicine.

Conch makes for peaceful rosaries
And is recommended for pacifying activities.
Golden rosaries are used for enriching activities,
While rosaries of coral accomplish magnetizing activities.

Rosaries of iron and turquoise are for wrathful activities.
Zi and agate are auspicious for various activities.
Clay and seeds are used for pacifying activities.
Apricot seeds accomplish enriching activities.

Soapberry is auspicious for magnetizing activities.
Nāga, garuḍa beak, and rakṣa are recommended
As rosaries for wrathful activities,
While bodhi seeds are auspicious for all.

Rosaries of bodhi tree and the kyenyen tree
Are auspicious rosaries for pacifying activities.
Mulberry and other fruit trees make rosaries
That accomplish enriching activities.

Rosaries of red sandalwood and tamarisk
Are recommended for magnetizing activities.
Teak and thorns are wrathful trees.
Rosaries of barlo tree

Are recommended for all activities.
Ivory rosaries accomplish all activities.
Clay balls make peaceful rosaries.
For enriching, stone rosaries are auspicious.

Rosaries of medicine accomplish magnetizing activities,
While rosaries of the great bone, such as skull,
Will accomplish wrathful activities.
Rosaries composed of a mixture
Are said to accomplish all activities.

In this way, certain substances and colors of rosaries are said to be auspicious for each of the four types of activity. In particular, the verse states that bodhi seeds are auspicious for all. Moreover, in terms of the way that rosaries multiply the effects of mantra recitation, it is said that the bodhi seed multiplies infinitely. Since the bodhi seed is auspicious for both peaceful and wrathful recitations, it is praised as the supreme substance.

You should not use a rosary that has been obtained from the hand of someone who has committed any of the actions with immediate retribution, nor from a butcher, samaya breaker, murderer, widow, or thief. This also applies to rosaries that have been obtained through robbery, offered to a deity by another, taken from a deity's ornaments, have an unsuitable number of beads, have been burnt by fire, stepped over by an animal, or nibbled on by birds or mice. It is said that such rosaries should be avoided since their use will lead to a lapse in the samaya vows related to mantra.

Instead, you should use a rosary made from a suitable substance and then wash it in water. You should also anoint it with the substances of a cow and perfume, as described in *The Root Tantra of Mañjuśrī*. *The Tantra of the Natural Arising of Awareness* explains:

For the rosary join three, five, or nine strings,
Symbolizing the three bodies, five families, and nine vehicles.
The knots are tied in three tiers, symbolizing the three bodies.

As stated here, even the string for the rosary must be made of threads that are suitable for the four kinds of activities. For example, for wrathful activity it is said that the string should be made of threaded intestines, tendons, and the like. *The Condensed Realization* explains:

> In all cases the thickness of the string
> Should fit the hole in the beads—
> Not too thick, not too thin;
> Not too long, not too short.
> If too thin, the activity will not succeed.
> If too thick, faults and obstacles will interfere.
> If too long, the deities are delayed and accomplishments fade.
> If too short, your life force will be impaired.
> If tangled, knotted, and uneven,
> Misfortune will follow.
> All these details should be understood.

The same scripture continues:

> If the string should break,
> Replace it swiftly, within a day.

The way to plait the threads is mentioned in *The Saṃbhuṭi Tantra*:

> The seeds of the Sanskrit alphabet
> Are strung with the thread of HŪṂ.

Thus, it is said that you should imagine that the thread of the rosary is the central deity and that the rosary that surrounds it is of the retinue of deities. You should also string the rosary while singing the syllable HŪṂ in a melodious manner. *The Condensed Realization* states:

> On the rosary of various activities are the central beads—
> The seal of enlightened body, speech, and mind.

As stated here, the central beads represent the three vajras of enlightened body, speech, and mind. It is said that the top bead should be blue, the middle red, and the bottom white.

A rosary with these qualities must then be consecrated. The way to do so is described in the following passage from *The Explanation of the Condensed Realization*:

> With the central beads in the middle standing upright, place the rosary in your left hand like a coiled snake.

As the text says, first bless your hands, then say and imagine the following:

> In the palm of the right hand is a sun disc marked with a HŪṂ.
>
> In the palm of the left hand is a moon disc marked with an ĀḤ.
>
> Next, with divine pride, purify all concepts of the rosary as being ordinary with the mantra OṂ SVABHĀVA ŚUDDHAḤ SARVADHARMĀḤ SVABHĀVA ŚUDDHO 'HAṂ. Imagine that a lotus with a seat of sun and moon discs appears within the state of emptiness. On this seat the central beads transform into the central yidam deity through instantaneous recollection and the rosary becomes the surrounding retinue. The seed syllables at the three places then project light, inviting wisdom beings that resemble the samaya being. With the mantra DZAḤ HŪṂ BAṂ HOḤ the wisdom being dissolves indivisibly into the samaya being and the seven vajra qualities become naturally and spontaneously present. The thus-gone ones, accompanied by their retinue of bodhisattva heirs, arise as the primordial essence of the rosary. Next, with the certainty of knowing things as they are, join your fingers, representing means and knowledge, and count the essence mantra. Doing so will bring about the power and potential to unimpededly attain all worldly and transcendent spiritual accomplishments.

After reciting the root mantra as much as you can, chant the "Essence of Dependent Origination" together with the Sanskrit alphabet. Then chant mantras over the ritual rice and scatter the grains on the rosary. In particular, you should recite the mantra that is given in your own scripture one hundred and eight times. In all cases, a specific point concerning the visualization is that you should visualize the deities you wish to accomplish dissolving into the rosary in the form of the syllables of the mantra, colored to correspond with the activity, like rain falling from the sky. Then recite the mantra OṂ RUCI PRAVARTAYA RATNAMAṆI DHARA JÑĀNADEVA ABHIṢIÑCA HŪṂ SVĀHĀ and chant the verses of auspiciousness.

When the time comes for applying the activity, first you should chant the three syllables one hundred and eight times, followed by the Sanskrit alphabet, the "Essence of Dependent Origination" and the mantras for blessing the rosary twenty-one times each. Following this, you should begin the relevant recitation. This is all very clearly explained in the relevant scriptures.

It is said that by using such a genuine rosary the effects of your mantra recitation will be multiplied by one hundred thousand. Moreover, the text continues:

> It is good to repeat the consecration from time to time.

And:

> It is, therefore, a key instruction to regularly repeat the blessing ritual.

For this reason, make sure to bless the rosary in this way at the beginning of your sessions.

The way to count the mantras is mentioned in the *Meteor Wheel That Tames the Haughty Ones*:

> The rosary for counting should be strung with several threads.
> The DZAḤ on the thumb projects a hook of light,
> Attracting the deity and bringing it to the navel and heart center.

How to Recite Mantras

Concerning the way in which mantras should be recited, the Great Master from Uḍḍiyāna explains:

> Count at your heart for peaceful activity,
> At your navel for enriching activity,
> At the secret place for magnetizing activity,
> Count with a wish to summon.
> For wrathful activity count near your knee
> At the point where the legs are crossed.
> For multiple activities count wherever is comfortable.

Explaining further, he states:

> When reciting peaceful mantras
> Count with the rosary on your index finger,
> And for enriching mantras, on your middle finger.
> For magnetizing, keep it on your ring finger,
> And for wrathful mantras, on the little finger.
> Always use your left hand;
> Never count with your right hand.

However, it is said that on some occasions you may count using both hands and that for wrathful mantras you can count using the thumb of the right hand. There is also a way of counting that expels, as is the case with averting mantras.

From a general point of view, an easy and effective way to practice is to place the rosary on top of the index finger, and then count with the thumb in the form of a hook. This holds for all four types of enlightened activity.

There are also samaya vows that must be observed. The great master Padmasambhava explains:

A genuine rosary should accompany you at all times,
Like the body and its shadow.
This is the fundamental samaya of the rosary.

Although a great many subsidiary samayas are taught,
In brief this is what you should know:
Do not show your rosary to others.
If you do not let it leave the warmth of your body,
Whatever you practice will quickly be accomplished.

Likewise, do not let anyone else hold it,
Especially, it is said, anyone with damaged samaya vows, obscurations,
Or with whom you do not share the same samaya.
It is important not to let it slip into the hands of such people.

Other than using it to count when reciting,
Do not hold it leisurely at inappropriate times.
Do not employ it for the sake of divination and astrology.
A rosary that has not been consecrated should never be held.

A consecrated rosary should be kept secret
And not used for other activities.
Do not place it on the ground or cast it aside.

Do not use a so-called "adulterated rosary,"
One mixed with inappropriate things.

Furthermore, the masters of mantra have taught that if you slip into conversation while counting the mantra, you must subtract some numbers, going back four beads on the rosary. If you cough, go back five, three if you yawn, ten if you sneeze, and one if you spit.

As described, first visualize the appearance of the deity, then the mantra chain, and finally the projection and absorption of light and so on. However, it is very important that these individual stages only be performed once you have reached stability in the visualizations of the preceding stage.

Concluding the Session

When the time comes to conclude the session, you must compensate for any additions and omissions in the recitation. To do so, chant the Sanskrit alphabet, recite the hundred-syllable mantra and the "Essence of Dependent Origination" three times each. Following this, make offerings and offer praise. The meaning of this meditation was explained above.

Should there be any auspicious sign when you arrive at the stage of accomplishment, you must immediately take the spiritual accomplishments or you will run the risk of it dissipating. Therefore, when you reach this stage of the practice, you should receive the spiritual accomplishments on a daily basis. It is especially important to do so at dawn on the final day of your practice. The meaning of this practice will be explained below.

Next, present offerings and praise as an expression of gratitude, then ask for forgiveness by supplicating in the following way:

> Ignorant and careless, we beginners have failed to develop meditative clarity in our visualization and have not recited the required number of mantras. In performing the ritual, we have added some things and omitted others. We have also failed to gather offering substances and ritual implements, and fallen prey to laziness. We now confess this and feel great embarrassment and remorse for all our confused errors related to the performance of the profound rituals of Secret Mantra. Please be forbearing and purify these errors.

Next, as you recite the hundred-syllable mantra, imagine that all transgressions are purified and cleansed.

Enlightened Mind

Thirdly comes the luminosity practice of enlightened mind. When there is a front visualization involved, such as during the accomplishment stage, the wisdom beings in front should be requested to remain in the support if there is one. If there is no support present, you should request them to depart into the natural basic space of phenomena. The samaya beings are then gathered into the self-visualization.

When there is only a self-visualization involved, the wisdom being within never departs. Thus, chant the verses of the dissolution while you visualize the following. First, imagine that the entire universe and its inhabitants melt into light and dissolve into the celestial palace. Next, the palace itself, starting from the perimeter, is gradually absorbed into the retinue deities. The retinue dissolves into the central male and female deities. The female consort then dissolves into the male deity, the male deity dissolves into the wisdom being in his heart center, and the wisdom being dissolves into the encircling mantra. Finally, the mantra dissolves into the absorption being—the seed syllable of the life force of enlightened mind.

Focus your attention on this syllable, which then dissolves, from the bottom up, until even the upper tip is gone. At this point, rest for as long as you are able in the nonconceptual state of emptiness free from dualistic observations. This clears away the extreme of permanence. Alternatively, you may also perform the dissolution that is likened to a rainbow vanishing in the sky. The first of these approaches is called the "subsequent dissolution," while the latter is known as the "complete dissolution." These are, in fact, very similar but for beginners it is very important to practice the subsequent dissolution. On this topic, the Great Omniscient One explains:

> The development stage ends the belief that appearances are real.
> The completion stage eliminates the belief that holds them to
>   be illusory.
> When free from believing that appearance and emptiness are real,
> You have reached the pure nature of indivisible development
>   and completion.

As stated here, the method for overcoming ordinary concepts, whereby we believe in the reality of the world and its inhabitants, is to dissolve the illusory perception of divine appearances into the space of luminosity. This is known as the completion stage. And since this practice is the key point for purifying the stage of death into the dharma body, it cannot be dispensed with.

Next, when emerging from this state of dissolution, recite the root mantra once. This creates the conditions for you to emerge as the single illusory form of the deity during the subsequent attainment, thereby eliminating the extreme of nihilism.

Sometimes it is taught that the three places should be marked with the three syllables that confer the blessings of vajra body, speech, and mind. At the crown of your head, visualize the syllable HAṂ, which melts and forms armor composed of crossed-vajras. At your fingertips, visualize two wrathful deities to protect the body. The head ornaments and crown should fit tightly and be very stable. Next, visualize the protective dome and chant the dedication, aspirations, and verses of auspiciousness.

When practicing the development stage it is important to understand each of the principles related to the object of purification, the process of purification, and the result of purification in relation to the practice of purification, perfection, and maturation. However, the details of these points should be learned from other sources.

Subsequent Practices

The subsequent practices constitute the seventh topic presented earlier [see p. 70], which is bringing the deity onto the path. This consists of the ten things to understand and the six fundamental samaya vows. Concerning the ten things to understand it is said:

> Treat the subsequent attainment like an illusion, a mirage,
> A dream, a reflection, the moon's reflection in water,
> A hallucination, an echo, a city of gandharvas,
> A bubble, and a magical apparition.

The six fundamental samaya vows are as follows:

> Not to abandon the guru and the yidam deity,
> Not to err about what should be accepted and abandoned,
> To observe meditative absorption,
> And to keep the object of your meditation and your conduct secret—
> These six are the samayas of the development stage.

As outlined here, you should adopt or abandon with respect to these. Moreover, you should also train in not parting from the three integrations by understanding the three seats to be the deity's maṇḍala.

The three seats are for the thirty-four deities. The aggregates and the elements are the seat of the male and female thus-gone ones, the sense fields are the seats of the male and female bodhisattvas, and the limbs are the seats of the male and female wrathful deities. The male and female bodhisattvas are buddhas from the perspective of their pristine fruition. They should not be mistaken for bodhisattvas that dwell on the levels of spiritual attainment.

In this way, whenever you engage in activities between sessions, or while moving around, sitting, eating, or walking, you should cultivate pure realms, transform sense pleasures into feast offerings, engage in the ten Dharma activities (such as prostrating, circumambulating, and reciting), and do anything that skillfully ripens the minds of others. Ensure that you do not let your body, speech, and mind slip into an ordinary state. It is said that if thoughts proliferate during the breaks, your sessions will become a farce. On the other hand, if you arouse renunciation, weariness with saṃsāra, and other such qualities during the breaks, and your mind is weary with cyclic existence when entering a practice session, that session will definitely be effective. If this then arouses a sense of enthusiasm, your subsequent sessions will also become increasingly endowed with good qualities.

Concerning the way to implement the practices associated with your behavior, such as eating, dressing, and so on, you may consult texts such as Dharmaśrī's *Inner Dharma Conduct*.

During the other sessions you should act in the usual manner, beginning with inviting the field of merit into the space within the protective dome, supplicating, going for refuge, and generating the mind of awakening, all the way up to the dissolution, arising, and other elements that take place at the conclusion, as well as reciting dedications, aspirations, and auspicious prayers.

In some approach manuals it is said that the practices of expelling obstructors, the protective dome, and so forth can be excluded in the later sessions of the day, and you may begin these sessions with offerings and blessings. Some approach manuals also say that you need not perform the stage of dissolution at the end of each session; if you do perform the dissolution, it is only performed at the conclusion of the evening session. However, it is better to do things according to the instructions outlined here. The rationale is that, in the context of approach, it is necessary to train the mind in the entire range of instructions related to purifying birth, death, and the intermediate state by means of the development stage ritual. On this point it is said:

> It is necessary to expel stray entities, protect against obstacles, and the like, which may occur in the context of the breaks.

If you dedicate a torma for obstructors on a regular basis, you should do so at the beginning of the morning session, but you will not incur the fault of omission if you do not. You should, however, dedicate a torma and perform a reparation feast offering of appropriate length in the evening session. In general, since evening and late night are vital times for reparation feast offerings, you should perform them at such times. Alternatively, because it may be easier to do so in the afternoon session, offering such a feast at that time does not present any problem either. Even without gathering regularly for a feast offering, doing it at the beginning and end of the approach and on sacred days will suffice. It is also permissible to omit a regular covenant proclamation and the Tenma goddess offerings.

Whatever the case, when you finish gathering the accumulations of offering the body after the evening session, you should perform the practice of sleep. Dharmaśrī taught this as follows:

> Outwardly, sleep in the style of a lion, facing west with your head to the north, your back to the east, and your right side down. With the right hand placed under your cheek, block the right nostril with your ring finger. Extend your left arm, resting it on your thigh. With the notion that you will wake up and engage in virtue, sleep while resting your mind in the spacelike nature of reality with the thought, "May I attain the dharma body of buddhahood."
>
> Internally, visualize the maṇḍala that is to be absorbed, then imagine that the entire impure universe and its inhabitants are struck with light from your heart center and are dissolved into the support. Next, the support gradually dissolves, all the way up to the uppermost tip of the life force of enlightened mind. This, in turn, is absorbed into nonobjectified basic space. Finally, fall asleep in the nonconceptual state. If you do not fall asleep, it will suffice to repeat this process.
>
> Secretly, at night you should "collect all objects of knowledge into a vase." In your heart center visualize a slightly closed red lotus with four petals, and within it a white letter A without any additional punctuation. This letter symbolizes the birthless nature and blazes like a butter lamp inside a vase. As you focus your mind on this letter, collect and retain the energies in your heart center with the sense that the upper and lower parts of your body have gathered there. By falling asleep in this manner your sleep will be dreamless and dawn as the luminosity of nonconceptual empty clarity.

When it comes time for the dawn session, imagine that you are awakened by the ḍākas and ḍākinīs who, accompanied by the sound of ḍamarus, bells, and cymbals, encourage you from the sky with this song: "Arise from luminosity as the form bodies!" Then, arising in the form of the deity in the context of the subsequent attainment, expel the stale winds and refresh your motivation. Next, bless your speech and then continue practicing up to the guru yoga and receive the four empowerments. Once these steps are complete, perform the dawn session as usual.

In this way you should practice the four sessions in a continuous succession until the approach is finished. The duration of the sessions is taught in *The Root Tantra of Mañjuśrī*:

> A series of one hundred finger snaps
> Is taught to be one circulation of the channels.
> Four circulations of the channels occur during a forty-five minute period.
> Four such periods are called a "session."
>
> Four sessions are taught to comprise a day.
> A night is taught to consist of the same.
> That which includes eight such sessions
> Is considered a day and night of practice.
>
> Ten blinks of an eye
> Is considered the duration of one second.
> "Ten seconds"
> Is considered a moment.
> Four moments are considered
> "One session" by those who know mantra.

To elaborate, the duration of an approach is threefold. There is a number-based approach, in which case the general approach is either to recite until you have reached a specific number that you have kept in mind or, if the mantra for the main deity is short, to recite one hundred thousand mantras for each syllable and, if it is long, to recite one hundred thousand of the entire mantra. Specific details can be found in the text you are using. It is also explained that the mantras of each member of the retinue should be recited one-tenth the number of recitations of the root mantra.

There is also a time-based approach. *The Tantra of the Emergence of Cakrasaṃvara* explains:

> In the complete epoch, a certain number of mantras is recited.
> In the threefold epoch, it is twice that number.

In the twofold epoch, it is explained to be three times that
number.
In the volatile epoch, four times that number must be recited.

Alternatively, the approach may last for one year, or six months, three months, or any other number of days, depending upon your inclination.

There is also a sign-based period of approach. This refers to continuing the approach until you have witnessed a sign of accomplishment either in actuality, in a meditative experience, or in a dream. Signs will be specified in the text you are using. On this topic, the Great Master of Uḍḍiyāna taught:

Joyous, ebullient, and with lucid awareness,
Your practice will develop and your mind and body will be
at ease.
In particular, afterward
Realization will dawn in your mind-stream and you will be
diligent.
You will no longer entertain mundane activities.

Thus, if the qualities of the path, such as renunciation, weariness, devotion, pure perception, compassion, and the mind of awakening, develop further while disturbing emotions, such as attachment and anger, gradually diminish, then the other signs in actuality, in meditative experiences, or in dreams are likewise authentic. However, if the opposite occurs, then even visions, prophecies, and the like are said to be demonic deceptions. With this understanding, it is very important not to entertain preferences, hope, or fear concerning signs.

Moreover, it is said in *The Tantra of Layered Lotus Stems*:

Thus, the master and the deity
Will be pleased because accomplishment is reached,
While the mother goddesses, ḍākinīs, and their servants
Will be enlisted in ritual actions because their wishes are fulfilled.

Thus, you should also understand that initiating ritual activity will be pointless prior to witnessing a sign of accomplishment.

Alternatively, when performing the reparation and supplication rite of the protectors in the evening or afternoon session, the protectors are to be visualized in the periphery surrounding the celestial mansion. Alternatively, you may visualize yourself as the heruka and visualize the protectors in the space in front of you, situated in the charnel ground surrounding the palace. Having done so, you may then present supplications and offerings. You may also follow these steps in the context of covenant proclamations and Tenma goddess offerings.

It will suffice to perform the departure and absorption of the protectors at the conclusion of offering the session torma, in the final section of the Dharma protector ritual. It is also suitable to perform these at the end of the entire ritual, together with the postritual proceedings.

When dispatching tormas, the person holding them should shift or move slightly away from the row. Finally, the ritual master should make the gesture of holding them aloft with his hands, and then scatter flowers. Then, on the roof of the retreat house, or outside to the northeast, they should be offered on a torma stand in the appropriate manner, facing either outward or inward depending on their mundane or transcendent character. The manner of hurling them as magical weapons, in the context of violent rites, should be performed according to the pith instructions.

In particular, there is a special ancillary practice that is to be carried out by those who wish to swiftly assimilate the two accumulations based on the skillful means of the ultimate, secret path of the uncommon vajra vehicle. This practice is the gathering offering. There are different categories according to who or what gathers. *The Vajra Explanatory Tantra of the Magical Web* explains:

> A gathering of all companions
> Is called a "gathering of an assembly of practitioners."
> A complete array of sense pleasures
> Is explained to be a "gathering of sense pleasures."
> An assembly of all deities and oath-bound protectors
> Is explained to be a "gathering of a great assembly."

Swiftly perfecting the two accumulations
By enjoying all of it without attachment
Is definitively explained to be a "great gathering."

If means and wisdom are inseparable, such an assembly is referred to as a "feast gathering." Just an equal number of means and wisdom, relying on an imagined wisdom seal, should be construed as a mere approximation. If means and wisdom have not been unified, such an assembly is not known as a feast gathering of ḍākas and ḍākinīs.

Moreover, an assembly of sublime beings who have unified means and wisdom in this manner is referred to as a "feast gathering of fortunate people." A gathering of the five materials for food and drink, clothes and jewelry, dancing and singing, ritual union and ritual liberation is a "feast gathering of pleasurable materials."

The wisdom maṇḍala, along with the support, the supported, and the protectors, is the support for spiritual accomplishments, which is also depicted as an image and meditated upon. This is termed a "feast gathering of delighted deities." The "great gathering" is added to these three, making four in total. The great gathering involves perfecting the collection of merit by partaking in the aforementioned gatherings without attachment and perfecting the collection of wisdom by embracing the gatherings with nondual wisdom.

The vajra siblings, an assembly without samaya breaches, should, moreover, relinquish heedless joking, commotion, and the like and, with the expression of the austerity of innnate awareness, take their seats after performing prostrations to the assembly of elders and to the maṇḍala. *The Compendium* explains:

Impure materials, which are connected
With misconduct and flaws from lapses,
Should be abandoned like a snake in your lap,
Banished far away with foxlike vigor.

Thus, impure materials, meaning types of material obtained from wrong livelihood and so forth, are unfit as feast substances and should be abandoned as such. Those who degrade the choice offering by, for instance, allowing the feast to be eaten before it is offered are referred to as "wolves of the feast gathering." Those who loot the leftovers are also termed this way. Thus, unerringly observe what is to be taken up and relinquished.

Since the five meats and the five nectars, or meat and beer, are indispensable, you should collect as much as you are able. These are mentioned by their secret names in *The Galpo Tantra*:

> Vajra life, galchi,
> Jamde, datrol, dagye,
> Tsetri, dzagad, dzakti,
> Branmo, shammo, kuntugyu,
> Amra, gundrum, agaru,
> Naling, gegye, and so forth are to be gathered.

And also:

> Appearance, great means, is the supreme life.
> Emptiness, knowledge, is the essential basis.
> Their nondual combination is the heart substance.

In this statement "life" refers to rice flour and so forth, "essential basis" refers to beer and so forth, while "combination" refers to food made from these two. To elaborate, Venerable Lord Atīśa said:

> There will be no merit in Tibet.
> They skimp on their torma ingredients.

Likewise, it is said that skimping on feast offering foods is also unsuitable. Rather, prepare exactly as much as you yourself would eat.

In the preceding quote "vajra life" is food. "Galchi" is a concoction of various spices. "Jamde" is milk. "Datrol" can refer to butter, cream cheese, or buttermilk. "Dagye" is curd and fried dough. "Tsetri" is a leafy vegetable. Madāna, pache, and "dzagad" are beer. Balom, "dzakti," and māṁsa are meat. "Branmo" is vegetable. "Shammo" is diluted beer. "Kuntugyu" is salt. "Amra" is human meat. "Gundrum" is elephant meat. "Agaru" is horse meat. "Naling" is cow meat. "Gegye" is dog meat.

In summary, collect whatever types of edible ingredients and beverages, such as garlic, herbs, and fruit, that your budget allows. The feast materials should not be placed on the bare ground. Instead, on the surface of flayed human skin, the pelt of a wild animal, or a drawing, arrange the edibles to your right and the beverages to your left using a skull cup, a jewel vessel, or the like. Anoint them with feast beer, and then with blessed vase water or clean water.

Next, purify them by anointing them with the nectar of the inner offerings and expel obstructors, thereby cleansing them of stains and faults and blessing them. However, it is said that the inner offerings are not to be sprinkled on the fivefold outer offering, nor on the rakta and the effigy. As indicated by this, it has been said:

> In general, even just anointing the torma and so forth with medicine and rakta has multiple functions. Like adding the active ingredient to a medicine, it will invoke the mind-stream of the yidam deity and the like, while cleansing away stains and impurities, removing obstructors, making offerings, and conferring blessings.

Following this, imagine the five syllables on a sun disc, representing the universe, and the food, representing its inhabitants; then purify, increase, and transform the food with the mantra and mudrā of the three syllables and so forth, thus blessing it as the sense pleasure goddesses. Next, emanating light rays from you, gather all the vital essences of the sense pleasures in the realms of the worlds and dissolve them into the feast substances. This is said to be an essential point.

In general, it is suitable even to offer a feast gathering, torma, and so forth by means of the deity of the session breaks. But if you perform an abridged version in the evening session, visualize an activity deity resembling the central deity, which emerges from the heart of the central deity, settles in the eastern foyer of the maṇḍala, and then performs a feast, leads the consciousness of obstructors and enemies to a higher state, and so on.

Alternatively, imagine that the same activity deity settles in the charnel ground in the outer northeast perimeter and there awakens the assembly of the three roots and guardians, which fill all of space like clouds amassing in the sky. This includes the deities of the maṇḍala and those deities who have been invited as guests from the buddhafields in the ten directions.

The Galpo Tantra explains:

> First, make offerings with the six sense pleasures.
> Second, make confession with the nectar of sacred substance.
> Third, give the form aggregate to enemies and obstructors.

Thus, it is said one should project in three parts the choice offerings that have been set aside, though four parts are also taught. Whatever the case, begin by imagining that the sense pleasure goddesses fill all of space and make offerings to the field of merit with an inconceivable variety of offering clouds. This pleases the deities and, in turn, perfects the two accumulations.

For the middle step of confession, visualize yourself confessing all degenerate, broken, faulty, and lapsed samaya vows while offering the five meats, the five nectars, and the like as samaya substances in form, but as the nature of wisdom nectar in essence. Through this, those of the field of merit are pleased and regard you lovingly. Imagine that all your faults are thereby completely cleansed, and that breaches with the wisdom deity are purified.

To conclude, if there is no separate effigy it will suffice to, at least, separate the makings for an effigy off from the feast food before blessing it. If this has not been done, then after offering the feast, as the nature of nectar, the effigy can be carved from the back of the feast dough and arranged facing upward. Next, imagine that through saying HŪṂ the sense pleasure goddesses of the feast gather into you, and summon, chain, bind, and intoxicate the enemies and obstructors. Finally, imagine that, after the consciousness has been delivered, the assembly of wrathful deities enjoys the remaining bodily support as vajra samaya food, then anoint it with nectar and offer it.

There is also a tradition in which a reparation rite is performed before the choice offerings are set aside. However, in this context, the practice tradition of Minling clearly makes more sense.

Jamyang Khyentse Rinpoche said, "The feast offering is like offering food and drink as hospitality for a guest, while the reparation is like giving wealth, meaning a gift of material goods."

The fourth part is the choice sky offering. For this offering anoint the arranged feast substances with medicine and rakta, make offerings to the protectors of the pure realms and so forth, and offer the choice sky offering in a clean place outside. In some treasures it is taught that this offering serves to bring about a fulfillment in the unity of the relative and ultimate truths. However, in the general transmitted teachings and treasures the fourth part is construed as the pure leftovers.

For the fifth part the ritual assistant holds the substances of means and knowledge with arms crossed and offers them to the ritual master, who first makes the circular lotus mudrā then accepts them with the three-pointed mudrā. Next, the assistant gradually distributes them to the entire assembly, starting from the front row. Imagining these to be the five meats and the five nectars, everyone enjoys them in the manner of an internal burnt offering rite. Thereafter, aspiration prayers are made.

Next, without hoarding anything, collect leftovers from those assembled, beginning from the last row. *The Galpo Tantra* states:

> In the intermediate direction of the northeast, the maṇḍala of leftovers is arranged,
> On flayed human skin, a half-moon of rakta, and an E . . .

Thus, it is said that to the northeast or southwest of the maṇḍala you should arrange a round disc of scented unguents for peaceful deities, or an image of the source of phenomena and a half-moon drawn on flayed human skin for wrathful deities. Upon it arrange the pure leftovers, which are the fourth part of the choice offering set aside earlier in the feast. Add to this half of the liberation section, together with the impure leftovers, placing them on the top and bottom, respectively. Present the choice offering to the seven upper objects. With the impure offerings of the

Great Glorious One and practitioners make offerings to the seven lower objects.

Visualize a celestial mansion, with gates, inside a vast dark-blue triangle that constitutes the outer perimeter of the maṇḍala of leftovers. Inside this visualize the thirty miraculous deities of the feast gathering, which are the five buddha families, the territorial entities, and the door guardians called the "seven upper objects." Imagine that an OṂ situated on a moon disc on the leftover torma radiates and absorbs light, causing the leftover torma to swell into a heap of nectar, the secret sense pleasures.

Imagine that the seven lower objects, such as Ḍākiṇī Gingling and the others, are invited with the sound of shrill whistling and the king-of-desire mudrā. They arrive inside the triangular perimeter in a dark flurry, like ravens descending on carrion. Overpower them with the mudrā of the heruka's vajra garuḍa wings. Offer them seats with the lotus mantra and mudrā. Make them subservient with the horse-faced mantra and mudrā. To the guests, seated in the five groupings of their respective families, make general offerings and sprinkle them with medicine and rakta. Arouse certainty through proclaiming the rationale. Then pour it on the many specific choice offering tormas and the impure tormas, thus connecting the choice offerings and the leftovers. Moreover, it is also said that you should blend below in the context of pacifying, enriching, and magnetizing, and blend above in the context of wrathful activity.

If the ritual master has realized the view, he or she should retain the pride of being the central deity and, while visualizing the upper palate as Hayagrīva, the lower palate as Yoginī, and the nectar of the mind of awakening as flowing from their point of union, he or she should spray the offerings with saliva. In the case of an ordinary ritual master, sprinkling the offerings with medicine and rakta will suffice, thereby blessing them.

At night place a candle in the torma to protect from confrontations during the night. Next, make offerings and entrust the lower objects with enlightened activity by calling them by name. Finally, the ritual assistant, wearing a hat and shoes, should carry the impure leftovers to a location seventy paces outside the retreat house, since this is where the demons eat, and clean off the torma tray there. It is said that the tradition of dedicating the water used to clean is not necessary. At the end, absorb the five buddha families of the upper objects into yourself. Let the other guests depart and the maṇḍala be reabsorbed.

A slightly different approach is taught in *The Maṇḍala Ritual of Viśuddha Heruka*:

> Vividly and clearly visualize the leftover torma as the seven upper deities. Imagine that various clouds of offerings appear from the assembly of torma deities and that you offer them to the deities. The torma deities then dissolve into you and the torma becomes a swirling ocean of nectar. Next, invite the seven lower objects and make offerings to the five groups of buddha families. Then spit on the impure torma and dedicate it.

In the context of pacifying, visualize the five male consorts of the buddha families with their respective seats in the center and four directions of the maṇḍala of the leftovers, and thus bless the torma. Invite the thirty-two ḍākinīs, imagining that they join with the five buddhas. Then, having made offerings with flowers and so forth, offer the torma.

The method for making offerings to the lower objects is taught next. Certain treasure teachings only teach how to dedicate to the lower objects and nothing more. Whatever the case, when practicing for a specific number of days, holding the leftovers in the northeast of the maṇḍala as ransom serves the purpose of hastening activity. In this context, the seven upper objects are as taught in *The Galpo Tantra*:

> That which is invoked from basic space,
> That which is properly blessed,
> Great means revealed as the male consorts,
> Knowledge present as the female consorts,
> The eight Kori wrathful goddesses,
> The local great Tramen goddesses,
> And the four wisdom-door guardians—
> This is the maṇḍala of the seven upper objects.

The Galpo Tantra also teaches the seven lower objects:

> The thirty-two that miraculously travel through the sky,
> The eight great Ging that take pleasure in union and liberation,
> The three Tsar of Laṅka that offer their full realization,
> The eight radiant goddesses that harm body, speech, and mind,
> The seven demons, rakṣasa, and mātṛkā, and the four sisters—
> The sixty-four beings are the objects who are messengers.
> They are also the six objects that have dominion over leftovers.
> Twenty-eight have dominion over the choice and leftover
> offerings.

In particular, in the context of accumulating one hundred feast offerings, you should repeat everything beginning from the blessing all the way through the conclusion of the leftovers. However, it will suffice to do the food offering just once afterwards. Alternatively, Goshi Geshe has said that, according to the practice tradition of Minling, there is also an approach to offering food in which offerings are presented to the ritual master and, immediately after imagining that he has partaken of it, the food is dedicated together with the leftovers. Goshi Geshe has said that it is good to accumulate numbers of such food offerings.

Jigme Lingpa has taught:

> It is said that such feast offerings involve six kinds of satiation. Those of the field of merit are satiated with offerings. The practitioners are satiated with vajra food and drink. The wheel of wisdom is satiated with the pure essence of nectar. The deities in the maṇḍala of the body are satiated with the wisdom of empty bliss. The outer and inner ḍākinīs are satiated with the melody of song. And the haughty, elemental spirits who perform activities are satiated with torma.

Finally, imagine that the mundane guests of the feast gathering and the wisdom beings depart. You reabsorb the samaya beings and then dissolve them into your heart center as the central deity. Alternatively, it is also suitable to perform the departure and absorption together with the postritual proceedings.

As for the benefits of the feast gathering, *The Vajra Net* states:

> Among all merits, the feast offering is supreme.
> In this life you will accomplish all you wish
> And obstructors and obstacles will be pacified.
> In a future life you will be born in a knowledge holder buddhafield
> Or attain the state of Samantabhadra.

Thus, the deities being practiced will be pleased, the two accumulations of the practitioner will be perfected, and all lapsed and broken samaya vows will be restored, such that you will become equal in fortune to the heruka.

Now I will offer a brief explanation of the topic of ritual liberation that occurs in this context. In general, there are many opinions about major and minor supreme objects of liberation. However, roughly speaking, a major supreme object is an auspicious and pure field, meaning a seven-times-reborn human, while a minor supreme object is a field of compassion, an enemy or obstructor included among the ten fields and the seven lapsed ones. The ten fields are outlined in *A Clarification of Commitments*:

> Enemies of the three jewels, opponents of the master,
> Violators, breakers, and transgressors of commitments,
> Those who arrive at the assembly, who are harmful to all,
> Those hostile to the commitments, wicked beings,
> And those in the three lower realms:
> These ten should the practitioner take on.

The seven lapsed ones are outlined as follows:

> Those lapsed from the sublime disparage the master and spiritual siblings.
> Those lapsed from the Buddha's word reject cause and effect.
> Those lapsed from the meaning view the two truths as separate.

> Those lapsed through action punish the blameless.
> Those lapsed through marks hold biases about the Dharma.
> Those lapsed through desire shamelessly steal and destroy.
> Those lapsed through being misguided cause sentient beings
> to suffer.

Taking any such enemy or obstructor as your model, sculpt a dough effigy with the appropriate characteristics. As an auspicious connection for the troops of saṃsāra to retreat, lay it down supine with its head facing southwest and its feet facing northeast or, alternatively, as though facing nirvāṇa and turning away from saṃsāra, lay it down with its head on the ground and its face directed toward you. Next, anoint it with rakta; then enter your protective citadel.

Then arrange the repelling vajra forces and make sure that the following nine factors are complete:

- The three types of bravery: the bravery of the body as divine form, the bravery of ineffable speech, and the bravery of nonoriginating mind.
- The three confidences: confidence in the view free of extremes, confidence in meditation beyond intellect, and confidence in conduct that is automatic.
- The three ferocities: an awareness sharper than a spear, which pierces through arrogant external entities; an awareness like a honed weapon, which cuts through internal afflictions; and an awareness like a strong wind, which scatters the cloud formations of concepts.

Replete with these nine factors, summon whichever enemy or obstructor is the target, imagine that he or she is actually present, then dissolve your enemy into the effigy. Next, commence the ritual of liberation based on the view comprising the fortress of suchness, meditation comprising a ravine of meditative absorption, and conduct comprising the life force of compassion. It is said in a tantra:

> The samaya vow of liberating with compassion
> Does not mean to kill and suppress.

Accordingly, keep compassion as your basic motivation and unimpeded anger as your temporary motivation. For the crucial point of irreversibility, visualize yourself as the heruka. For the crucial point of invincibility, visualize the ritual dagger as the Supreme Son. For the sake of hostility, visualize the effigy as the actual target.

Now, to cleanse away the target's lifespan, visualize that inside the heart of the visualized target is consciousness, the substance of life force, which is the pure essence of blood the size of a sparrow's head. At its center is the support of the target's lifespan, a white A in the nature of light. At the center of that is a drop, inside of which is the support of consciousness, the life force syllable, a green NRI. Visualizing three HŪṂ syllables at the point of the ritual dagger and three PHAṬ syllables underneath them, strike the lifespan support at its heart center with the dagger. The NRI, together with the A, collect on the point of the ritual dagger with a white flash. Then, by pointing the ritual dagger back toward yourself, the A syllable dissolves into a HŪṂ at your own heart, causing you to become brilliant and radiant. This is the command over lifespan.

Next, imagine that the life force syllable NRI dissolves into the three HŪṂ syllables at the point of the ritual dagger and is projected to the Great Glorious One in Akiniṣṭha by the three PHAṬ syllables underneath. The NRI then dissolves into his heart center. Following this, from among the three HŪṂ syllables, the blue HŪṂ of the all-ground, together with the HŪṂ that is the life force of enlightened mind, melt into light. Together with the red HŪṂ of the afflicted mind, they dissolve into the A at the throat. Both the A and the white HŪṂ of the mental consciousness then dissolve into the OṂ at the crown, which itself melts into light. Fused together, this descends to the space of the mother by way of the horse of the spinal column. It is thus born as the son of the Victorious One. This is the command over purification.

Following this, imagine that the physical support left behind is gradually dismembered, starting from the right foot for men, and from the left foot for women, and anointed with nectar. Next, imagine that, while dancing, the devourer, the lotus Gingmo, along with its emanations, gives the liberated offerings to the deities of the maṇḍala, thereby pleasing and delighting them. The offerings should be made as taught by Minling Terchen:

> One part is to be given as an averting torma. One part is to be offered when inciting the deities to avert. One part is to be mixed in with the pure and impure leftover tormas.

In this way, as the results of liberation there are three satisfactions: (1) you are satisfied by the vital essence of life, (2) the enemy is satisfied by having his or her consciousness elevated, and (3) the deities are satisfied through being given flesh and blood. Thus, the procedure for the ritual of killing is to rend asunder the three unions of deity and support, body and mind, and flesh and bones. Kongtrul has said:

> The main factor in such violent activity is the end of the three activities of protecting, averting, and killing. You should conclude protecting with suppressing, averting with hurling, and killing with burning.

When invoking the deities, invoke their enlightened mind-streams by visualizing the torma as the deity and anointing it with medicine and rakta. Imagine that, from the basic space of the great peace of the dharma body, the form bodies arise in a wrathful manner for the benefit of beings and unflaggingly carry out enlightened activity with ferocity and urgency.

In the context of a covenant proclamation as well, bless the torma by anointing it with medicine and rakta and regularly offer it in the manner that you offer torma to the male, female, and hermaphroditic oath-bound protectors. During the special circumstances of wrathful ritual activity you should hurl the torma as a magical weapon. Anoint the torma of the local Tenma goddesses with the water used to cleanse the torma tray, invite the twelve Tenma goddesses to the outside of the retreat house with light rays from your heart center, and please them with suitable substances. Thereafter, have the ritual assistant go to a place seventy paces away and dispose of the torma, then send the guests back to where they came from. Next, put the torma tray upside down at the end of the row and upon it visualize the world system of the universe in the form of the syllable E and a triangle, and that the enemy or demon is suppressed there. Following this, visualize the torma tray as Mount Meru and, on top of it, the sentient beings that inhabit the universe as the Supreme Steed Heruka. With this, imagine that he performs a vajra dance, thus concluding the ritual.

Some additional minor points are mentioned in *The Condensed Realization*:

> Do not wear another person's clothing until reaching accomplishment or your accomplishment will dissipate. If you eat food from the hand of someone possessed by a demon, accomplishment will be delayed. Do not move your seat or the signs of heat will vanish. If you protect another, your power will deteriorate. If you wash your old clothes or your body, spiritual attainments will vanish.
>
> If you cut your hair or nails, the power of mantra will deteriorate. If you converse with others, mantras will not accrue in number. Especially, do not converse with those with lapsed samaya vows, those who commit misdeeds, those who are polluted, and the like. If you do recitations in a loud voice, their potency will deteriorate and the subtle elemental spirits will fall unconscious. Thus, recite in a whisper. Do not count prayer beads on your chest while lying on your back. Do not blow on your prayer beads. If the Dharma is preached in the retreat house, signs of accomplishment will not appear.
>
> If you make a commitment for a long duration obstacles will arise. Thus, start with short periods and extend them. Except for during killing and averting rites, do not expel saliva and mucus or a breach of samaya vows will enter into the mantra. Do not expel them on a passageway or your voice will be overpowered. Do not sleep during the day or there will be many problems. Do not expel bodily waste where people can see it or on a passageway.
>
> Do not show the accomplishment substance to others. Do not give away the substance of spiritual accomplishment. When finished, give a thanksgiving offering. Do not

> abruptly leave the retreat. Do not be distracted, disturb the body, speech, and mind, or do busy work. To be distracted by ordinary activities is referred to as "being impervious in a negative way," while being distracted by other virtuous activities is termed "being impervious in a positive way."

Furthermore, it is also said:

> If the tongue is not agile when reciting mantra, bathe and observe proper cleanliness. Thoroughly scrape the phlegm off the tongue and, each session, apply either long pepper or black pepper powder to the tongue. With the second-to-last finger completely smear the powder all over the top of the tongue. Doing this for a few days will help.
>
> Regularly replenish the offerings, but do not replace them. On sacred days, collect the old offerings that have not been thrown out and replace them. If torma and offerings are not blessed as soon as they are set out, obstructors will enter into them. Thus, anoint them with clean water and bless them. Ensure that there is nothing between you and the torma. Ensure that the torma is not too far away, that it has a stand, is not crooked, and that its vertical arrangement is not in disarray, and so forth. Do not place an empty vessel on the grass. By holding the collateral torma the deity and spiritual accomplishments will gather. By holding the Dharma protector torma in the morning and discarding it in the evening activities will be swift and spiritual attainments will be conferred. When discarding the torma do not let it face outward. Offer it on an outside torma stand with the torma facing inward. Do not direct the torma tray outward either and do not wash it until accomplishment has appeared.
>
> In the context of a magical weapon rite, face the torma outward and also clean the tray of the tormas related to ransoms, karmic debts, and so forth. In general, do not hurl a pacifying torma as a magical weapon. Do not carry enriching and

magnetizing tormas far away. In order to remove obstacles related to travel, discard the torma in the direction you will travel. Discard tormas for deceiving death and karmic debts in the four directions. Place the expelling tormas that remove obstructors farther away. Hurl wrathful tormas as magical weapons to liberate enemies and obstructors.

In particular, offering Dharma protector offering tormas and so forth in burnt offering rites, such as during a smoke offering, is extremely profound. Even if you do not, carry them to a clean place where there is no bodily waste from humans, dogs, or pigs and clean them there. Do not leave them for the poisonous fangs of dogs, rats, and the like. Do not exchange items with anyone else. If something must come inside the retreat space, wait a day and bring it in gradually. At that time, if you have various dreams early in the retreat, they are deluded appearances. Thus, focus on meditative absorption. If they occur later, they are signs of pollution. Thus, assiduously recite the hundred-syllable mantra.

Now I will explain the meanings of mantras that occur in some ritual texts. E means "here." ARALI means "play." HRĪNG HRĪNG is a symbolic phrase that means "assemble." SAMAYA means "commitment." TIṢṬA means "firmly." LHAN means "reside!" PŪJA means "to offer." HO means "delight." SARVA PAÑCA AMṚTA means "everything as the five nectars." KARAM means "power." KAHĪ means "partake." MAHĀRAKTA PŪJA KAHĪ means "Partake of the offering of great blood." BODHICITTA is "the mind of awakening." MAHĀSŪKHA is "great bliss." DHARMADHĀTU is "basic space of phenomena." MAHĀPŪJA is "great offering." OṀ VAJRA AMṚTA KUṆḌALI HANA HANA HŪṂ is "Strike, strike where the vajra nectar collects!" SARVA ŚATRUM is "all enemies." MĀRAYA is "Totally kill!" A is "nonorigination." HO is "pleased." MAHĀ is "great." SŪKHA is "bliss." Alternatively, in Avabhraṁśa, ALI is "cooked food." ULI is "drink." TALI is "raw food." TAPALI is "to mix."

Now, for the four lunar sacred days when virtuous activities are multiplied. From the first to the fifteenth of the final winter month of Māgha, the first Mongol month, is the sacred time frame when Buddha showed miracles. The seventh day of the final spring month of Vaiśākha, the fourth Mongol month, is the sacred day when Buddha was born. The fifteenth day of that month is the sacred day when Buddha became enlightened and passed away. The fourth day of the middle spring month of Āṣāḍha, the sixth Mongol month, is the sacred day when Buddha turned the Wheel of the Dharma. The fifteenth of that month is the sacred day when Buddha entered the womb. The twenty-second day of the middle autumn month of Āśvina, the ninth Mongol month, is the sacred day when Buddha descended from the god realm. The entire months in which these days occur are sacred periods. Moreover, the third day of the middle spring month of Caitra, the third Mongol month, is the time when Buddha preached *The Wheel of Time*. The fifteenth of that month is the time when Buddha preached the Perfection of Wisdom Sūtras and others, in addition to many tantras. It is said that the full moon, new moon, and eighth days of the lunar month are always sacred days of Amitābha, Buddha Śākyamuni, and Medicine Buddha, respectively. Alternatively, Lochen Dharmaśrī said:

> Externally, during the three days of the eighth, fourteenth, and fifteenth of the waxing period and during the twenty-fifth, twenty-ninth, and new moon days of the waning period the ḍākinīs circulate to the three external places. Internally, these are times when there is a special circulation of energies in the channels. In particular, on the tenth during the day and on the twenty-fifth during the night the accomplished ḍākinīs convene at the places of practitioners. Thus, in order to accomplish whatever ritual you initiate, exert yourself at those times.

CONCLUDING RITUALS

Choose an auspicious day to end your retreat. In the last session of the day, before you plan to leave the retreat, begin by setting out a fresh offering torma along with other excellent offerings, such as the materials needed for a gathering offering. Following this, perform an extensive gathering offering, fulfillment and confessions, and other such rituals. In the early morning session on the following day, get up early and perform the ritual as it is laid out in the text you are using. Next, perform a gathering offering, fulfillment ceremony, and dedication of the torma. Then take the Dharma protector torma that you have been using on a daily basis and either burn it or take it to a clean place and perform the covenant proclamation and Tenma goddess offerings, along with the dance of Hayagrīva.

When taking the spiritual accomplishments, replenish the offerings and place a kapāla filled with fermented liquor, Dharma medicine, and dairy products on the shrine. Then light the offering lamp that you use on a daily basis. Dedicate a torma to the obstructing forces and, after they have been expelled, visualize a stable protective dome, consecrate the offerings, and perform the descent of blessings. Once these steps are complete, imagine that all the spiritual accomplishments of the enlightened body, speech, and mind of the victorious ones throughout the ten directions and their heirs coalesce in the form of the three syllables and white, red, and dark-blue nectar, which rain down upon the torma and nectar, dissolving into them.

Next, recite the approach mantras of the main deity and the entire retinue and recite an appropriate addendum to the mantra, such as KĀYA VĀKA CITTA SARVA SIDDHI PHALA HŪṂ. At the break of day, instantaneously visualize the old offering tormas as the deity. Alternatively, in this context you may also separate the wisdom maṇḍala from the samaya being and merge it indivisibly with the torma.

With the knowledge that the torma is the deity, think of it as the source from which you receive empowerment and spiritual accomplishments. To begin, present offerings and praise, and perform general confessions, such as the "Supreme Wisdom Form," along with the confession liturgy from the text you are using.

Following these steps, purify whatever enmity may be present by reciting the hundred-syllable mantra twenty-one times and confess any impaired or broken samaya vows, thereby purifying your mind-stream and making it a fit receptacle for spiritual accomplishments.

Next, recite an appropriate supplication prayer to invoke the enlightened mind of the deity. Hold the torma in your hands and recite the liturgy for invoking the spiritual accomplishments. Then offer the following prayer with intense devotion:

> Supreme deity, I have shared a connection with you in my previous lives. Now, once again, I have completed the samaya vows of approach and accomplishment. I have completed the proper number of days and, with daybreak near, now the time to bestow the spiritual accomplishments has arrived. In accordance with the pledges you have made in the past, please pacify adverse conditions and hostile forces with the boundless blessings of your wisdom, love, and power. Please cause all positive qualities to develop fully and grant me mastery over the splendor and riches of saṃsāra and nirvāṇa. Please vanquish all harmful forces, enemies, obstructive forces, and demonic beings. Please bestow upon me the common spiritual accomplishments, including the unobstructed accomplishment of the infinite activities subsumed within the four forms of enlightened activity. In particular, please grant my main objective: the fruit of the culmination of abandonment and realization, the embodiment of the spontaneously accomplished twofold benefit, the unsurpassed spiritual accomplishment of the Great Seal, the union of bliss and emptiness, inseparable in essence from your own vajra body, speech, and mind, supreme yidam deity! Please bestow these upon me this very moment, without delay!

With these words, imagine that all the supreme and ordinary spiritual accomplishments emerge in the form of rays of light from the three places of the assembly of deities. Dissolving into your own three places, the light rays bring you all the spiritual accomplishments you desire. Touch the torma to your three places and take the four empowerments. Imagining that the torma deity then dissolves into light and becomes nectar, dip the material torma into the nectar and drink the nectar with the conviction that you are equal in status to the yidam deity.

Alternatively, when there is a frontal visualization, there is no need to separate the wisdom being of the self-visualization. In such cases you should hold up the substances of the spiritual accomplishments with your hands. Invoked by the blissful sounds of the passionate union of the assembly of deities visualized in front of you, all the victorious ones throughout space gather and their bodhicitta, transforming into the essence of nectar, rains down. The nectar completely fills up the bodies of the deities in front and their bodies begin to emit the common and supreme spiritual accomplishments.

The spiritual accomplishments of enlightened form emerge as deities, enlightened speech as seed syllables, enlightened mind as symbolic implements, and their bodhicitta, the nature of pristine great bliss, takes the form of five-colored rainbow light. Inseparable from the torma, all of these dissolve into the four places of the self-visualization, bringing with them empowerments, blessings, and the common and supreme spiritual accomplishments. Imagining all this, enjoy the consecrated substances.

Following this, present offerings and songs of gratitude and, in this particular context, offer a peaceful fire puja offering to make up for any omissions or additions made during the recitation. Offer the substances using only the primary mantra. To petition for the retreat, recite the following:

> May any lack of clarity in my meditative absorption, impurity in the ritual, errors with the mantra and mudrā, and any additions, omissions, contradictions, or confusion be cleansed and purified.

In this way, ten percent of the recitation should be performed as a fire puja offering that utilizes substances and mantra. Since fire puja offerings are praised in all the higher and lower classes of tantra as important for the development of your practice, the fire puja offering must not be dispensed with.

During the dissolution stage, dissolve the visualization beginning with the protective dome and complete the concluding rituals. This comprises the completion of the retreat on an inner level. Next, maintain an uninterrupted schedule of practice sessions for three, seven, or another appropriate number of days. As a gesture of gratitude, perform as many gathering offerings, fulfillment ceremonies, and so forth as you can, along with dedications, aspiration prayers, and so on. When you physically complete the retreat, arise as the deity in the ensuing attainment, don armor, and protect the body. Go to the boundary of the retreat and set out a white torma and offering cup in front of the poles of each of the guardian kings. Then present offerings and praises of gratitude, request them to depart, and dismantle the poles. You may then proceed to meet a few of your companions who have received the same teachings and who abide by the samaya vows. These and other such details can be understood according to the system of *The Universal Secret*. If you are able, you can make offerings, as represented by presenting "The Smoke Offering to the Kings," and other such offerings, in an uncovered space to the lords of the four places, in general, or to specific deities, as well as offering alms to the destitute.

In some recitation manuals, it is taught that the substance of the spiritual accomplishments should be divided into four portions and enjoyed by your guru, the knowledge holders, yourself, and companions with whom you share samaya vows. After daybreak, perform the rituals for the daily torma, the torma for the protectors, and so forth.

The residual that has been imprisoned should also be offered here. Of the three portions of the practice torma, one part should be hidden as treasure in the retreat space, one part should be offered as material for the fire puja offering, and one part should be mixed with another torma and left outside. Remind the Tenma of their oath and complete their practice in its entirety, then proceed with the stages of dissolution and so on, up to the prayer of auspiciousness. Next, perform the amending fire puja, take down the guardian kings' poles, and present offerings to the local protectors. Though it is taught that you should perform these steps in this order, in practice it suffices to use whichever structure is most convenient.

Concerning the dedication, the unique feature of the skillful means of Secret Mantra is that you accumulate as much merit by performing the ritual one time each session as you would normally accumulate in an entire great eon. For this reason, dedicate all the virtue you have gathered, are gathering, and will gather—as exemplified by the basic virtues you have already accumulated in the past—as causes of enlightenment. To do so while imbuing the dedication with the knowledge that does not conceptualize the three spheres is the way to dedicate in a completely pure manner. Nevertheless, for beginners it is unlikely that such a dedication free from poison will occur, so you may also dedicate in a manner that simulates this state, thinking to yourself, "Just as the victorious ones throughout the three times and their heirs dedicated, likewise I now dedicate this merit as well." Reciting the dedication liturgy with this attitude is a unique method that will ensure that the basic virtues will not go to waste, but instead will develop further and further.

Concerning aspiration prayers, since the enlightened activity that benefits others is the culminating result that you seek through the path of the supreme vehicle, give voice to whatever aspirations you bear in mind. Recite any appropriate aspiration prayers, whether long or short, and attune your mind to the words you chant. With the superior attitude of wishing to benefit the teachings and beings, recite pure aspiration prayers to ensure that the temporary and ultimate benefit and happiness will be vast and unceasing. It is the unfailing reality of the interdependence of cause and result that whatever aspirations are made will be fulfilled accordingly.

For auspiciousness you may recite words of auspicious interdependence while thinking to yourself, "Through the power of the blessings, compassion, and truth of the host of deities that have been approached and accomplished—the three roots and three jewels—may all harmful and malevolent forces be pacified, may all positive qualities increase and develop, and may the fruits born of this virtue manifest vividly, beautifying the universe and its inhabitants and bringing the sublime glory and auspiciousness of benefit, happiness, virtue and goodness." At the same time, imagine that the victorious ones and their heirs appear in the space above you, proclaiming the auspiciousness with vajra songs and sending down a shower of flowers from all directions. These dissolve into you, your surroundings, your things, and so on, imbuing you with positive qualities and causing your body to take on a radiant glow. Scattering flowers brings virtue, and goodness to all times, places, and situations.

In this way, the basis for purification is your own buddha nature, which is referred to as "potential" and "element." The objects of purification are all the incidental impurities, while the process of purification is the path that unites the two stages. Following that path, you actualize the result of purification, which refers to all the qualities of the ground.

Moreover, the various forms of absorption serve as a skillful means. When you train in each of these absorptions and subsequently master them, you will gradually progress through the five practices of the defiled paths of accumulation and joining, as well as the undefiled states of the four knowledge holders. This comprises the definitive perfection, practice through actualization. One who practices in this manner is referred to as a "mature student."

Nevertheless, even if you have yet to attain stability in meditative absorption, there is also the approach of devoted training. This involves simply meditating on the mere forms of the development stage to the best of your ability. In that way you can complete the preparation, main practice, and concluding activities of the development stage in each session, from the protective sphere to the concluding steps of donning armor and protecting the body. The Great One of Uḍḍiyāna taught:

> The view relates to scripture and reasoning. Meditation relates to experience. Secret Mantra relates to empowerment. Blessings relate to devotion. Experience relates to realization. Conduct relates to time. Spiritual attainments relate to the samaya vows. The fruition relates to benefiting others. Practical instructions relate to the guru. Practice with these nine relationships.

In particular, tantra relates to practice manuals. Practice manuals relate to liturgical arrangement. Liturgical arrangement relates to the practice tradition. The practice tradition relates to the key instructions of the lineage gurus. Accomplishing the yidam deity via these relationships is the very essence of the infinite victorious ones.

Hence, with certainty about these relationships, exert yourself without partiality. *The Condensed Realization* states:

> Accomplish one buddha and you accomplish all others without practice.
> Hence, exert yourself in practicing one deity without partiality.
> Should you practice many with an attitude of partiality,
> You will have accomplished none, and it will wear you out.

In particular, it is important to arouse faith and devotion in the yidam deity. You should not have any doubt that the yidam is, in essence, your own guru, the embodiment of all the buddhas, who has shown you the three forms of kindness. A tantra states:

> But the spiritual accomplishments linked to that
> Are still imminent for a simpleton who has faith.

And Patrul Rinpoche taught:

> That which opens the door to all dharmas,
> Clears away adverse circumstances for all practices,
> And enhances all the instructions
> Is said to be devotion. This you should know.

Once you have entered into the profound practice of approach and accomplishment in the appropriate manner, it is important to arouse the compassion of the buddhas with heartfelt yearning.

Generally speaking, the compassion of the buddhas enters sentient beings in a particular manner. First, their compassion is everlasting and continuously unfolds like a flowing river. It is natural and instinctive, occurring without effort or thought, like sunlight. Still, when aroused and prayed to, their compassion is like the response of a compassionate person to a beggar asking for money and when meeting with an appropriate object—someone in need of guidance—their compassion resembles that of a parent seeing his or her child racing toward a precipice. In this way, it allows for the victorious ones and their heirs to view you as their child and kin, and for the ḍākinīs and Dharma protectors to see you as their companion and master, respectively. That provides a unique circumstance for you to receive their blessings. Consequently, if you arouse the compassion of the buddhas and pray to them with intense, heartfelt longing, they will be powerless not to grant you the two spiritual accomplishments, just as the result occurs once the right causes and conditions have come together.

At that point, there are lesser, middling, and great spiritual accomplishments. The lesser spiritual accomplishments are the four enlightened activities: pacifying the eight fears, increasing the six riches, magnetizing based on the four kinds of devotion, and the four types of wrathful activity. The eight fears are those of fire, water, lions, elephants, snakes, flesh-eating demons, shackles, and thieves. Alternatively, the eight fears can be listed as illness, famine, fire, water, war, weapons, imperial punishment, and untimely death. The six riches are longevity, merit, glory, splendor, retinue, and wealth. The four kinds of devotion are when others feel affection toward you as though seeing you as their parent, respect for you as though seeing you as their guru, fear of you as though seeing you as a king, and love for you as though seeing you as a friend. The four wrathful activities are to annihilate by wrathfully instilling fear in hordes of enemies, banishing them, killing them, and summoning them. The four enlightened activities, counted together with these four subcategories of wrathful activity, are referred to as the "eight great activities." The middling spiritual accomplishments are mentioned in the following song:

> Eye medicine, swift-footedness,
> Sword, unearthing,
> Pills, flight, invisibility,
> And extracting essences . . .

The great spiritual accomplishments are the eight qualities of mastery, as outlined in the following passage:

> Subtle body, lightness to the touch,
> Pervasiveness, genuine attainment,
> Complete manifestation, stability,
> Mastery, and control over desirable things . . .

The supreme spiritual accomplishments are the four unique enlightened activities: pacifying the obscurations of karma, the afflictions, and the all-ground; increasing the qualities of scripture and realization; magnetizing the wisdom of liberation and omniscience; liberating yourself through realization and others with compassion. It also refers to mastering all the qualities of the paths and levels, such as the powers, clairvoyance, retention, and eloquence. Moreover, the supreme spiritual accomplishments in the temporary context of the path of joining are to attain the illusory form of the matured knowledge holder; on the path of seeing, to attain the form of luminosity of the knowledge holder with power over longevity and to attain the unified form of training of the Great Seal knowledge holder. Ultimately, the supreme spiritual accomplishment is to attain the unified form beyond training of the spontaneously present knowledge holder.

The glorious Ngawang Trakpa writes:

> Complete enjoyment, integration, great bliss, lack of inherent existence,
> Being completely filled with compassion, uninterrupted, and unceasing . . .

Having actualized the state of the unified vajra holder with these seven unified features, the twofold benefit will certainly be perfected.

> The treatises of the learned and the key instructions of the accomplished
> Are an ocean of eloquent expositions of the profound and vast,
> Billowing with countless waves of scripture and reasoning.
> Inferior minds can hardly fathom its depth.

Still, hoping to benefit a few with a fortune like mine,
I have compiled the oral instructions of realized beings.
These are droplets of nectar, written with devotion and faith.
Any mistakes that I have made, I confess to the masters of the
three lineages.

May the wish-fulfilling cloud of virtue gathered through these
efforts
Forever appear above all beings
And shower them with unceasing benefit and happiness,
Bringing forth the sublime result of the twofold benefit.

At the request of some devoted students, and motivated by the wish to help those with inferior minds like my own, I gathered together these instructions from the recitation manuals of various indisputably learned and accomplished masters, along with the oral instructions of my own supreme and noble guru. I, the ignorant one with the title of tulku, Kunkyen Tenpe Nyima, compiled these notes in my own retreat hut at Ngepa Dongyi Gatsel Chokhor Namgyal Ling. Śrīyantu. Virtue, virtue, virtue.

Illuminating Jewel Mirror

A Brief, Clear, and Comprehensible Overview of the Development Stage

Shechen Gyaltsap Pema Namgyal

Namo Guru Deva Ḍākinīye!

> Just to hear or remember your name
> Instills in us the vajra wisdom—
> Guru, sublime deity, I bow to you
> As I set out to briefly describe the development stage.

The great vajra-holding Conqueror has taught uncountable gateways to the Dharma in accord with the capacities of beings to be guided. The goal of all of these is the resultant supremely secret vajra vehicle, a path that has two stages: the development stage of means and the completion stage of knowledge. Here, with the intention to help beginners, I will set aside extensive quotations and verbosity and describe in a very concise and comprehensible way the theory and practice of the first level, the development stage, in connection with its ritual enactment.

The vajra vehicle is a part of the Great Vehicle, in fact it is its pinnacle, so first of all it is vital to be grounded in the motivation and conduct of the Great Vehicle. It will not suffice to delve haphazardly straight into mantra and claim to be doing recitation practice. Instead, we should consider this: for once, we have now attained something so rare and valuable, a precious human life with its freedoms and advantages. It will, however, not last long since we are not immortal. When and where we will die is unsure, and there are so many ways death can happen. We have only a few things to help us stay alive, and many of them can cause our death as well. When death suddenly comes around, no one can stop it. When we die, we can take nothing along with us but our positive and negative actions. If the ripening of our tainted, unwholesome actions carries us then into the lower realms, we will face the endless suffering of heat, cold, starvation, thirst, and enslavement. Even if wholesome, tainted actions propel us into the higher realms, we will not remain there forever; they are still conditioned states and will end at some time. Thus, any type of birth we may take within existence will be characterized by the three types of suffering, and will leave us without the slightest chance of real happiness.

Now we are at this juncture of paths that lead up or down, whereby our future fate, either good or bad, lies before us. Here we should reflect on the futility of all the pain and happiness, victory and loss, joy and sorrow that occur in our lives and conclude that the only thing for us to do is reach the fruition—liberation from this perpetual suffering. If we cannot sincerely engender such an attitude of disenchantment, our path will not even qualify as that of the Lesser Vehicle, let alone the Great Vehicle. Beyond this, as followers of the Great Vehicle, it is vital to have the noble wish to help others. We should thus consider the great kindness of every single being throughout the reaches of space, without distinction regarding friend or enemy, connected as they have been to us as our fathers, mothers, friends, and relatives in past lives. Though all of them want only happiness, they are unaware of the means to achieve it and instead perpetuate the causes and effects of suffering. How sad! If only they could be happy and never suffer; and how wonderful if they could swiftly attain unsurpassed, complete enlightenment! Whatever the cost, we alone must bring them to that state. However, in order to have the power to do so, we must, by all means, first reach the level of complete enlightenment ourselves. To that end we must harmoniously integrate the profound key points of the paths of sūtra and mantra and put them into practice.

It is important to have a foundation in these special points of motivation and conduct, so train by repeatedly applying them to your personal experience. Always maintain mindfulness and attentiveness, and give up the self-centeredness that impedes them. If we do not know how to continuously use all our physical, verbal, and mental endeavors for altruism and transform them into the seeds of awakening, we will never enter the ranks of the Great Vehicle. This precise type of mind training is crucial at the beginning since it will not be enough just to proclaim oneself a Great Vehicle practitioner.

When a person is well grounded in the Great Vehicle attitude and behavior, and is ready to enter the resultant vajra vehicle of Secret Mantra, it is first of all necessary to receive the ripening empowerments. Without that, we are not permitted to even hear the teachings, let alone practice them. It also does not suffice just to receive empowerments; we must adhere to the commitments, which constitute their life force. If we do not adhere to them, whatever we set out to do will go wrong—it will lead us to misfortune in this life and, afterwards, land us directly in vajra hell. It is said, however, that if one is able to keep them correctly, one will be liberated within seven lifetimes even without practicing.

The root of these commitments is to never transgress the bonds related to the guru's body, speech, and mind. If we are able to constantly supplicate the guru, his blessings will automatically penetrate us and all the qualities of experience and realization will emerge like ice melting in springtime. All the major and minor qualities that emerge on the Great Vehicle path are said to depend on the guru, our spiritual guide. Thus, it is important to consider whichever main part of practice we are doing—whether the development, recitation, or completion stage—as an expression of the guru's body, speech, and mind.

Those who lack the fortune to already be motivated by this sort of renunciation, enlightened attitude, and devotion may nonetheless wish to strive in the practice of the two stages. For them there is no way around first reaching some degree of practical understanding of the presentations of the ground, path, and fruition continua, just as in archery one must first identify the target. One should learn the elaborate version of these from the profound sūtras and tantras on the definitive meaning as well as their commentaries and instructions. We can then also learn the specific details from the oral teachings of a qualified master who holds a lineage for them. I will definitely not be able to present them here in just a few words.

THE BASIS OF PURIFICATION

To provide a mere kernel of the basic principles for beginners, the basis of purification—as it is commonly taught in sūtra and mantra—is the reality of suchness, or the essence of the bliss-gone ones. The nature or definition of suchness is resolved in the Victorious One's middle wheel of teachings in terms of the empty essence, the natural state endowed with the three liberations. In the final wheel of teachings suchness is expressed in terms of the manifest aspect of luminous wakefulness indivisible from the undefiled enlightened attributes. In mantra, however, suchness is described as vajra mind, which is the unity of these two. This refers to the intrinsic wakefulness beyond expression that is the innate luminosity of one's own mind.

Moreover, the basis of purification can also be described as the ultimate *evaṃ*, emptiness with all supreme qualities, the thoroughly immutable great bliss, indivisible unified wakefulness, the all-pervasive identity, the essence that is beyond destruction and separation, and the unconditioned nature. Everything that manifests arises from this basis. This includes the impure delusion we initially experience as a sentient being, our mixed pure and impure experiences while a practitioner on the path, and also the entirely pure experience of enlightened bodies and wisdoms at the fruition of buddhahood.

It is said that no matter how things temporarily appear, in their true and ultimate condition they remain primordially as the infinitely pure circle of deities. This is what is seen by the eyes of a buddha whose obscurations have been purified, similar to how a pair of healthy eyes perceives the white color of a conch.

THE OBJECT OF PURIFICATION

This essence is primordially pure in nature, and its identity is beyond the changes of the three times. By not recognizing suchness, however, we ascribe self-entity to its manifestations, and out of the full-blown force of erroneous fixation confused experiences emerge adventitiously. Similar to how the sun can be covered by clouds, the true face of our essence becomes obscured, while the appearances of environments, objects, and bodies emerge unendingly. This is the object of purification—the aspect of the truth of origin, which is karma and disturbing emotions, as well as the resulting defilements. This includes, in short, all coarse and subtle obscurations of adventitious unreal appearances down to their most subtle aspects. These are overcome by wisdom at the consummation of the path, whether that of sūtra or mantra. In the present context of mantra, the development stage purifies the gross aspects, while the completion stage purifies the extremely subtle aspects, such as the obscuration of transference related to the three appearances.

THE PROCESS OF PURIFICATION

The process of purification, generally speaking, is any degree of goodness that is created through the Great Vehicle. It constitutes the cause, or method, for purifying the fleeting stains that obscure our potential. From the perspective of the resultant Secret Mantra, however, it refers specifically to perceiving how everything within appearance and existence, saṃsāra and nirvāṇa, is primordially the nature of enlightenment, the inseparability of the truths of purity and equality, never apart from the great sublime dharma body. Having resolved this as the view, the process of purification is to strive in both the development and completion stages of the path, method and insight, which harmonize with this view.

THE RESULT OF PURIFICATION

As the path is completed by training in this way, we become free of the cloudlike, adventitious obscurations that appear, yet do not exist. At that point we transform and become the essence of the twofold purity. This is the identity of the three bodies of enlightenment and the actualization of all the qualities that abide within the ground. It is known as the effect of separation.

Therefore, from the perspective of the essential reality of things, our essence does not change during the occasions of the ground, path, or fruition. In this sense, it remains without increase or decrease; nothing is ever removed from nor added to it. Furthermore, relative saṃsāric phenomena are unreal adventitious appearances that never have existed and never will. This being the case, they are empty forms—nonexistent deluded appearances emerging out of the power of habit—and are always devoid of reality. Just as a child in a dream, never having been born will also never die, the intrinsic nature never increases nor disintegrates. This is the meaning of equality. I have heard the omniscient Mipham Rinpoche himself say that comprehension of this is a crucial point in both the systems of sūtra and mantra. We should therefore understand it to be the single intended goal of the Great Vehicle paths, whether sūtra or mantra, which uniformly hold this as the single path to liberation.

In short, the ground of purification is the naturally present ground, which is primordially beyond being bound or liberated. The object of purification consists of fleeting and nonexistent appearances, which are the basis of deluded imputation. The path, or process of purification, is everything included in and associated with the truth of the path, the wisdom that serves as a remedy by purifying these appearances. The effect of separation is the quality of having purified delusion. In this way we should properly understand the key points of how these relate to one another. The ground and path are connected as that which we should know and what brings about this knowledge. The fruition and the path are connected as that which we should attain and that which causes this attainment. The ground and fruition are connected in being of a single essence and identity. Without understanding these principles we will take the essential nature to be merely a provisional reality and focus on it as a conditioned phenomenon, hoping that our present practice will create the cause for achieving it as a result in the distant future. Separating appearance and emptiness in this way, we will not form even a basic understanding of the view, meditation, conduct, or fruition of the resultant path of unity, and our path will become an artificial fabrication. Therefore, it is of utmost importance that, if nothing else, we gain some familiarity with this topic at the outset.

After gaining this conviction we can enter the path. There are many suitable teachings directed toward this, such as the "five things to take as the path," but here I will instead summarize the core points and consider the principles of outer, inner, and secret approach and accomplishment as they are described by the omniscient master Jampel Gyepa.

First is the deity to be accomplished. The ultimate deity of reality, itself, is naturally-existing wakefulness, the maṇḍala of the mind of awakening. Within this state, all phenomena of appearance and existence are primordially beyond union and separation. Beings who do not realize this, however, experience themselves as different from the deity, and so become enveloped in the thoroughly binding shroud of karma and disturbing emotions. On the contrary, the deity, with its liberated wisdom body, has manifested true reality and thus fulfilled its own benefit. By means of immeasurable wisdom, love, and ability, it appears for others' sake in a form that may be peaceful or wrathful, representing its great aspiration and wisdom, such as Mañjuśrī or Yamāntaka, along with its emanated maṇḍala. It carries out enlightened activity unfailingly by means of the features of its form, the knowledge mantras of its speech, and by entering into absorption mentally, thus granting any spiritual accomplishment desired and establishing beings definitively in the state of the lasting happiness of liberation.

To practice this imputed deity in an outer way, we visualize it, perform its recitation, and make offerings to it.

To practice the deity on an inner level, consider the deities to be the pure essential wisdom energies and essences in the citadel of your own central channel. Your own impure body, speech, mind, and field of experience, on the other hand, are merely the magical display of the fluctuating energy of karma. Therefore, visualize the circle of deities as they naturally dwell in the central places of your channels, and practice energy and mantra indivisible. Accomplishment is then reached by focusing on the root of all this, which is the luminous dome of the heart, also known as the sphere of awakened mind, immutable great bliss, and unconditioned self-display.

On a secret level, when you realize the truth that your own mind is originally unborn, naturally existing wakefulness, the primordially equal basic space of all saṃsāra and nirvāṇa, there is no other deity to accomplish whatsoever. The deity is thus accomplished spontaneously and without effort; it is nothing more than a magical display that appears out of that basic space of saṃsāra and nirvāṇa. Therefore, to practice by resting evenly in natural awareness, originally beyond effort or cultivation, is the ultimate point of the profound Dharma. If you train by applying these instructions in accord with your meditative experiences as a practitioner, you will reach the utmost limit, the perspective of the great, primordial indivisibility of your mind and the deity. At that point it is said that you yourself become a greatly accomplished one.

In short, the ground is your innate mind, intrinsic wakefulness that is originally beyond being bound or liberated. The ultimate fruition is whichever deity you are practicing, such as glorious Vajrasattva, dwelling in the Unexcelled Realm. The path consists of the practitioner appearing in the form of the deity by means of the imaginary development stage. If you understand that these three are naturally indivisible in the play of the guru's mind—the manifest aspect of empty bliss, great wakefulness—then every true key point of practice is complete.

The Great Lord of Secrets states, "Its rituals are unique in that they integrate the development stage rituals taught in the tantras," which means that the development stage, with all its facets, is a complete path for purifying the habits for the four modes of birth.

The text also teaches that, "Its unique result is the capacity to develop the power of mantra." This is true although, generally speaking, a path that is merely development stage will lead, at best, to achieving the level of knowledge holder in the desire or form realms—up to great supreme worldly attribute—and accomplishing the eight qualities such as lightness and subtleness. However, if we use the authentic path of definitive perfection as it is laid out in the unique teachings of the Early Translation School on the *Secret Magical Web*, we can train in the path of unified development and completion from the outset, beginning with the three samādhis and progressing through the perfection of the five experiences. In doing so, we can connect to the actual luminosity, the unified form of the deity, at the path of seeing. This is logical considering the explanations that even the ordinary sūtra path can eventually lead one to the actual luminosity at the path of seeing.

The text furthermore states that, "Its unique essence is the nature of blissful melting and emptiness." This means that, when following the authentic path of means, the form of the deity appears as the natural expression of the emptiness produced by the blissful melting. Otherwise, for a follower of the path of liberation, it appears as the natural expression of the union of utterly immutable bliss and emptiness that is complete with all supreme qualities.

Finally, the text mentions that, "Its unique function is the completion of purification, perfection, and maturation." In being a process of purification, the development stage path refines away and purifies the objects of purification, such as the three phenomena of cyclic existence, by manifesting in a similar way to them. The visualization of the seed syllable for the three enlightened bodies perfects the fruition within the ground by resembling the nature of nirvāṇa, the result of purification. Finally, by laying the foundation for extraordinary wisdom to dawn in one's mind-stream, the development stage matures one for the completion stage. Thus, the development stage practice is unique in four ways.

With conviction in these principles, we begin the main explanation, which integrates them with a ritual structure. Here there are three divisions: (1) the preliminaries, (2) the main part, and (3) the conclusion.

THE PRELIMINARIES

The preliminaries consist of (1) the general and (2) the unique preliminaries.

The General Common Preliminaries

Refuge

The practice of taking refuge comes after we have engendered the genuine disenchantment and noble attitude described above. In this case, we and all other sentient beings are those who take refuge in the guru, three jewels, and the host of maṇḍala deities. We do so because we recognize the qualities of the objects of refuge, and seek protection from the suffering of cyclic existence in general, from selfishness in particular, and especially from ordinary, deluded, fixating thoughts. On a relative level, we take refuge by accepting the refuge objects as teacher, path, and companions, and on an ultimate level by understanding that they are inseparable from our own minds. They then remain our refuge until we become enlightened or, in other words, until the objects of refuge have manifested in our mind-streams. With this understanding, visualize the objects of refuge in the sky before you in the usual manner, and chant aloud the refuge verses in your text three times.

Arousing the Mind of Awakening

To arouse the mind of awakening in aspiration we make a commitment to the result, wishing to attain the goal of unexcelled fruition for the sake of all beings. To arouse it in application we make a commitment to the cause of that fruition. These two aspects together constitute the relative type, which is taken symbolically. The ultimate type, which emerges from the power of meditation on ultimate reality, is to bring to mind an insight, a recognition of the fact that we and all other beings are equal in our primordially enlightened nature, and then to remain in meditation within that recognition without adding or omitting anything. This mind of awakening is, in short, emptiness that is intrinsically compassionate. Bring these points to mind and say the verses for arousing the mind of awakening according to your text while taking the field of accumulation as a witness. Afterward, train your mind in the four immeasurable qualities of: (1) love, wishing beings to be happy; (2) compassion, wishing them to be free from suffering; (3) joy, wishing them happiness devoid of suffering; and (4) equanimity, wishing them to remain with neither attachment to friends nor hatred toward enemies.

The Meditation of Vajrasattva

Next is the meditation and recitation of Vajrasattva, which clears away adverse circumstances. Visualize Guru Vajrasattva above your head as the "power of support." Then give rise to the "power of remorse" as you sincerely regret the negative deeds you have carried out in the past. Pledge henceforth to refrain from them at the cost of your life, which is the "power of resolve," or "restoration." For the "power of applying the antidote" imagine that your recitation of the hundred syllables causes a stream of nectar to flow down from the mantra circle in Guru Vajrasattva's heart center. Entering you, and all others, through the crown of your head, it fills your body and purifies you of all your damaged and broken vows as well as concepts and obscurations. While integrating the four powers of the antidote in this way, recite the hundred syllables as many times as possible. At the end, supplicate with a sense of shame and regret, and imagine that doing so leads Vajrasattva to melt into light and dissolve into you. At that point, rest evenly in the state in which misdeeds and downfalls have no inherent existence.

Maṇḍala Offering

The maṇḍala offering creates conducive circumstances. On an outer level the maṇḍala consists of the central mountain, continents, sun, moon, and the riches of the universe and its inhabitants. On an inner level it includes whatever you own—your home and valuables—while on an innermost level it refers to your body with its collections of aggregates, elements, and sense bases. Mentally transform all this into a "Samantabhadra offering cloud" that is, by nature, great wisdom. Then offer it a suitable number of times, while reciting the corresponding verses, and while bringing to mind the ultimate level of offering, the nonconceptual primordial state free from subject and object of offering.

Guru Yoga

Guru yoga infuses our mind-streams with extraordinary blessings. To practice this, resolve, once and for all, that your root guru is, in fact, the embodiment of all buddhas, as it is taught in every sūtra and tantra. Recognize that your guru has the same qualities as the Buddha, while his kindness towards you is even greater, and then let your mind be overcome with devotion. In this passionate state of mind, visualize your guru in the style of the "all-embodying jewel" or, alternatively, together with all the lineage gurus, whether they appear in tiers or surround him like a marketplace crowd. Then, along with all beings, make a genuine offering of the seven branches, with your body, speech, and mind in unison. In this way you bow down, make offerings, confess to harmful deeds, rejoice in what is virtuous, request the turning of the Dharma wheel, supplicate the buddhas not to pass from their form bodies into nirvāṇa, and dedicate all virtue to unexcelled enlightenment. If there is a lineage prayer, recite it while still overwhelmed by intense devotion. At the end, use the visualization for receiving the four empowerments and imagine that your guru melts into light and dissolves into you. Then rest evenly, for as long as you can, in the natural state in which the guru and your own mind are indivisible, the basic nature of great bliss, the nonconceptual state of empty luminosity beyond words. This is the ultimate guru yoga; afterwards you should make dedications and the like.

The meaning of the preliminaries, the method for practicing them, as well as their precepts and benefits can be studied in the various other texts where such things are already described in detail.

The Unique Preliminaries

The unique preliminaries have two parts: (1) removing adverse circumstances and (2) creating conducive circumstances.

Removing Adverse Circumstances

This section has two parts: (1) expelling obstructors and (2) drawing the boundary.

Expelling Obstructors

Like a fish leaping out of the water, visualize your mind, as the natural expression of emptiness, instantly in the form of a boundary deity, such as the wrathful king Hayagrīva or Vajra Rage. Cleanse and purify the obstructors' torma into emptiness, and imagine that within emptiness appears a jewel vessel holding the torma substance replete with nectar of the five sense pleasures. With OṂ, purify any impure stains, with ĀḤ, multiply the substances, with HŪṂ, transform them into whatever enjoyments are wished for and, with HOḤ, remove any defiling stains. In this way the torma is consecrated and transformed into radiant wisdom nectar.

With light rays from your heart center summon the obstructors before you and offer them the torma with the mantra and mudrā. Command them with words of truth and, using the verse in your text, order them not to make obstacles to your attainment of awakening; then toss the torma outside. There may be certain beings who do not heed your command and set about making obstacles. So next, as you continue to visualize yourself as the Wrathful King, imagine an overwhelming torrent of wrathful deities, weapons, and fireballs, numerous as the particles in the universe, streaming out of your heart to expel those obstructors far, far away. Fumigate using resin, scatter with charmed mustard seeds, chant fierce mantras, and put on a wrathful and terrifying air.

Drawing the Boundary

Second is to draw the boundary, which is analogous to locking the door after you have chased out a thief. At this point the wrathful deities and weapons you have just emanated now gather back, and as if melding together, coalesce to form a vajra ground everywhere beneath you. Surrounding you like an iron mountain range in every direction is a high and vast circular fence made of intertwined vertical and horizontal vajras. A vajra dome that is fixed to the fence like a lid encloses it above. Resembling the upper part of an Indian tent, it has a high peak that gradually slopes downward. Extending inward from the junction of the fence and the dome, a vajra lattice forms a sheltering canopy. Outside, a vajra lattice made of interlocking, linked vajra chains covers the enclosure. At the apex of the dome is a half-vajra top ornament. The fence is secured on the outside at its midpoint by a vajra chain. All of the vajras in this visualization are blue. Imagine that wrathful deities, weapons, fireballs, and vajra sparks emanate from this, shooting outwards to guard against any obstructors or obstacles, so that even the wind at the end of an eon cannot pass through.

These are the general features of the protection circle. It should be understood that there are other specific details, for instance the ten wrathful deities arrayed on the spokes of the wheel of the protection dome. There are also visualizations for the domes of weapons and the protection circles of the four elements, which are outside the main protection dome, and which should be applied, by context, according to the central figure. Chant the verse from your text while imagining yourself contained within this along with the other people and valuables to be protected, including your retinue. Afterward, seal this with the insight that holds no reference points of a self to be protected, wrathful deities and weapons doing the protecting, or of an act of protecting; this is the protection circle of suchness, which is the most supreme form of protection of all. Subsequent to this certain liturgies may include other parts, such as a confession of damaged and broken vows in order to clear away any wrongdoing in relation to the deity, or a vajra pledge never to transgress these vows again. If so, you should be able to understand the visualization according to its context by deriving the meaning from the verses.

Creating Conducive Circumstances

Second, in order to create conducive circumstances, there are two parts: (1) the shower of blessings and (2) consecrating the offering articles.

Shower of Blessings

Here those that "shower down" are the great blessings, the resplendence of the wisdom deities' five qualities of fruition. You, the practitioner, are the recipient, as well as your dwelling place and practice articles, for the purpose that you may connect with the shower of blessings of the wisdom deities' three vajras. This instills you with a resplendence that enables you to bring all spiritual accomplishments within reach, foremost of which is your own inherent wisdom. The process of the shower of blessings begins with you making an invocation with heartfelt devotion. This causes the blessings of the three vajras of all three root deities—who now fill the sky like sesame seeds bursting from a pod—as well as all spiritual accomplishments, to take the shape of deities for enlightened body; of seed syllables, for enlightened speech; and of symbolic implements, for enlightened mind. Imagine that these shower down like snowflakes on a vast lake, dissolving into and blessing you as well as your dwelling place and practice articles. Chant the verse for the shower of blessings, fumigate with special substances, and invoke with the music of the hand drum and other instruments.

Consecrating the Offering Articles

Second, consecrating the offering articles has two parts: (1) the general cleansing and purification and (2) the individual consecrations.

The General Cleansing and Purification

While visualizing yourself as the deity, the syllables RAṂ, YAṂ, and KHAṂ are projected out of your heart center. From RAṂ appears fire, burning away any impure defects in the offering substances. From YAṂ wind arises, scattering fixation on things as being real, while from KHAṂ appears water, cleansing away habitual tendencies. Finally, using the SVABHĀVA and other mantras, transform everything into the nature of emptiness, and rest evenly in spacelike emptiness.

The Individual Consecrations

For the individual consecrations there are two parts, one general and one special. The general consecration applies to both the outer and inner offering materials. First, the syllable BHRUṂ projects a wide and vast jewel vessel, which contains an OṂ, or else the individual seed syllables, meaning the first letters in each word marked with a dot. The syllables produce the outer offering materials, such as beautiful divine flowers, and the inner offerings, the naturally occurring substances, including the flowers of the five sense organs. Also emanated are the five sense pleasures, the auspicious articles and symbols, the seven royal possessions, and every other possible offering. Every one of these offerings emanates countless goddesses, each bearing its respective offering item. Thus, recite the mantra and the rest while visualizing that clouds of offerings stream out to fill up all of space.

There are then three special individual consecrations: one for medicine, one for torma, and one for rakta.

Medicine

Medicine refers to the nectar in the naturally present, bliss-sustaining vessel of the skull cup. It consists of the commitment substances of the five families of male and female bliss-gone ones. There is human flesh and excrement in the center, cow flesh and semen in the east, dog flesh and the human brain in the south, horse flesh and menses in the west, and elephant flesh and urine in the north. For each of these there is a syllable, respectively: HRĪḤ and BAṂ, HŪṂ and LĀṂ, TRĀṂ and MĀṂ, OṂ and MŪṂ, and ĀḤ and TĀṂ. Each of these syllables produces one of the five male and female buddhas, who then join together, inviting the victorious ones and their children throughout time and space with their blissful sounds and light rays from their places of union. The fire of intense passion causes the victorious ones to melt into light and then dissolve into the five pairs of male and female buddhas. This, in turn, causes the secret spaces to flow with white and red nectar, filling the skull cup. Finally, the male and female buddhas of the five families also melt into light and dissolve into the nectar, which is transformed into the essence of the five wisdoms, perfect in color, fragrance, taste, and potency. Imagine all of this as you recite the mantra.

This description is based on the lotus-speech family, so here Vairocana and Amitābha have been switched. Otherwise, vajra-family practices, such as the "Magical Web of Vajrasattva," should be applied to Akṣobhya. Practices related to the other four families should be applied to the buddha family if it is of the family of Vairocana, and so on. In any case, there is no contradiction, and you should correlate it according to context with your text.

Torma

For the torma, visualize a torma vessel as wide as the earth made of jewels. Within it is the torma substance, an inconceivable conglomeration of sense pleasures that appears as anything that delights the deities, emanated and amplified to fill the reaches of space. Though it is generally explained that there are three meanings of "torma," in this context it is understood to mean an offering substance.

Rakta

For the rakta, imagine a fresh skull cup with the hair still on it, which symbolizes the space of the female consort. Within it gather all concepts that cling to and fixate on the desire, form, and formless realms or, in other words, fixate on body, speech, and mind: those that cling to the body and appearance of the desire realm; to the speech and semiappearance of the form realm; and to the mind and nonappearance of the formless realm. These all coalesce and are purified into the nature of detached great bliss, a swirling ocean of rakta, which spreads throughout all of space while emanating clouds of desirable things.

These are the preliminary practices of engagement and counteraction. Collectively, they purify, perfect, and mature in a way that correlates to the link between object, process, and result of purification. First, they *purify* and protect against the objects of purification—the adverse circumstances of the saṃsāric condition. These consist of the tainted modes of birth that cause us to enter into existence in the desire realm, as well as the abodes, bodies, and enjoyments that subsequently unfold. They also refine the conducive circumstances that consist of accumulated meritorious actions. Next, they *perfect* the fruition by paralleling the actual results of purification. These include the defeat of the four demons that obstruct enlightened activity, the gathering of the two accumulations, the bestowal of empowerment with great flashes of light, and the actualization of the absorption that purifies enlightened realms. Finally, they *mature* us for the completion stage by means of the process of purification. This refers to the incredible method whereby these preliminaries clear away the obstacles and pitfalls in the practices of the channels, energies, and essences, and also produce within us the strength of experience and realization.

Please keep in mind that the descriptions throughout this text regarding how the principles of purification, perfection, and maturation can be integrated come largely from *The Great Commentary on the Ritual of the Profound Path, The Assembly of Bliss-gone Ones of the Great Compassionate One*, composed by the sun of the teachings of the Early Translations, Minling Lochen Rinpoche.

THE MAIN PRACTICE

The main practice in absorption has three parts: (1) the visualization practice of enlightened body, (2) the recitation practice of enlightened speech, and (3) the luminosity practice of enlightened mind.

Enlightened Body

The visualization practice of enlightened body has five aspects: (1) the cause: setting up the framework through the three samādhis; (2) the result: developing the support and supported maṇḍalas; (3) inviting and welcoming the wisdom beings into the support; (4) the activity stage of homage, offering, and praise; and (5) focusing on the deity's appearance, the primary focal point.

The Three Samādhis

The Samādhi of Suchness

Of the three samādhis, the first is the "samādhi of suchness," which purifies the death process. When embodied beings die, their internal earth, water, fire, and wind elements successively dissolve into consciousness. At the same time, external visible forms, sounds, smells, tastes, and textures also successively dissolve, and breathing ceases. The essences in the left and right channels then coalesce at the upper and lower endpoints of the central channel. At that point, texture dissolves into mental objects and consciousness merges with luminosity. The two essences residing at the A and HAṂ dissolve at the heart into the sphere that is a nexus of five essences, at which point all coarse and subtle thinking ceases. In a process of progressive magnification, the stages of appearance, increase, and attainment dissolve the coarser thoughts, and the stage of full attainment dissolves the subtler ones. If you fail to recognize empty luminosity through all of this, it will now dawn for a brief moment—lucid, empty, and free of thoughts, unobscured like space and free of the three discordant, polluting conditions. This is the actual luminosity of death, which is the basis of purification. If you recognize it, you are liberated without passing through the intermediate state. A resemblance of this luminosity is also present, for instance, during our sleep at night. For this reason, there is an instruction on recognizing luminosity at that time and then resting within that state without dreaming. Thus, the object of purification here is the extremely subtle habitual tendency to regress when we fail to recognize suchness.

The result of purification is the dharma body of enlightenment, a wakefulness that is utterly free of conceptual constructs. The process of purification is the meditation on all phenomena as being empty and devoid of self-entity. Moreover, apart from all phenomena of saṃsāra and nirvāṇa being merely the self-display of mind and wisdom, they do not possess an atom's worth of true existence. Wisdom, moreover, is the true nature of mind and cannot be found elsewhere. Thus, the intrinsic nature of our minds right now is unconfined wisdom, empty and lucid, the equality that is, by nature, free from any marks of conceptual elaboration.

If we relate this to the three gates of liberation, the gate of emptiness refers to the fact that the nature of mind is not something created but is naturally unconditioned, its essence empty. The gate of marklessness refers to the cause, and means that the nature of this emptiness is beyond the scope of conceptual mind's ability to characterize it as existing in such-and-such a way. The gate of wishlessness refers to the fruition, and means that, within the equality of that intrinsic nature, there is no fruition to attain and no process by which to attain it, and thus there is nothing at all to wish for. In this way, by settling your mind nonconceptually within the intrinsic nature that is beyond concepts, there is nothing to add or remove, accept or reject. This is the samādhi of suchness, which is primordially pure like the center of vajra space.

To use this type of meditation to progress on the path, rest evenly within emptiness for the main practice, free of elaboration and without concepts. This is in tune with the luminosity of dying as well as the dharma body at the fruition. Immediately afterwards, think, "This is the dharma body, death purified," and with such conviction in the purification and perfection, rest assured in the link between the ground and the fruition. On a downward level, practicing in this way purifies and refines away the stains of cyclic existence, the death state, the view of eternalism, fixation on appearance, and the formless realms. On an upward level, it nurtures the seed of the luminosity that manifests the dharma body, thus setting in place a link for perfecting the fruition. It also matures you by creating a foundation for the actual luminosity associated with the higher path of the completion stage to dawn in your mind-stream.

The Samādhi of Total Illumination

The object of purification at this stage is what occurs just after the fourth moment of the dying process. At that time the manifest realms of the five wisdoms magically appear as clusters of the five buddha families within the luminosity of the spontaneously present form body, which is similar to the autumn sky free of clouds. However, unless you have experience in the key points of practice, you will not recognize this. Thus, your conceptual mind, riding on energy, will progressively undergo the three experiences, which in turn give rise to the extremely fine and subtle mental body of the intermediate state. It has all the senses, is unimpeded, possesses subtle clairvoyance, and experiences magical karmic displays. Sustaining itself on the scent of burnt offerings, it experiences everchanging, fluctuating, and flickering dreamlike experiences that are terrifying and painful; thus, it is also called "the perpetuating disembodied consciousness."

The result of purification is the buddhas' enjoyment body adorned with the major and minor marks of enlightenment. It resides in the ultimate, self-manifest Unexcelled Realm, where it performs the dance of magical wisdom. The process of purification is to cultivate all-pervasive illusory compassion for beings who have not realized the way things are. To describe this in more detail, colors of rainbow light appear incidentally out of the pure expanse of space, though they are nothing but the nonexistent magical displays of space itself. Thus, in the natural state of emptiness and suchness, there is no duality of saṃsāra and nirvāṇa. Still, while there is never any parting from nonduality, beings are deceived by not recognizing the trick of the illusion. Confused, they regard these manifestations as real and proceed to wander helplessly throughout the realms of cyclic existence. Toward these beings we form a nonconceptual, illusory compassion, which we extend to sentient beings in every realm, wishing them permanent freedom from suffering.

In order to take this onto the path, practice the samādhi of total illumination as an illusory experience that, in the way it appears, accords with both the intermediate state and the resultant enjoyment body. Be confident that the intermediate state, in its pure form, is the enjoyment body. The samādhi of total illumination purifies the intermediate state, the view of nihilism, fixation on emptiness, and the form realms. It sets in place, moreover, a link for perfecting the resultant enjoyment body. Finally, it matures you by creating the foundation of great compassion, which is the cause for emerging in the unified, luminous state of the deity.

The Causal Samādhi

When intermediate-state beings approach their future place of conception, they develop craving toward it, whether it is the location of miraculous birth, the scent and taste in the case of birth from heat and moisture, or the copulation of their parents in egg- or womb-birth. The object of purification by the causal samādhi is this intermediate-state energetic mind, precisely in the moment before it connects to its imminent place of birth due to such craving. The result of purification is said to be the display, in physical manifestation, of coarse emanation bodies of perfect enjoyment to guide beings according to their needs. The process of purification is to meditate on your own awareness, the union of emptiness and compassion, as a particular seed syllable. This syllable, such as ĀḤ, HŪṂ, or HRĪḤ, has the nature of bliss, clarity, and emptiness, and is identical in color to the primary deity.

Train progressively in the previous two samādhis until you reach familiarity with them. Then proceed to the causal samādhi, the cause for accomplishing the realization of the emanation body, with which it is in tune. As the unity of the former two, it is the intrinsic, unchanging great bliss, the essence that pervades and extends throughout everything in existence as well as peace, both the animate and inanimate universe. Its nature is indestructible like a vajra, and it is the support for the mind of awakening. It is the subtle, great awakened life force, appearing in a way that is extremely fine yet vivid. Totally immutable, it has the features of clarity and stability, and can manifest as anything whatsoever. This seed syllable, manifesting as the identity of the indestructible great essence, is what emanates the entire maṇḍala. Meditate on it as the nature of bliss, clarity, and emptiness. This will create the causes for manifesting any maṇḍala as the magical display of bliss and clarity with the nature of emptiness.

Just as the causal samādhi provides the seed for the unfolding of the entire maṇḍala, the energetic mind in the intermediate state at the moment of entering the place of birth provides the seed for future existence. Similarly, a buddha's emanation body displays an array of manifestations to guide beings. These three are, in this sense, a congruity, so in order to take the causal samādhi onto the path, take assurance in the knowledge that birth in its pure form is the emanation body.

The causal samādhi purifies and refines away the craving consciousness at the moment of entering the place of birth. It also purifies the desire realm, and the concept that appearance and emptiness differ. In addition, it establishes a link for manifesting, out of the enjoyment body, resultant emanation bodies to guide beings according to their need. Finally, it also ripens you by creating the basis, in the context of completion stage, for emerging in the form of the deity out of bliss and the energetic mind.

In this way the three samādhis purify their objects: the habits associated with death, the intermediate existence, and rebirth. Their collective process of purification and the identity of their path as a whole is compassionate emptiness, which is, in fact, the single mainstay of the entire Great Vehicle path. It is vital that we focus our energy wholly on this at the outset since, in its absence, any path is just artificial. Whether or not we practice the later aspects of the development stage ritual in all their details is unimportant compared to having some degree of understanding and experience of this principle, as every key point is included within it.

The Maṇḍalas of the Support and the Supported

There are two aspects to the support and supported maṇḍalas: (1) visualizing the support, the celestial palace, and (2) visualizing the supported deities.

The Celestial Palace

Here there are also three parts: (1) visualizing the basis, the levels of layered elements, (2) visualizing the celestial palace, and (3) visualizing the seat.

The Basis

In this stage the object of purification includes several things. First, it includes the space element, which is the basis for the formation of the world, or the "container," where sentient beings take birth. It also includes the main cause for the formation of the world, which is mind. In addition, it includes the habits of shared karma that sentient beings have commonly gathered and ingrained in their minds, which eventually ripen into common outer appearances. Finally, it includes the maṇḍalas of the four elements as well as the central mountain. The result of purification is the basic space of phenomena, the realm where all buddhas become enlightened, symbolized by the pure expanses of the five female buddhas.

For the process of purification, begin with the causal seed syllable suspended in space within the protection circle. This then projects the syllables E, YAṂ, RAṂ, BAṂ, LAṂ, and SUṂ, which in turn send out light rays, purifying the five elements as well as thoughts that fixate on them. The syllables then gather back the pure essences of those five elements, which are all the qualities of the five wisdoms. In doing so, they dissolve and become the progressively layered elements. E gives rise to space in the form of a deep blue pyramid, "the source of phenomena." The broad side faces upwards and the tip points downwards. Above that, the green wind maṇḍala emerges out of YAṂ in the shape of a vajra cross, surrounded by a ring of smoky, dark-green light. Next, RAṂ transforms into the fire maṇḍala, a red triangle surrounded by a chain of blazing flames. BAṂ becomes the round, white, and swirling maṇḍala of water, encircled by white light. LAṂ gives rise to the earth maṇḍala, a square made of gold and surrounded by yellow light. Finally, SUṂ becomes the square-shaped central mountain made of the four types of precious substance. It has four terraces and is entirely surrounded by iron mountains. Visualize all of these touching one another but without being joined. Feel confidence in the link between the ground and the fruition, meaning that the five elements in their purity are the female buddhas of the five families.

This explanation applies to peaceful deities, but for wrathful ones you should visualize a sea of blood, a ground of human flesh, a mountain of skeletons, etc. in accordance with your practice text.

The Celestial Palace

Here the object of purification is the fixation that sentient beings have for the places where they live and the homes they inhabit. The result of purification is the wisdom of the basic space of phenomena, free of all elaboration, which is said to be the dwelling place of all buddhas. This wisdom is, by nature, a celestial palace, which is described symbolically as "the expanse of the vajra queen's womb." It is the celestial palace of delight in the sublime secret and supreme liberation, the great citadel of passing beyond suffering, the ultimate Unexcelled Realm of the natural state just as it is. This immaculate, self-manifest celestial palace is the essence of Vairocana, and thus thoroughly pure.

Here the process of purification is to take the self-manifest palace of buddhahood as the path. At this point imagine that the causal seed syllable projects a five-colored syllable BHRUṂ, which descends onto the top of the central mountain. After projecting and absorbing light, it dissolves into light and becomes the celestial palace composed of the two accumulations of merit and wisdom. In essence it has the nature of the five wisdoms, while its appearance is that of a celestial palace, with perfect design and decorations.

At the outermost level is an immense and vast protection dome. Inside of it is the central mountain, the top of which is a perfectly even ground consisting of miniscule vajras. At the periphery is a vajra enclosure resembling a fence of iron mountains, which emanates masses of five-colored fire. Within that enclosure, forming a perimeter, are the eight charnel grounds composed of all their awesome attributes, including stūpas, trees, fires, clouds, rivers, spiritual adepts, the guardians of the directions, gods, and nāgas. In the center of these is a thousand-petalled lotus made of a variety of jewels; its center is round, green, and level, and its red pistils are moist with dew. This lotus supports a bright and resplendent sun disc that spans the width of the pistils. At the center of the sun is a double vajra. The hub of the vajra is a deep-blue square, and its spokes are the color of their respective direction—the three extending eastward, for instance, are white. The celestial palace, which is perfectly square in shape, rests on this foundation. It has five consecutive layers of walls, each made of different types of jewels, the innermost of which is the color of the family of the main deity.

A ledge of red jewels surrounds the external foundation of the celestial palace, which protrudes at the base. On this ledge, the "platform of delights," are the offering goddesses, gathered in pairs and facing inward. Beginning at the far northern corner of the eastern side and continuing clockwise, they are: the blue lute goddess, the yellow flute goddess, the red round-drum goddess, and the green clay-drum goddess. Each of them holds her particular implement. Then, continuing on the southern side are: the blue goddess of beauty and the red goddess of laughter, both bearing their emblems; the yellow goddess of song, holding miniature cymbals, and the green goddess of dance with the emblem of dance. To the west are: the yellow goddess of flowers, the black goddess of incense, the red goddess of lights, and the green goddess of perfume, all bearing their emblems. To the north are: the red goddess of visual form, bearing a mirror; the red goddess of taste, with a tray of food; the green goddess of texture, carrying garments; and the white goddess of basic space, holding the triangular "source of phenomena." They are all adorned with silks and jewelry and have a serene and graceful countenance.

At the corners of the porticos and in each corner—the southeast, southwest, etc.—of the palace itself there is the seal of a half-moon and vajra. At the top of the palace walls runs a yellow frieze trimmed with inlaid jewels resembling frost. Above that run beams, which are supported by posts, also called pillar stabilizers. On top of these are the rafters that support the roof, on the tip of each of which is a "face of glory." From the mouths of these hang garlands and tassels made of jewels, as well as flower garlands, silk streamers, mirrors, crescents, and tail fans, all fluttering in the breeze. The roof rests on the rafters and extends out to the edge of the external foundation. Beneath, on the underside of the roof, is a line of rainspouts made of white gemstone which look like anointing vases turned upside down. Between them run garlands fastened directly to the lower ends of the rafters. Holding down the base of the roof from above is a parapet, also called a *lenken*, which has a stūpa design and consists of three or four levels of upright, white jewel planks. This is also referred to as the "half-lotus petal."

Inside the celestial palace there are eight pillars that support four interlocked beams, upon which twenty-eight rafters rest. The rafters support the ceiling, which is made of jeweled planks, except for a skylight in the center. A layer of jewels covers this entire level. The so-called "central chamber" is formed by an arrangement of pillars or wooden posts at each of the four corners of the skylight. They support the roof, the peak of which is adorned with a jewel-vajra top ornament.

In the exact center of the walls in each of the four directions there is an entrance with an outer vestibule. The upper parts of the vestibules have two protruding corners, while the lower corners connect with the external foundation. Each has four pillars, upon which are four interlocked beams. Each vestibule also has an architrave consisting of two parts, one "causal" and one "resultant." The causal architrave consists of stairs leading into the entrance. There are eight of these, two at the left and right sides of the roofed entranceway, and four at the midway point of the entrance itself.

The resultant architrave rests on top of the four interlocked beams mentioned above, and may consist of either four or eight constituent parts. If we consider one with eight, they are, sequentially: the horse ankle, lotus, casket, lattice, cluster ornament, garlands, rainspout, and roof. The horse-ankle ledge consists of a row of upright golden vajras set against a blue background. The lotus ledge is a row of lotus petals made of red gemstone. The casket ledge is a flat box made of various jewels inserted between small pillars. The lattice is a net of white jewels hanging down from the ledge of hanging clusters. The cluster-ornament ledge is similar to the frieze. The garland ledge consists of jewel garlands and tassels which hang from the mouths of lions against an even background.

The rainspouts and roof of the portico are similar to those described above, but the portico roofs furthermore are adorned with garuḍa heads at their four corners. From the necks of these garuḍas hang bells with strikers that make them ring in the breeze. In the middle of the architrave's facade there is a trefoil-shaped gap resembling an elephant from the back decorated on the inside with jeweled garlands and tassels.

On top of the portico roof, on the center of a lotus, is a golden wheel. It is supported on either side by two deer, a horned male representing method, and a hornless female representing knowledge. Finally, a decorative white parasol made of jewels surmounts it. Beyond this, the space in and around the palace is decorated with a variety of beautiful things such as jeweled canopies, banners, pennants, tail-fans, and bells strung on golden thread that ring as they flutter in the breeze. All of this is clear, translucent, and unobstructing.

This has been a mere overview. If you wish to study further details, they can be learned from other more specific texts, such as the *Magical Web*.

In the case of wrathful maṇḍalas, the palace is in the structure of the "blazing charnel ground palace," which functions to tame disciples of a less tractable nature. It has walls made of alternating dry, fresh, and rotting skulls, pillars made of the eight great gods, and beams made of the eight great nāgas. Its ceiling consists of the twenty-eight lunar mansions, while the skylight is made up of the eight planets, the sun, and the moon. The lattices and tassels are made of snakes and skulls. The palace architraves are ornamented with fingers, skulls, the five major organs, and garlands of the sun and moon. Its rainspouts are arm and leg bones, and its ledge is made of backbones. The roof consists of the hollow skull of Mahādeva and a heart adorns its pinnacle. The palace's banner is a human corpse. Its canopies are made of human skin, its tail-fans are made of corpse hair, its wreaths are made of intestines, and it is ornamented with pendulant lungs and hearts. Inside and out, the whole area is filled with charnel grounds and swirling lakes of blood, while terrifying fires and fierce storms rage everywhere.

In certain tantric scriptures you will see the phrases "beams of great excellence" and "rafters of lesser excellence." Guru Rinpoche explains in his commentary on Vajrakīlaya that "great excellence" refers to human corpses. He then comments that "lesser excellence" refers to: people who have deviated from the royal caste and become rock-dwelling lizards, people who have deviated from the priestly caste and become meadow-dwelling marmots, people who have deviated from the merchant caste and become forest-dwelling monkeys, and people who have deviated from the untouchable caste and become water-dwelling frogs. Beyond this, nothing more can be described here, as you must look to your particular text to understand the inner chamber and divine abode associated with a specific maṇḍala.

When practicing in this manner, if you fail to recall the purity of each individual element of the visualization, the object of your meditation will stray into your ordinary state of mind. Therefore, keep in mind that it is the qualities of enlightenment—the phenomena related to complete purification, consisting of inconceivable compassion and activity—that appear as the celestial palace in order to guide disciples. Composed of a variety of jewels, it is enlightened wisdom manifesting in shape and color in order to fulfill disciples' wishes.

The fact that the palace is square in shape shows there is no unevenness whatsoever in the basic space of phenomena. Its four doors represent the four activities of pacifying, increasing, magnetizing, and subjugating, or else, the way that the four boundless qualities, love and the rest, lead into the palace of great bliss. They also represent entrance into the palace of the nonarising basic space of things from the levels of the four liberations: the emptiness of cause, result, action, and essence.

The eightfold raised architrave entranceways represent the eight vehicles: of gods, humans, listeners, self-realized buddhas, bodhisattvas, action tantra, performance tantra, and yoga tantra. Otherwise they may symbolize passage through the eight effortful vehicles up to anuyoga and onto the effortless, nondual vehicle of ati. The four resultant architraves represent the four means of magnetizing: giving, speaking nicely, behaving consistently, and acting meaningfully. The eight parts of each of these symbolize the perfection of the qualities within the systems of the eight vehicles to complete liberation, or else, if there are four, the four vehicles of listeners, self-realized buddhas, bodhisattvas, and Secret Mantra. The uninterrupted spinning of the wheel of the Dharma is shown in the wheels and other such things.

The "platform of delights" represents the four applications of mindfulness: of the body, sensation, mind, and mental objects. The four pillars in the architraves symbolize the four right exertions: to prevent nonvirtue from happening, restrain existing nonvirtue, create virtue where there is none, and increase existing virtue. The four vestibules represent the four bases of miraculous power: intention, diligence, attention, and discernment.

The five-layered walls symbolize the five faculties that govern complete purification: faith, diligence, mindfulness, concentration, and knowledge. The frieze, top border, rainspouts, eaves, and central chamber symbolize attainment of the five strengths; when the same five (faith and the rest) become strengths, they cannot be overcome by their opposing factors.

The decorative jewel lattices, tassels, flower garlands, silk streamers, mirrors, half-moons, and tail-fans symbolize the seven factors of enlightenment: mindfulness, discernment of phenomena, diligence, joy, pliancy, concentration, and equanimity. The eight internal pillars symbolize the eight aspects of the path of the noble ones: right view, thought, speech, action, livelihood, effort, recollection, and concentration.

The pillar capitals symbolize the eight emancipations: (1) to perceive forms with regard to one's own body, (2) to perceive forms other than one's own body, (3) beauty, (4-7) the four sense spheres such as infinite space, and (8) the serenity of cessation. The four beams symbolize the four types of fearlessness: to proclaim that all has been abandoned and realized for one's own benefit and to show the path and its obstacles for others' benefit.

The twenty-eight internal rafters symbolize the eighteen types of emptiness and the ten perfections. The eighteen types of emptiness are: (1) emptiness of the outer, (2) emptiness of the inner, (3) emptiness of the outer and inner, (4) great emptiness, (5) emptiness of beginning and ending, (6) emptiness of the conditioned, 7) emptiness of the unconditioned, (8) emptiness of emptiness, (9) emptiness of what is beyond limits, (10) emptiness of nature, (11) emptiness of the unobserved, (12) emptiness of the ultimate, (13) emptiness of nonabandonment, (14) emptiness of nonentities, (15) emptiness of all things, (16) emptiness of individual characteristics, (17) emptiness of entities and nonentities, and (18) emptiness of essence. The ten perfections are: (1) generosity, (2) discipline, (3) patience, (4) diligence, (5) concentration, (6) knowledge, (7) method, (8) power, (9) aspiration, and (10) wisdom.

Otherwise, the twenty-eight rafters can be said to symbolize the buddhas' ten powers along with their eighteen unique qualities. The upper flat panels symbolize inconceivable qualities. The four posts supporting the central chamber symbolize the four correct discriminations: of Dharmas, meanings, language, and confidence. The crowning ornament symbolizes that all maṇḍalas of the enlightened ones coalesce in the expanse of naturally aware wakefulness.

Furthermore, the canopy represents the utter purity of true reality. The parasol symbolizes protecting beings with great compassion, while the pennant symbolizes great compassion itself. The banner represents victory over the demons and the prevailing of the Dharma. The bells resound with the sounds of the teachings of emptiness. The light that radiates in all directions represents the eternal adornment wheel of enlightened body, speech, and mind. The palace's nonobstructing appearance, utterly clear and bright while at the same time translucent, shows how everything is none other than the expression of wakefulness.

The crossed-vajra that forms the ground symbolizes wakefulness whose nature is indivisible from emptiness. The twelve enclosures symbolize the complete purity of the twelve links of interdependent origination: (1)

ignorance, (2) formation, (3) consciousness, (4) name and form, (5) the six sense bases, (6) contact, (7) sensation, (8) craving, (9) grasping, (10) becoming, (11) birth, and (12) old age and death.

The sun seat represents the natural luminosity of true reality. The lotus garlands show that true reality is unstained by any faults. The eight charnel grounds represent the innate purity of the eight collections of consciousness: the (1) eye, (2) ear, (3) nose, (4) tongue, (5) body, (6) mind, (7) disturbed mind, and (8) all-ground consciousnesses. They also represent the eight analogies of illusion: (1) illusion, (2) dream, (3) reflection, (4) mirage, (5) the moon's reflection in water, (6) visual distortion, (7) echo, and (8) apparition. The vajra fence symbolizes nonconceptual wakefulness, by nature utterly indestructible. The masses of flames symbolize the fire of wakefulness consuming wayward demons and disturbing emotions.

All of these qualities mentioned here—from the applications of mindfulness onward—are part of the extraordinary transformation that constitutes the undefiled state of enlightenment. Although it is important to remember the purity of each symbol as well as what it represents, as a beginner you may not be able to bring all of this to mind in a single practice session. If this is the case, you can approximate the recollection of purity by thinking to yourself that all the features of the celestial palace represent the buddhas' inconceivable qualities of abandonment and realization. We visualize the supporting maṇḍala, in short, so that we may take the self-manifest palace of the buddhas as our path. Through this process—by feeling confidence in perfect purity, the fusion of ground and fruition—we take the realms of all buddhas as our path as well.

Moreover, these visualizations ripen the practitioner for the subsequent practices due to a series of correlations. The stacked elements and the central mountain correlate to the five cakras and the central channel. The basis of the maṇḍala, the lotus, sun, and crossed-vajra, correlate as well to the energies and essences at the center of the cakras. Finally, the mind that mingles with all these in one taste—with its aspects of clarity, emptiness, and bliss—correlates to the celestial palace. Thus, by training properly in the supporting maṇḍala, the channels, essences, and energies will become pliable and under control. It thus matures you for the higher path by setting a foundation for the completion stage wisdom to dawn in your being.

The Seat

By visualizing the seat, the object of purification consists of sentient beings' fixation or habitual tendency toward a particular place of birth, such as the mother's lotus, the semen and ova, heat and moisture, etc. The result of purification is to manifest enlightened emanation bodies within saṃsāric states that guide beings according to their needs while being unstained by flaws such as the four modes of birth. Another result is to perfect the wisdom of luminosity—unified means and knowledge—through the natural purity of enlightened mind.

The actual procedure, or process of purification, is to visualize the seats of the central figure and retinue each in their respective manner. One common presentation, for instance, is to have a lotus in the center of the celestial palace, surmounted by a red sun disc and a white moon disc equal in diameter to the center of the lotus.

Otherwise, in the *Magical Web* for example, the central deities of the five buddha families have seats with five layers: an animal throne with a surface of jewels surmounted by a sun, a moon, and a lotus. The bodhisattvas have a seat of three layers: a sun, moon, and lotus. The six sages merely have a lotus for a seat, while the wrathful gatekeepers only have a sun. Finally, the doer and deed have a four-layered seat made of a sun, moon, lotus, and jewels.

This is just one example, however, and we must follow our own particular text. Wrathful deities have their own distinct thrones, which may consist, for instance, of Rudra, Mahādeva, male and female direction guardians, the major and minor bases of deliverance, and beasts.

In any case, with regard to the purity of the various seats, the animal thrones represent guiding beings by means of the four types of fearlessness, the ten strengths, the four bases of miraculous power, the ten powers, or the four activities. These are symbolized, respectively, by the lion throne, elephant throne, horse throne, peacock throne, and the half-bird, half-man *shang shang* throne. The sun and moon represent the luminosity of awakened mind in its natural purity, the unity of means and knowledge. The lotus is a symbol of flawlessness, while the jewels represent the fulfillment of beings' aspirations. The wrathful deities have seats that symbolize the defeat of ignorance, dualistic concepts, karma and disturbing emotions, as well as the four demons. However, for specific details, once again we must look to our particular scripture. While the other principles have been sufficiently described above, the ten strengths and the ten powers are as listed in the summary of *Introduction to the Way of the Learned*:

> The ten strengths are: the correct and incorrect,
> Ripening, elements, inclinations, faculties,
> Absorptions, paths, previous states, death and transference,
> And knowing the extinction of defilements.
>
> The ten powers are to have power over:
> Life, mind, materials, karma,
> Rebirth, intention, aspiration,
> Miracles, wisdom, and dharmas.

Finally, the lotus seat is related to the channels and the cakras, the sun to the fire of inner heat, and the moon to the syllable HAṂ at the top of the head. Therefore, visualizing the seat ripens you for the higher paths by creating a foundation for attaining the immutable bliss based on the melting bliss of blazing and dripping.

The Supported Deities

The visualization of the supported deities has two parts: (1) the actual visualization procedure and (2) the blessing and bestowal of empowerment.

The Actual Visualization Procedure

The visualization procedure has three aspects: (1) a general explanation of how to purify the habits of the four modes of birth, (2) a specific application of the visualization ritual of the three vajras, and (3) the characteristics of the deities.

Purifying the Four Modes of Birth

The Glorious Magical Web describes:

> To purify the four types of birth
> There are four types of development:
> The very elaborate and elaborate,
> The simple and the completely simple.

Purifying Birth from an Egg

The first of these four—the very elaborate and extensive style—refers to the procedures called *one's own children* and *another's child*, which purify birth from an egg. It has both an extensive and a concise version.

The extensive version is described according to the tradition of the sādhana section in *The Complete Secret of the Eight Sādhana Teachings*, which explains the general meanings of *one's own children* and *another's child*.

In the practice of *one's own children* you visualize your mind, the nature of the bliss-gone—the essential awareness that constitutes the basis for all appearances within saṃsāra and nirvāṇa—as the central male and female deities. These then give birth to other thus-gone ones, who become your children and are established within your retinue.

In *another's child* all the other thus-gone ones who previously dissolved into you in the context of *one's own children* and then exited the womb to manifest like children in your retinue now merge with the heart of the central deity. At that point all your conceptuality takes the form of a syllable, which descends into the consort's space. In this way you are born as her child and join the retinue.

Furthermore, there are five steps in making others *one's own children*. (1) First, the causal seed syllable descends onto the seat, projects and absorbs light, and then transforms, emerging as the causal heruka, the central male deity with consort. (2) Next, the light of bliss that shines where the male deity's secret vajra joins the female deity's space invokes all buddhas in the ten directions, who then enter the male consort through his crown and dissolve into the space of the female. (3) Once again, light rays are projected, summoning sentient beings and purifying their obscurations. They then dissolve into the female consort's space. (4) One then engenders the great pride of being the nondual identity of saṃsāra and nirvāṇa, thinking, "I am the Great Glorious One, head of all saṃsāra and nirvāṇa." (5) Finally, the assembly of deities emerges from the secret space and they take their respective seats.

Another's child is similar, for instance, to birth from an egg whereby first the egg is laid and then hatches so that the sense organs and limbs fully develop. This process has eight parts: (1) The primary male and female deities first dissolve into light and become a sphere of light, together with the seed syllable and symbolic implement. (2) This then transforms and emerges as the resultant heruka with consort. (3) Next, all the male deity's conceptuality is transformed into the essence of syllables while he thinks, "I am not able to produce a child." (4) Light rays of invocation then stream out of the female deity, and the deities in the retinue are supplicated to take birth as their children. (5) The retinue deities then delightedly melt into light and dissolve into the heart centers of the primary male and female deities. As they merge with the heart of the central deity, one takes pride in being the identity of great wisdom, the universal lord of every maṇḍala. (6) Next, the secret space where the male and female consorts are joined is consecrated and the maṇḍala emerges within the space of the female, complete with the celestial palace and throne. (7) You then visualize your own forty-two concepts, which abide essentially as syllables, transforming into the complete assembly of primary and retinue deities, which emerge from the space of the female consort. (8) Finally, you invite the wisdom deities from basic space so that they dissolve into the samaya being, and your three places are sealed with the three vajras. The retinue deities are then established on their thrones, the primary deity dissolves into the resultant heruka, and the celestial palace and thrones each dissolve into themselves.

There is also a concise version, which follows the tradition of the tantra section and accords with the *Magical Web*. There are, in fact, many points of discrepancy when comparing the extensive and concise styles of this meditation and the various expositions of the sublime beings of the past. However, they should be studied elsewhere.

Here, in our version of the concise method, you should begin by going for refuge and engendering the mind of awakening. Then visualize two stages, as occur in egg birth. First, visualize yourself instantly as the primary male and female consorts and then invite and visualize the maṇḍala you are practicing within the space before you. Next, make offerings, praise, supplications, daily confessions, and so on. Once this is finished, use VAJRA MU to rest evenly in emptiness again. This, in itself, is the unique feature of this approach—if you understand that, you can apply this presentation generally to the very extensive and moderately extensive development stage approaches for purifying womb birth.

In the majority of practices that outline a procedure such as the three vajras, the process of developing the deity is, in fact, as follows. Begin by visualizing the field of accumulation and go through the steps for gathering the accumulations; then dissolve the field into yourself, settling without any reference point. Next, carry out the various ritual procedures such as the expulsion of obstructors before proceeding to meditate on the samādhi of suchness and so on.

Whichever style of development you use, whether extensive or brief, its purpose is to purify your fixation on empty appearances. In the extensive style, the central deity and the entire retinue—*oneself* and the *children*—melt into light, while in the concise manner, both are left within the state free of concepts. Both methods purify the death state, in which all concepts and outer appearances temporarily cease. They perfect the dharma body—the basic space in which all habitual tendencies are purified—within the ground. They mature one for the completion stage of luminosity, which abides within the wisdom state that eradicates dualistic thought. They lead to the remanifestation, at the time of enlightenment, of the assembly of *another's child*, the primary and maṇḍala deities.

When we use the concise style and train according to our specific practice manual, there is a complete purifying and refining away of both the intermediate state—which follows the death state and the subsequent, progressive flaring of the energetic mind—as well as the vastly unfolding experiences of the birth state. There is a perfection within the ground of the divine form in the unified state beyond training. Manifesting out of the dharma body as the form bodies, it appears infinitely throughout the basic space of phenomena. Finally, there is a maturation of the completion-stage practitioner so that he or she can emerge out of luminosity as the divine form in the state of unity in training. This was the explanation of my teacher, Guṇa, lord of the tantra section of the great secret and a supreme expert in the definitive meaning.

Purifying Womb Birth

There are three ways to purify womb birth: (1) the four manifestations of enlightenment, (2) the ritual of the three vajras, and (3) the five manifestations of enlightenment.

The Four Manifestations of Enlightenment

The Heruka Galpo describes the four manifestations of enlightenment:

> First, emptiness and the mind of awakening,
> Second, the occurrence of the seed,
> Third, the complete form,
> Fourth, setting out the syllable . . .

The first manifestation of enlightenment, as explained here, is to rest evenly in the nonconceptual meditation of simplicity, and then cultivate the mind of awakening within that state. This is an illusory, unattached compassion toward all those who are unable to realize such a state themselves. On a downward level, this purifies the death state, in which all of the eighty intrinsic thought states subside due to confusion, as well as the indistinct appearances that unfold in the intermediate state as the karmic wind flares up again. Upwardly, it perfects the dharma and enjoyment bodies within the ground. In between, it matures one for the practices of luminosity and illusory body.

The second manifestation of enlightenment is to visualize the form of the deity's seed syllable, which is essentially the wisdom of unified emptiness and compassion. This purifies and refines away the stage at which the intermediate state consciousness, in the form of a disembodied perpetuating spirit, merges with the parents' semen and ovum. It perfects the emanation body within the ground, and matures one for emerging out of the symbolic wisdom in the illusory body of the deity.

The third manifestation of enlightenment is to visualize the seed syllable transforming into the symbolic implement of vajra mind, and then from that into the complete bodily form. This purifies and refines away the process of fetal development, beginning with the coalescence of the semen, ovum, and energetic mind, progressing through the embryonic stages: the oval, thickened, elongated, round, and solid phases. This would also include Viṣṇu's "fishlike" and "turtlelike" stages, as well as the complete development of the eyes, the other sense organs, and the limbs. It perfects the unified essence body within the ground, and matures one for emerging out of ultimate luminosity in the unified form of the deity.

The fourth manifestation of enlightenment may entail the projection of the seed syllable for producing the deities, or else the act of sealing via placement of syllables in the deity's three places. This purifies the fixation the newborn infant has on engaging with various things when it begins to explore objects with its senses. It also perfects the fruition of spontaneously present enlightenment within the ground. Finally, as one emerges in the unified form of the deity through completion stage training, it matures one to enjoy the experience of sense pleasures without any attachment as they have become the adornments of awareness.

The Ritual of the Three Vajras

The second method, the ritual of the three vajras, will be explained below [see p. 175].

The Five Manifestations of Enlightenment

The Hevajra Tantra explains:

> The moon is mirrorlike wisdom,
> The seven of seven, equality.
> Discernment is said to be the deity's
> Seed syllable and symbolic implements.
> All becoming one is perseverance itself,
> And perfection, the pure expanse of reality.

In this regard, the "ground manifestation of enlightenment" refers to the fact that, in the context of the ground, the white essence, red essence, energetic mind, and their collections are primordially enlightened as the essence of the five wisdoms. The "path manifestation of enlightenment" refers to the symbolic wisdom on the paths of accumulation and joining, and the fourfold unified emptiness that manifests the actual luminosity on the paths of seeing and cultivation. In order for this to develop in one's mind-stream there are the development stage visualizations of the moon, sun, symbolic implement, etc. The "resultant manifestation of enlightenment" refers to the five bodies, five wisdoms, and all of the qualities of the unified state beyond training at the fruition.

With this understanding of how the manifestations of enlightenment are linked to the ground, path, and fruition, we now turn to the specific way of training in the five path manifestations of enlightenment.

(1) The basis of purification for the first manifestation includes: the aggregate of form, the element of space, the body, the all-ground consciousness, the disturbing emotion of delusion, the male element in womb birth, the moisture in heat-and-moisture birth, the male element in egg birth, and the empty aspect of miraculous birth. The process of purification is to visualize the first manifestation of enlightenment, the moon disc, which is the essence of Vairocana and mirrorlike wisdom and emerges from the vowels.

(2) The basis of purification for the second manifestation includes: the aggregate of sensation, the element of earth, the disturbed consciousness, stinginess and pride, the red female element in womb birth, the female element in egg birth, the heat in heat-and-moisture birth, and the luminous aspect of miraculous birth. The process of purification is to visualize the second manifestation of enlightenment, the sun disc, which is the essence of Ratnasambhava and the wisdom of equality and emerges from the consonants.

(3) The basis of purification for the third manifestation includes: the intermediate-state consciousness (the disembodied perpetuating mind) merging with the semen and ovum, the aggregate of perception, the element of fire, speech, the mind conscious-

ness, the disturbing emotion of desire, and the intermediate-state consciousness as it enters into one of the four modes of birth. The process of purification is to visualize the third manifestation of enlightenment, the seed syllable combined with the symbolic implement, which is the essence of Amitābha and discerning wisdom.

(4) The basis of purification for the fourth manifestation includes: the coalescence of the semen, ovum, and mind into one; the aggregate of formations; the element of wind; the actions of body, speech, and mind; the five sense consciousnesses; the disturbing emotion of envy; and, in terms of the four modes of birth, the coalescence of the intermediate-state consciousness with semen and ovum in egg and womb birth, with heat and moisture in heat-and-moisture birth, and with merely empty luminosity in miraculous birth. The process of purification is to visualize the fourth manifestation of enlightenment, the coalescence of the moon, sun, symbolic implement, and seed syllable into one taste in the form of a spherical orb, which is the essence of Amoghasiddhi and all-accomplishing wisdom.

(5) The basis of purification for the fifth manifestation includes: birth from the womb after the period of gestation has culminated, the aggregate of consciousness, the element of water, the mind consciousness, the act of grasping at the reality of the eightfold collection, the disturbing emotion of anger, and the state in which the physical sense fields associated with taking birth in one of the four ways are fully developed. The process of purification is to visualize the fifth manifestation of enlightenment, the complete bodily form, which is the essence of Akṣobhya and the wisdom of the basic space of phenomena.

The three principles of purification, perfection, and maturation also apply to the five manifestations of enlightenment. Someone with a special physical support, such as a human body made of the six elements, can reach liberation by applying skillful means. Such a body has the bases for purifying the elements—the coarse aspects of the channels, essences, and energetic mind—fully manifest.

A person with this type of body must first be matured via empowerment. Then he or she should train in the five manifestations of enlightenment in the context of the conceptual path of the development stage. The main emphasis at that level is also the white essence, red essence, and mind. Therefore, by taking something that in appearance accords with saṃsāra as the path, one can thoroughly purify all aspects of semen, ovum, energy, and mind, which are the nature of existence and object of purification. Furthermore, by training on the path of devoted intent, which is in harmony with the true state of the victorious ones, one can perfect within the ground all the qualities of the five factors of fruition as well as the five wisdoms. Both of these mature one for aspects of the completion stage, such as appearance, flaring, near-attainment, luminosity, and union.

Purifying Birth from Heat and Moisture

Third is the simple style of development stage. This practice is based on the intent of anuyoga and serves to purify birth from heat and moisture. It says in *The Magical Key to the Treasury*:

> In the anuyoga vehicle, without developing it,
> But merely uttering the essence mantra,
> The complete form of the deity is visualized.

Unlike in womb birth, which involves a lengthy gestation, all the body parts of those taking birth from heat and moisture are fully formed as soon as the consciousness enters the combination of heat and moisture. Similarly, here, there is no need to make use of the details explained in mahāyoga, such as the five manifestations of enlightenment, nor the elaborate descriptions found in extensive development rituals. Instead, bring to mind the view of the great anuyoga scriptures, according to which all things are naturally enlightened as the fundamental maṇḍala of awakened mind—the great bliss child of nondual basic space and wakefulness. Without wavering from this view, direct its expression, the force of compassion, toward purifying the habitual craving toward the bodies and abodes of birth from heat and moisture. Then simply utter the essence mantra of the deity you are going to visualize. As you do so, visualize in completeness the form of the supported deity along with its support. This is the manifest aspect of relative truth that appears from the ultimate basic space of wisdom—Samantabhadra's expanse of emptiness. In this way you should train in the path of indivisible bliss and emptiness. This is known as "the magical development stage of insight into the unreality of appearances."

Purifying Miraculous Birth

Fourth is the completely simple style of development stage, which complements the pith instructions of atiyoga and serves to purify miraculous birth. Even faster than in birth from heat and moisture, the body of a being born miraculously is fully formed as soon as its consciousness enters into empty luminosity. The path that purifies this type of birth is a similar process, as Master Ganthapāda explained:

> Meditate without any seed,
> Like a being taking birth miraculously.

All sights, sounds, and thoughts—which is to say, all phenomena—are primordially enlightened as the vajra essence of the body, speech, and mind of the victorious ones. For this reason, the spontaneously perfect maṇḍala is already present right now in the state of fruition, effortlessly and without being created. This is the view of the atiyoga pith instructions, within which we visualize the maṇḍala of support and supported perfectly complete in an instant, like a fish leaping from the water. The knowledge holder Jigme Lingpa has described this:

> Those of the very highest acumen practice the development stage ritual of complete simplicity by developing the mind's inner potential. This potential is linked with the universal view of the king of vehicles, the natural and supreme yāna. The momentum that ensues from this process allows one to train in the indivisibility of development and completion. Without having to verbalize anything, the mind's nature is visualized in

its innate state, as the complete form of the deity. This occurs in a manner similar to the way a reflection can suddenly appear in a mirror. The following passage illustrates this approach:

> The deity is you and you are the deity.
> You and the deity arise together.
> Since samaya and wisdom are nondual,
> There is no need to invite the deity,
> Nor to request it to take its seat.
> Self-emanated and self-empowered,
> Awareness itself is the Three Roots.

In this form of development stage practice, the nature of the deity is inherently and perfectly present within illusory wisdom. This purifies miraculous birth. Explaining further, the omniscient Longchenpa writes, regarding the effortless approach of atiyoga:

> In the same way that miraculous birth occurs instantaneously,
> There is no need to start from nothing and then meditate
> On development and completion in stages.

General Remarks on the Development Stage

Moreover, it is said that each aspect of development stage, completion stage, and union possesses, in itself, these three aspects, creating a progression from the development stage of development stage to the union of union. Thus, every practice that involves visualizing the form of a deity need not be categorized as only development stage, i.e., as one part of a pair, opposed to completion stage. Nevertheless, when considering the development as one of only two stages, the development stage is the first step for someone who has not engendered the wisdom of the completion stage. Such a person trains in the development stage in order to mature for the completion stage practice. First he or she must gain conviction in the view of mantra and then proceed to cultivate the appearance of the deity's form as a conceptual imitation. Later, when the special realization of the completion stage emerges, the form of the deity appears as an expression of wisdom. This constitutes a direct cause of the unity in training.

In light of this, even though as beginners our development stage practice is only a conceptual imitation, we can nonetheless embrace it with confidence in the view, so that it will be in harmony with the true wisdom. On the other hand, if we fail to do that, it will neither lead to nor ripen us for that wisdom. That is why both the stake of absorption and the stake of unchanging realization are so crucial. For this reason, the practice of the two stages does not always unfold precisely as described in the scriptures and practice manuals. A beginner, for instance, may try to rest evenly in the wisdom of the completion stage, but it will be nothing more than holding something conceptually in mind. On the other hand, someone with superior realization can meditate on the complex details of the development stage in such a way that they manifest as the natural expression of wisdom.

Furthermore, when someone who has not engendered the wisdom of the completion stage visualizes the deity in practices related to the channels, energies, and inner heat, it may be a conceptual imitation. However, it is still considered the completion-stage form of the deity because it is a way for intrinsic wisdom to emerge. Lastly, those who have realized a high view may still meditate on highly elaborate forms of development stage. In their case, it is not out of personal necessity, but rather for the sake of their disciples. Specifically, it is to underscore to their students the auspicious coincidence made by entering into and being ripened within a particular maṇḍala. This is how my teacher Guṇa explained it.

Moreover, when we train in the development stage as beginners and first bring out the appearance of the deity's form, we should investigate where the deity we visualize first appeared from, where it currently remains, where it will go afterward, and what its essence really is. We will then come to an understanding that it did not come from anywhere in the beginning, does not remain anywhere in the present, and will not go anywhere in the end; it is a projection of our own mind. After this, we can proceed to analyze the essence of our own mind in the same way and conclude that its true state is originally devoid of the marks of arising, dwelling, and ceasing. With this understanding, we can perceive the secret key point of unity, that the form of the deity in development stage is inseparable from our own mind, appearing while not being real, like a rainbow or moon reflected in water.

Having gained such an insight, we can apply it to all our experiences and activities, and train progressively until all appearances arise, without fixation, as the empty yet luminous development stage of magical illusion. We will also come to some understanding—whether as an idea or in experience—of the key point that the deity we are visualizing, our guru, and our own mind are indivisible. What I share here comes from my own experience, limited though it may be. I impart it with the intention to benefit my present vajra brothers as well as sādhana practitioners of future generations.

In this way there are four styles of development stage practice related to the four modes of birth. We should practice primarily the one among them that corresponds with our own type of birth, but above all the style that is in accord with our mental capacity. The Omniscient Lord of Dharma has mentioned this:

> Though there are four ways to meditate, you should use
> The one that addresses the type of birth that predominates.
> To purify habitual patterns meditate accordingly using them all.
> In particular, meditate in harmony with egg birth as a beginner,
> And when this is somewhat stable, with womb birth.
> Once very stable, meditate in harmony with heat-and-moisture birth,
> And when completely habituated, use this true stability
> To develop instantaneously, in harmony with miraculous birth.

The Ritual of the Three Vajras

Let us now look closer at the practical application in terms of the ritual of the three vajras. While in *Ladder to Akaniṣṭha* the meditation begins with the symbolic implement, we will instead follow the more commonly known approach, the concise practice to purify womb birth as it is used in the majority of the treasure texts within the tradition of the Early Translations.

According to this approach, the object of purification encompasses the entire process that begins with the intermediate-state consciousness entering in between the father's semen and the mother's ovum, on through the complete development of the body. The various parts of the visualization, then, correlate to the stages of this process. The sun disc in the seat purifies the mother's ovum, while the moon disc purifies the father's semen. The descent of the seed syllable (the causal samādhi) onto the seat purifies the intermediate-state consciousness as it enters into the combination of red and white elements within the mother's womb. When the seed syllable transforms into the symbolic implement of a particular deity, it purifies the coalescence of mind, semen, and ovum after the consciousness has entered between the red and white elements. The subsequent projection and absorption of light rays purifies the fetal development of aggregates, elements, and sense bases through the workings of the four elements. The symbolic implement transforming into the complete form of the deity purifies the habits associated with the period from the complete development of the fetus until the time of birth.

This style of visualization can implicitly purify the habits for the other modes of birth as well. In terms of egg birth for instance, the seed syllable purifies the disembodied consciousness; the symbolic implement purifies its entrance between the semen and ovum; the projection, absorption, and transformation into a sphere purifies the development of the egg; and that sphere transforming into the bodily form purifies the development of the body out of the egg. Likewise, in terms of birth from heat and moisture, the sun disc in the seat purifies the heat aspect, while the moon disc purifies the moisture aspect; the seed syllable and symbolic implement purify the intermediate-state energetic mind; the projection, absorption, and completion of the bodily form purify the body materializing out of heat and moisture when the mind, heat, and moisture coalesce. Finally, in terms of miraculous birth, the seat purifies the place of birth; the seed syllable and symbolic implement purify the intermediate-state energetic mind; the projection and absorption purify the craving for a home and body, which is further sustained by grasping; and the completion of the bodily form represents and purifies the instantaneous creation of the body.

The result of purification for the ritual of the three vajras is to manifest enlightened emanation bodies to guide whoever is in need, acting out the process of entering into the womb and taking birth. The process of purification begins with the ritual of the seed syllable of enlightened speech, in which the causal seed syllable suspended in space descends onto the seat. Then, in the ritual of the symbolic implement of enlightened mind, it transforms into the symbolic implement of a particular buddha family, marked in the center by the seed syllable. This then projects countless light rays, inviting the buddhas of the ten directions into the sky before you, who then dissolve into the syllable-marked implement in the form of light rays. Finally, in the ritual of the complete enlightened body, the symbolic implement with its seed syllable transforms into the resultant vajra holder, meaning the bodily form of a visualized deity, vivid and complete with the major and minor marks.

This is a way of taking the emanation body, the pure form of the birth state, as the path. It also matures one for the completion stage. For instance, the sun and moon united upon the lotus seat represent the blissful heat in the context of the higher paths where the blazing and dripping converge in the cakras of the central channel. The seed syllable and symbolic implement represent the energetic mind dissolving into the central channel. The projection and absorption of light and the subsequent transformation represent the empty bliss produced by the melting bliss. The completion of the bodily form represents the ability to manifest out of empty bliss in the form of the wisdom deity, the natural and innate empty bliss.

This explanation has been in terms of a single primary deity but can also be applied to the development of the other, secondary deities. For this there are five steps. (1) First, visualize the complete form of the central deity. (2) Next, visualize the female consort's seed syllable, and then (3) as it transforms, the female consort. (4) Then visualize the three-tiered beings, and finally 5) seal with the lord of the family.

With regard to the ground, these five stages purify, respectively: (1) birth as an infant; (2) engaging in courtship, once one has come of age and feels the pangs of lust; (3) the act of taking a wife; (4) the progressive development of one's physical, verbal, and mental abilities; and (5) mastery over one's family trade. With regard to the fruition, they correspond respectively to: (1) taking birth as an enlightened emanation body; (2) becoming a renunciant and undergoing hardship in pursuit of enlightenment; (3) emerging from austerities and going to Bodhgayā; (4) taming the demons and developing concentration; and (5) gaining the wisdom of complete omniscience.

With regard to the higher path, the five steps mature the practitioner to accomplish the empty and blissful form of the wisdom deity. They do so by laying the foundation for manifesting out of the blissful energetic mind in the form of the deity. This involves relying on either one of the two seals in pursuit of the supreme spiritual accomplishments and thereby gradually cultivating intrinsic wisdom. In this way one swiftly connects to the supreme spiritual accomplishment.

Likewise, when there is a visualization of retinue deities, the object of purification is the previous child conceiving its own sons and daughters. The result of purification is to project, through the great bliss of all buddhas, infinite emanations out of delightful clouds of music. It is also to establish one's retinue at the level of enlightenment, indicated by their birth within one's buddha family. The process of purification is to visualize the deities in the retinue who develop from their seed syllables. This is the most that can be said about this here; you should also look to the specific details described in your particular text.

The Characteristics of the Deity

The third section concerns the characteristics of the visualized deity. At this point a definitive description of the object of meditation cannot be made above and beyond what appears in the practice manual of the deity that is being visualized. We can, however, identify meditation deities in general as being either peaceful or wrathful, and then describe the nine traits and thirteen enjoyment body ornaments of peaceful deities (the latter of which apply generally in the Early Translations), as well as the nine expressions of the dance, glorious attributes, and charnel ground ornaments, which apply to wrathful deities.

The Nine Traits of Peaceful Deities

1. Peaceful deities have soft bodies, arms, and legs, symbolizing the purification of birth and the fact that pride is naturally purified without being given up.

2. They are well proportioned, with thin waists and smooth curves, showing that anger and sickness are naturally purified.
3. They are not slack, but firm, showing that desire and death are naturally purified. This may also be shown in the embrace between means and knowledge.
4. Their bodies are straight, and their joints amazingly flexible, showing that envy is naturally purified.
5. They are supple and have a youthful demeanor, showing that delusion and aging are naturally purified. These are the five essential qualities.
6. Furthermore, being free of ignorance, their bodies are immaculate, with hues that are vivid and distinct.
7. Having unfolded the wisdom that perfects the sphere of totality, they are radiant, while glowing and emanating countless light rays.
8. Being beautiful and dignified, they are majestic, replete with the flowers of the major marks and the fruit of the minor marks.
9. Finally, since they have perfected all supreme qualities, their magnificence overwhelms the beings in need of guidance.

The Thirteen Enjoyment Body Ornaments

Among the thirteen enjoyment body ornaments, the first five are the five garments of divine silk, which symbolize the eradication of the disturbing emotions that afflict beings. These include: blue silk ribbons with white patterns that dangle down the back; a five-colored silk diadem, a set of fluttering silk ribbons strung over the ears; dancing sleeves that come to the shoulders; a shirt of white silk embroidered with gold; and a dhoti, a multicolored type of lower garment, which sometimes appears instead as a skirt that is entirely maroon.

Since they have refined sense pleasures into ornaments without giving them up, they also wear eight jeweled ornaments, which symbolize the fulfillment of beings' wishes. On their heads they wear a crest-shaped hollow crown of precious metal with a jewel at its peak. On each ear they wear earrings of precious materials inlaid with gems. They wear necklaces of three lengths: a choker strung with various alternating jewels, a similarly-made necklace that hangs down to the upper chest, and a long necklace that hangs down below the navel. They also wear jewel-inlaid armbands, as well as two bracelets, two anklets, and rings on their fingers and toes, all similarly designed. Lastly, they have a belt decorated with studded gems.

These ornaments are sometimes counted in slightly different ways. For instance, some count the necklace and long necklace together, or the bracelets and anklets together, while counting the rings separately. Some even exclude the rings and instead count each of the first eight individually. In any case, the ornaments themselves are just as described here.

Moreover, in terms of the seven factors of enlightenment, the jeweled necklace represents mindfulness, the crown represents the discernment of phenomena, the bracelets represent diligence, the earrings represent pliancy, the armbands represent concentration, the long necklace represents equanimity, and the flower garland represents joy.

In addition, the six perfections can be linked to the bone ornaments of the male deity, in the sense that the necklace represents generosity, the bracelets discipline, the earrings patience, the crown wheel diligence, the belt concentration, and the offering thread, known as the *serka*, knowledge.

In terms of the female deity, her nakedness represents freedom from the obscuration of conceptual thought. Her age of sixteen years represents immutable great bliss endowed with the sixteen joys. Her hair hangs loose, symbolizing the boundless unfolding of basic space and wisdom. She is also adorned with five bone ornaments: the wheel of bones representing the wisdom of basic space, the necklace representing the wisdom of equality, the earrings representing discerning wisdom, the bracelets representing mirrorlike wisdom, and the belt representing all-accomplishing wisdom.

The male and female embrace each others' bodies, symbolic of the fact that emptiness and compassion are not separate. Their mouths are joined in a kiss, symbolic of one taste, the simplicity of flawless great bliss. They remain indivisible with vajra and lotus joined in union, symbolic of the unity of calm abiding and insight.

The Nine Expressions of the Dance

Wrathful deities convey the nine dancing expressions.

1. The first of these is *captivating*, which is an expression of passion. It refers to the essence of Vairocana, which is the deities' seductiveness, as they are adorned with jewelry, the male and female consorts are embracing, etc.
2. They are also *heroic*, an expression of wrath, referring to the essence of Ratnasambhava, the fact that they are so powerful as to be invincible.
3. They are *terrifying*, an expression of stupidity, referring to the essence of Akṣobhya, the way that they instill fear merely upon sight.

These first three are their three physical expressions.

4. They are *laughing*, the essence of Amitābha, emitting sounds of laughter like "Ha ha!" due to their state of passionate, haughty glee.
5. They are *ferocious*, the essence of Amoghasiddhi, berating with abusive words like "Capture! Strike!"
6. They are *fearsome*, the essence of Māmakī, as they overwhelm with fierce roaring sounds similar to thunder cracks.

These three are their verbal expressions.

7. They are *compassionate*, the essence of Samayatāra, taking ignorant beings and realms under their care with nonconceptual compassion.
8. They are *intimidating*, the essence of Pāṇḍarāvasinī, meaning they are capable of anything necessary to tame incorrigible beings with their wrath, their state of mind being overcome by passionate wrath.
9. Finally, they are *peaceful*, the essence of Locanā, referring to their nonconceptual realization that everything is the same taste in true reality.

These are their three mental expressions.

The Eight Attributes of the Glorious One

The eight attributes of the Glorious One are so called because they are primordially and intrinsically present on the body of the Great Glorious One. It seems, however, that there are some slight discrepancies in the ways these are identified. Nevertheless, *The Divine Realization Tantra* describes these clearly and also mentions their symbolism. According to this scripture they are:

1. Hair tied in a knot for reversing cyclic existence
2. Vajra garuḍa wings of method and knowledge
3. A dark-blue diadem for overpowering eternalism and nihilism
4. A vajra at the crown indicating supreme awareness
5. A mighty coat of armor to advance in splendor
6. The knowledge consort with whom the deity is in nondual union
7. The iron of a hero for repelling harm and malevolence
8. Vajra fire for incinerating disturbing emotions

The Eight Charnel Ground Ornaments

The eight charnel ground ornaments are decorations representing triumph and heroism. In the past they were the spoils of the liberation of Rudra, donned by the Great Glorious One as ornaments on his body. They include the three worn garments, the two fastened ornaments, and the three smeared things.

The three garments are:

1. The entire skin of a human
2. An upper garment of elephant hide
3. A skirt of tiger skin

The two fastened ornaments are:

4. Skull ornaments, which consist of:
   a. A crown of five dry skulls
   b. A necklace of fifty fresh skulls
   c. Armbands of skull fragments
   d. Bracelets and anklets

5. Snake ornaments, which are types of jewelry resembling venomous snakes:
   a. A white hair band of the royal nāga caste
   b. Yellow earrings of the merchant caste
   c. A red choker of the priestly caste
   d. Green bracelets and anklets of the peasant caste
   e. A black necklace of the untouchable caste

The three smeared things are:

6. A clot of human ash on the forehead
7. Drops of blood on the cheeks or, alternatively, on the cheeks and tip of the nose
8. Smears of grease on the chin

Certain deities are of a semiwrathful type. They wear an elephant skin upper garment, symbolizing the defeat of ignorance by means of the ten powers of knowledge. They are swathed in a tiger skin skirt, representing the defeat of anger by means of heroic wrathful activities. They are adorned with silk streamers, symbolizing the defeat of desire by the mind of awakening. They have a crown of five dry skulls, the identity of the five buddhas, which represents the defeat of pride. They wear a necklace of fifty fresh heads strung together as a garland, symbolizing the purity of the fifty mental states after envy has been defeated. Finally, their bodies are adorned with the bone ornaments, which have the nature of the six perfections. You should visualize all this as it is described in your particular text.

Blessing and Empowerment

This section covers (1) bestowing blessings and (2) conferring empowerment.

Blessing

When blessings are bestowed, the object of purification is the stage of maturation of the infant's physical, verbal, and mental abilities. The result of purification is the attainment of mastery over the inconceivable secrets of enlightened body, speech, and mind at the time of awakening. The process of purification utilizes the samaya maṇḍala you have already developed. You next visualize a white syllable OṂ, representing vajra body, clear and glowing, in the skull palace cakra at the crowns of both the central and retinue deities in the maṇḍala. At their throat cakras visualize a clear and glowing red syllable ĀḤ, representing vajra speech. In their hearts visualize a clear and glowing blue syllable HŪṂ, representing vajra mind. It should be in front of the wisdom being in the hearts of the primary male and female deities, while in front of the awakened life force syllable of the others. There are sometimes other details as well, such as visualizing these syllables within a wheel, lotus, and vajra at the three respective places, and visualizations of the forms of Vairocana, Amitābha, and Akṣobhya. For these you should follow your text.

In any case, take pride in joining the ground and fruition by having solid conviction that body, speech, and mind in their pure state are the three vajras of all the thus-gone ones. In terms of the higher path, the three elements of semen, ovum, and energy correlate to enlightened body, speech, and mind. By eradicating their impure aspects, you set a foundation for the dawning of the wisdom that emerges when their pure aspects flourish.

Empowerment

During empowerment the object of purification consists of the coarse, disturbed thought processes that come about as the infant's channels and elements develop. The result of purification is to be empowered, at the time of awakening, as the Dharma King of the three realms and sovereign of all thus-gone ones. Here the process of purification entails the bestowal of empowerment, with mantra and gesture, upon the five places of the heads of all the deities: the crown, forehead, tip of the right ear, nape of the neck, and tip of the left ear. Place the lord of the particular family in primary position in the middle, exchanging his place with Vairocana.

When empowerment is granted, the male and female buddhas appear out of seed syllables and join in union. A stream of nectar of the mind of awakening, the nature of the five wisdoms, then pours down from the places of union. This fills up your body, cleanses away obscurations, and purifies the five poisons into the five wisdoms. As the excess liquid overflows above and dissolves into the intrinsically present lord of the family, take pride that you have realized the goal of your inherent wisdom. There are a number of stages here, such as inviting the empowerment deities and the actual bestowal of empowerment, which you should apply according to context. In relation to the completion stage, this process matures you for the higher path by creating the cause for the empowerment of the five poisons that takes place through the progression and reversal of the four joys. It also creates the cause for the energetic mind to dissolve into the crown protuberance.

Inviting and Welcoming the Wisdom Beings

Here the object of purification is the child's process of gaining the same aptitude as others in his caste before him. The result of purification is to unite with the wisdom of all the thus-gone ones at the time of awakening, thereby arriving at an equal experience, inseparable from their realization. The process of purification consists of inviting and dissolving the wisdom beings, and has two parts: first inviting and then welcoming the natural wisdom maṇḍala.

To invite the wisdom maṇḍala, you, as the samaya being, project light rays in the shape of hooks from your seed syllable, the awakened life force. These light rays permeate all the naturally and spontaneously present pure realms, where they cause the thus-gone ones of the four times and ten directions to manifest in a skillful dance of form bodies without leaving the great equality of the dharma body. As they take the forms of the deities in the maṇḍala you are practicing, complete in its supporting and supported aspects, imagine that they actually arrive in the sky in front of you. Fumigate with incense made of special substances and play various instruments. Then, with your mind in a state of one-pointed faith, chant the invitation verse in a melodious way. While still visualizing yourself in the samaya maṇḍala, imagine that they arrive in the sky above you at the place where the flames of the protection circles meet.

Second, to welcome the wisdom deities you have just invited into the samaya maṇḍala, say the general mantra DZAḤ HŪṂ BĀṂ HOḤ. With DZAḤ, you summon the wisdom deities into the samaya maṇḍala; with HŪṂ, they dissolve indivisibly; with BĀṂ, they are bound by an indestructible oath to remain until your aspirations are fulfilled; and with HOḤ, you welcome them to remain, continually and joyfully. This serves to remove any fixation on the samaya being as inferior and the wisdom being as superior, and confirms that the wisdom maṇḍala is inseparable from your mind. It also serves as a way for you to receive the blessings of all the buddhas. Finally, it replicates the way the symbolic luminosity points out the actual wisdom in the context of the higher paths, while laying a foundation for the wisdom of the nonduality of saṃsāra and nirvāṇa to emerge in your being.

Offering and Praise

Next, the description of the offerings and praise to the nondual maṇḍala has two parts: a general explanation of the principles of purification, perfection, and maturation, and then a description of the actual practice.

For the first, the object of purification is the frivolous pleasure the child takes in things such as food, drink, dress, jewelry, and houses, its partiality with regard to property and possessions, and efforts to attain fame, fortune, and a certain economic status. The result of purification is to become, at the time of awakening, an unsurpassed object of reverence and veneration, always surrounded by infinite clouds of offerings. This is what is perfected. The process of purification consists of the procedures for homage, offering, and praise. This process matures you by forming a basis for you to revel in the play of awareness discipline during the higher path.

Secondly, the actual practice process involves three stages: homage, offering, and praise.

Homage

Generally speaking, the superior mode of practice is the "homage of resolute unity": to realize that you are inseparable from the deity and then remain in the nondual equality in which the samaya and wisdom beings have merged, like water poured into water. This can be applied to the offering and praise as well; in fact, if you realize this, it is fine to forgo any separate conventional, conceptual homage or offering. Still, in a mere relative sense, you can follow in the manner of common respect and conform to the style of the outer tantras by paying homage and making offerings, etc. This is the approach of the unexcelled practice system where one resolves that the displays are merely self-projections and recognizes their nondual nature. Just as the gods in Delightful Emanations revel in their own magically-created pleasures, imagine that either a second bodily form like yourself or else emanated goddesses emerge from the heart of the central deity and offer the homage. They say, "ATIPU HOḤ," representing their homage, and the deities accept the homage by responding, "PRATĪCCHA HOḤ."

Offering

The offering has four aspects: outer, inner, innermost, and suchness.

Outer Offerings

For the outer offering, visualize yourself as the central deity and imagine that clouds of goddesses of the sense pleasures project out of your heart. In the manner of deities worshipping deities, these fill up the infinitude of space and bestow offerings. Recite the offering verse from your text and imagine that the emanated goddesses, holding their respective offerings, present them and then dissolve into their respective places.

The offerings include: a beverage of sweet, cool, and pure drinking water; clean and refreshing bathing water for the hands and feet; brilliant and beautiful flowers for the eyes; fragrant incense for the nose; illuminating lamps for the eyes; cool, fragrant perfume for the heart; rich, nutritious food for the tongue; and lovely music for the ears.

These all have a particular symbolism. The flower is a symbol of the beauty and brilliance of wisdom awareness. Incense symbolizes the way nonconceptual compassion burns away concepts. The lamp is a symbol of intrinsic luminosity dispelling the darkness of ignorance. The perfume is a symbol of the extremely profound unconstructed wakefulness of spacious awareness unfolding and pervading all things. The bathing water symbolizes wakefulness cleaning away the stains of concepts. The food and drinking water are symbols of the taste of untainted concentration. Finally, the music symbolizes the perpetual, audible, yet empty sound of mantra.

Also included here are the five sense pleasures—visible form, sound, smell, taste, and texture—in the way that they create pleasure as objects of the five senses. On an inner level, when male and female join together and share in ecstasy, there are also visible forms to behold, laughing sounds of union, the scent of satiation with bliss, the taste of the melting bliss, and texture in the contact between the secret vajra and space, as well as the white and red substances. These are inner sense pleasures in the sense that they are phenomena that cause all inner and outer phenomena to arise as empty bliss. They appear in the forms of goddesses who express the sixteen types of joy—four times the four of joy, supreme joy, extraordinary joy, and intrinsic joy.

Inner Offerings

The inner offering is divided into two: a common and a special type.

The common type includes certain symbolic offerings, such as the flowers of the five senses, which are the sacred substances of the eyes, tongue, ears, nose, and heart, naturally present in a clean corpse. In addition, there are: incense made of human fat for fumigation and burnt offerings, butter lamps fueled by human oil with wicks of corpse hair, perfume made of bile, and food offerings of human flesh.

These all have a particular symbolism as well. The brilliant and beautiful flower represents the five subtle physical faculties that are inherently present in the bodies of living beings. These faculties form the support for the five sense consciousnesses and relate exclusively to their respective objects. The incense offering of burnt human fat represents the odor that comes from the impure aspect of flesh, which is the source of the fatty tissue. The oil lamp represents the fluid that results from human oil, which gives the body its radiant complexion. The perfume represents the gall bladder, a repository of odor. Finally, the food offering consists of the nutrients that come from digesting food and drink and which develop one's flesh and blood. Here it is used to feed the deities of the aggregates, elements, and sense sources.

Beyond this, you can make actual or mentally created offerings of the outer and inner sensual pleasures, offer things you do not even own, and imagine countless clouds of offerings produced through the power of aspiration.

The special inner offering consists of medicine, torma, and rakta.

For the medicine offering consider that everything within saṃsāra and nirvāṇa exists as an unfabricated, naturally present nectar. For this reason the sacred substance composed of the proper combination of the eight primary and one thousand subsidiary ingredients can emerge from the equality of true reality. It is the identity of the five wisdoms and the five buddha families, an essential extract of medicinal nectar that dispels thoughts of dualistic fixation.

Take this nectar with your thumb and ring finger—the amulet of the sun and moon—and offer it, imagining that you have delighted the deities. Then imagine that the deities project all spiritual accomplishments and the blessings of enlightened body, speech, and mind from their three places in the form of the three seed syllables, which land upon the nectar. Again, take some nectar between your thumb and ring finger and touch it to your three places and then your tongue, while thinking that you have attained the accomplishments of the three vajras.

In the secret meaning, the five nectars refer to the pure essences of the five aggregates, while the five meats refer to the pure essences of the five senses. They constitute an ambrosia nectar because the accomplishment of immortality is gained by retaining them without letting them leak out.

Next is the torma offering. Imagine that the outer container of completely pure space is the torma vessel, which contains the edible and drinkable torma substances along with everything desirable. Then offer it while you emanate it out in the form of vast clouds of the five sense pleasures. Imagine that tubes of light emerge from the vajra-shaped tongues of the deities with which they draw up and imbibe the contents, so that your bond with them is mended. You should also bring to mind the true meaning that the foods are the five sense objects and the drinks are the consciousnesses. In this way the contents are imbibed and subsequently dissolve within the expanse of luminosity.

For the rakta offering consider that the root of the disturbing emotions is our conceptual grasping and attachment to the three realms, which in fact creates cyclic existence. To cut cyclic existence from the root, condense all attached thoughts into the form of blood and vanquish them into unattached great bliss. Thereafter, within the basic space of the equality of saṃsāra and nirvāṇa, offer this sacred substance, gathered into an ocean of pure essence and liberated within the nonarising expanse of saṃsāra. The real meaning here is that the course of the sun and moon is arrested at the tip of the secret space, whereby the continuity of saṃsāra is cut. Think that by making this offering saṃsāra, as an ocean of blood, is consumed, so that the realms of cyclic existence are emptied.

Innermost Offerings

Third, the innermost offering has two aspects: union and liberation.

For the offering of union one should consider that all of appearance is of the nature of skillful means, the male aspect, while emptiness, in its entirety, is knowledge, the female consort. These two in essence remain indivisible. The fact that all phenomena are, in this way, naturally a nondual union constitutes the view of appearance and existence being a primordial unity. As an expression of this, while sustaining the three notions, visualize yourself as the male and female deities in union. Through their union, as the four joys unfold in forward and reverse order via descending flow and ascending stabilization, the offering cloud of stainless nondual bliss and emptiness is established. This pleases the perfect circle of the deities, who are themselves the original purity of the aggregates, elements, and sense sources.

In the liberation offering the enemies that one seeks to liberate are the disturbing emotions, which come about through strong dualistic fixation and belief in a self. These emotions prevent our liberation and lead us into bondage in the three realms of cyclic existence. They are all liberated by the sharp weapon of nondual wisdom, the perfected essence of natural awareness, into the expanse of great equality, empty awareness itself, the basic space of the sense sources' primordial purity. This is the true meaning of the triple world being primordially liberated.

As a manifestation of this primordial liberation, one should give rise to great compassion and then liberate, in an illusory way, the beings who lack this realization. Such beings are of ten types, including malevolent demons and *rudras,* impelled as they are by the ripening of vicious karma. Liberate their supported consciousnesses into basic space and place them within the circle of great bliss. Then offer their aggregates of flesh, blood, and bones—impure residue of the three poisons—as food to the deities and imagine the deities are delighted.

Suchness Offerings

For the offering of suchness consider that all phenomena contained within appearance and existence, saṃsāra and nirvāṇa, are primordially the nature of enlightenment—perfect within the single sphere of equality free of elaboration. Therefore, there is no duality in terms of an object to whom we offer, a person making the offering, and an act of offering; these are indivisibly of one taste in the maṇḍala of the mind of awakening. Thus, to offer all of appearance within the seal of Samantabhadra's conduct, the great bliss of unity, is the most eminent offering of all.

Praise

It says in the *Karmamāla*:

> Wield the vajra and ring the bell,
> Make the whirling gestures of the five families.

First, make the relevant gestures. Then join your palms, bow, and offer praises while bringing to mind the buddhas' supreme qualities.

To describe these in brief, the ultimate dharma body of the buddhas is endowed with the twofold purity—both the primordial, natural purity of the basic space of phenomena and the freedom from all incidental conceptual elaborations of subject and object. While not wavering from this vast equality, the buddhas appear to disciples in the symbolic forms of great wisdom, in whatever way is befitting. They manifest the various displays of the central and retinue deities, whether peaceful and adorned with the major and minor marks or wrathful and terrifying, mesmerizing with their dances.

However, although they manifest in this way, the buddhas ultimately lack even the slightest material existence, both in appearance and in essence. With one instance of their perfectly melodious speech they can instantaneously reveal the countless ways of the Dharma to their innumerable disciples, each according to the disciple's inclination. At the same time, their speech is ultimately the invincible voice of indestructible resonance, beyond words and effort. With their wisdom mind that knows things both as they are and in their extent they instantaneously perceive all that can be known in the three times. In essence, nonetheless, they never waver from resting evenly in equality, the nature of which is beyond perceived and perceiver.

They have mastery over inconceivable qualities such as the ten powers, the fearlessnesses, and the unique attributes. Still, essentially they remain in one taste, inseparable in the three times from undefiled basic space. Their inconceivable enlightened activity to benefit beings in any way necessary extends constantly and spontaneously to the innumerable beings in need of guidance for as long as cyclic existence lasts. At the same time, they are utterly free of any effort or thought-movement.

These constitute the supreme qualities of the inexhaustible ornament wheel of enlightened body, speech, mind, qualities, and activity, while the supporting and supported maṇḍalas manifest as their specific expression. Here you should bring to mind the symbolism of every aspect of these maṇḍalas as described in your particular text, and while doing so, sing vajra songs of praise.

Furthermore, it is crucial to understand the inherent equality of the object being praised, the subject offering the praise, and the act of praising, considering that in ultimate truth it is the innate, intrinsic wisdom of your own mind—great bliss, simplicity, awakened mind without beginning or end—that appears in the symbolic form of the maṇḍala circle.

The Appearance of the Deity

The training in holding the appearance of the deity, the primary object of focus, has four aspects: (1) vivid appearance, (2) stable pride, (3) recollection of purity, and (4) manifesting as bliss, clarity, and emptiness.

Vivid Appearance

In terms of the authentic path of definitive perfection, vivid appearance includes seven aspects:

1. Holding the deity in mind
2. Correcting faults that involve change
3. Parting from the deity
4. Taking the deity onto the path
5. Mingling with the deity
6. Connecting the deity to ultimate truth
7. Taking the deity as the path

These, however, can all be understood by reading the detailed explanations in *Illuminating Jewel Lamp: Essential General Points on Approach and Accomplishment*, composed by the lord guru of unmatched kindness, whose very name is difficult to mention, the true and definite great vajra holder Pema Garwang Lodro Thaye. Since I am writing this text as a supplement and act of reverence to it, I hesitate to say anything more.

To summarize though, all of these points come down to visualizing the supporting and supported maṇḍalas perfectly complete in a single instant. At first, hold in mind the general appearance of the central figure's form, and then scan through the specific features, from the crown protuberance down to the throne, including the subtle details of the body, symbolic implements, ornaments, and garments. When these appear vividly, visualize the central figure completely in one moment. Then proceed from there until you can rest evenly while keeping the entirety of the supporting and supported maṇḍala in one-pointed focus, like a star or planet appearing in a clear lake. Otherwise, beyond the fact that you should begin by concentrating on whatever is easiest to keep in mind, there is no particular fixed order or session length, so practice in accord with your individual temperament.

After you have become adept in this practice, train in acquiring the eight measures of clarity and stability. Among these, first are the four measures of clarity. The visualization should be *distinct*, meaning it should be unblurred down to the pupils of the eyes. It should be *alive*, meaning there should be the sharpness of awareness, empty and lucid with an awake quality, rather than a lethargic state that lacks the intense clarity of awareness. It should be *vibrant*, meaning it is not made of mindless matter like a rainbow, but rather all features, even down to the pores of the skin and single strands of hair, are suffused with omniscient wisdom. Thus, it is radiantly present, with the bright quality of the senses manifest a hundredfold. Finally, it should be *vivid*, appearing to your mind as if it were directly in front of you, rather than a conceptual speculation concerning the deity's form.

Of the four measures of stability, the first is *unwavering*, meaning not wavering due to laziness, absent-mindedness, etc. The visualization should be *unchanging*, meaning that it does not become, for instance, blurry or vague. It should be *utterly unchangeable*, meaning though you remain composed for a long time, subtle thoughts will not disturb you. Finally, it should be *flexible*, meaning that you are able to visualize anything just as it should be, such as the color of the body, the face, arms, movement or stillness, or the projection and absorption of light rays.

Vivid appearance refers to having attained these eight measures of clarity and stability.

Stable Pride

Stable pride refers to the pride we take in joining ground and fruition, as was explained in detail above. The main point, in short, is to take pride in being the deity you are practicing, the universal splendor of the wisdom of all buddhas, who has eradicated all flaws and perfected all qualities. This is not a simple pretense but an acknowledgment of how things are. Our innate body, speech, and mind are primordially the essence of the three vajras, and so everything that manifests out of them—our concepts, aggregates, elements, and sense sources—are primordially pure, nothing other than the manifestation of the deity. Therefore, since there is no deity to meditate on and accomplish elsewhere, we can have pride—i.e., confidence—in the realization that we, as the meditators, are no different from the deities we are practicing. If in this way we understand how to reach the innate by keeping such pride continuously, vividly, and without clinging to it, we can follow the authentic swift path.

The object of purification, in this case, includes ordinary, impure experience, as well as grasping pride that fixates in an impure manner. The former is purified by vivid appearance, and the latter by recollecting purity; training in these transforms them respectively into pure vivid appearance and pure stable pride.

Recollecting Purity

The general points for recollecting purity were discussed earlier in the section on the development of the deity, in the context of the purity of the supporting and supported maṇḍalas.

In terms of specific details, though, if a meditation deity has one face, it represents the single sphere of the dharma body, while one with three heads symbolizes the three bodies of enlightenment, or the three gates to complete liberation. Two arms symbolize the unity of method and knowledge, four symbolize the activity to benefit beings via the four immeasurables, and six symbolize the six wisdoms, which are the five plus inconceivable wisdom. Two legs represent not dwelling in either extreme of existence or tranquility, while four represent the four legs of miracles.

Being white in color symbolizes the mirrorlike wisdom and being unstained by faults. Yellow represents the wisdom of equality and the unfolding of the supreme qualities. Red represents discerning wisdom and a loving, compassionate concern for the welfare of the beings in need of guidance. Green represents all-accomplishing wisdom and the spontaneous accomplishment of unobstructed enlightened activity. Blue and black represent the wisdom of the basic space of things and immutable true reality.

In terms of the symbolic implements, the vajra is a symbol of the unconditioned, the wheel symbolizes cutting through disturbing emotions, the jewel signifies qualities emerging, the lotus is a symbol of being unstained by defects, and the crossed-vajra and sword indicate unobstructed activity. The bell is a symbol of emptiness, nonarising basic space. The kapāla symbolizes sustaining bliss and nonconceptual wisdom. The khaṭvāṅga staff shows liberation within the expanse of the three bodies of enlightenment. The curved knife symbolizes cutting birth and death at the root. The large horn is a symbol of conquering the four demons with great wisdom and then subduing, or offering up, cyclic existence. When the deity has a male appearance it represents skillful means and immutable great bliss, while a female appearance represents knowledge and emptiness suffused with the excellence of all aspects. The union of male and female symbolizes that bliss and emptiness are beyond unity and separation. Beyond this, you should meditate on the specific associations of purity as described in your particular text.

In conclusion, the main point is that the qualities of enlightenment are naturally and spontaneously present within our innate nature. Whatever qualities a deity may have, they are pure as the essential nature of that deity. In short, your thoughts are pure as the deity, the deity is pure as wisdom, and wisdom is the dharma body of enlightenment, discernment free of subject and object. While the dharma body has no characteristics whatsoever, such as a face or arms, its inconceivable qualities can still manifest with features of a face, arms, and ornaments. In this way, the dharma body is the dominion of spontaneously accomplished enlightened activity. You should, therefore, keep in mind that the deity you are concentrating on in meditation is pure and free from the slightest concrete, material existence. You should, of course, remember these points about purity when you are chanting through a liturgy, but in this context in particular you should train in the specific points of purity with sincere conviction. After developing a solid conviction in them, rest evenly in meditation while maintaining the pride and vivid appearance of the deity as they were described above.

Bliss, Clarity, and Emptiness

The basic identity of the meditation deity is the wisdom of bliss, clarity, and emptiness, which relate to three aspects of training. First is to draw out the melting bliss by meditating on the male and female deities joined passionately in union. Second is to train in the clear appearance of the deity's form within that physical and mental experience of bliss. Third is to train in vivid pride unspoiled by clinging. When you seal your practice with these key points, it is an incredible method for letting any maṇḍala manifest as the dharma body.

Even if you are unable to do this, when you are training in the development stage of vivid appearance, recollection of purity, and stable pride, it is vital to be free of thoughts that cling to something as truly there. You should do this with an understanding that the visualization is empty, in essence, while by nature it is like a rainbow or a moon reflected in water, appearing while lacking real characteristics. Sealing the development stage with the completion stage, in this way, is the method for manifesting any maṇḍala as the dharma body. It becomes a path that joins the two accumulations since the appearances of the relative development stage gather the accumulation of merit while the ultimate accumulation of wisdom is accrued through embracing those appearances with thorough insight into their nature, the unconditioned absolute. Moreover, it is a complete and unmistaken path in which method and knowledge are unified. This is to say that it incorporates the two bodies of enlightenment—the appearing form body and the empty dharma body—as well as the two truths: the method of relative appearance and the knowledge of ultimate emptiness. Understand that this is the special quality of the profound and swift path of mantra.

If you lack this understanding and take up a one-sided development stage as if it were concrete and material, it will not become a path to enlightenment, but only a terrible impediment that binds you to cyclic existence. If you meditate on a peaceful deity as if it were materially existent, you will be born as a god in the desire realm, while if you meditate on a wrathful deity in this way, you will be reborn as an evil worldly spirit or a powerful demon like Rudra. In the annals of the Secret Mantra tradition there are stories of this actually happening.

To conclude, it is important to practice the development stage with the three elements of vivid appearance, recollection of purity, and stable pride for as long as possible without becoming weary and fatigued. When you do become weary, begin the recitation.

In most unelaborate daily practices and in the tradition of the higher yogas, the section from blessing and empowerment up until the praises is often omitted. This is not problematic since the identity of the wisdom being is sublime ultimate truth, the innate essence of your own mind, in which the seven riches—basic space, wisdom, enlightened body, speech, mind, qualities, and activities—are spontaneously present. As well, all conceptual phenomena that manifest as its expression—including the aggregates, elements, and sense sources—are the sublime relative truth, remaining primordially as the circle of the deities in the three seats of completeness.

Furthermore, when you take this as the path and meditate on the maṇḍalas of support and supported, that is the samaya being. The wisdom being and samaya being remain primordially indivisible, like gold and its golden color or turquoise and its blue color. To train in meditation in accord with this fact is the absorption being. Therefore, if we can understand that these three are, by nature, one identity, we will not fixate on the wisdom being as superior and the samaya being as inferior. Once we no longer make such concepts, the act of sealing, receiving empowerment, and the other parts of the process of purification are not necessary; the invitation, offering, praise, and so on are complete within the essence. *The Secret Essence* proclaims:

> Everything that exists, without exception,
> Is nothing other than the Buddha.
> The Buddha himself cannot find
> Anything that is not the Buddha.

In *The Marvels* it is explained:

In the recognition and practice of the maṇḍala
Of primordial, spontaneous equality
There is no need for conceptual stages
Like inviting and requesting to depart.

Similarly, *The Two Segments* declares:

The deity is you, and you are the deity.
You and the deity are coemergent.
So there's no need to invite, nor request to remain.
Visualize your mind as the divine master.

It also says:

The deity and mantra truly dwell
In the nature free of constructs.

In short, we should see the vital point expressed by the Omniscient Lord of Dharma in *Resting in the Nature of Mind*:

Your mind is originally the nature of the deity.
Your body is the maṇḍala, words are Secret Mantra.
When everything is great wisdom, spontaneously perfect,
There are no separate samaya and wisdom beings, no invocation
or welcome,
No need to request them to depart.
Nothing good you should do, or bad you should not.
When you bring to mind the fact that the maṇḍala
is primordial,
And that that maṇḍala is within you,
There is no need to create what was never created.

Enlightened Speech

The recitation practice of enlightened speech has three divisions: (1) a general presentation of the key points of the four stakes that bind the life force, (2) a specific explanation of the relevant visualizations, and (3) a description of the extra concluding rituals.

The Four Stakes That Bind the Life Force

The thirty-ninth chapter of *The Tantra of the Perfect Secret* says:

> Whether wisdom or mundane, if the four stakes
> That bind the life force are not planted,
> Practice will never be fruitful, like running in place.
> The way to capture the life force of all glorious ones
> Is to understand one point and attain the life force of all,
> Just as Rahula swallows the sun out of the sky,
> And, without having to catch its reflection
> In all the thousands of pools of water,
> Attains the life force of them all.
> Thus, the four stakes that bind the life force are vital.

In this quote, "running in place" means to undergo a pointless hardship, like a child who is tricked with an empty promise. The life force of the entire development stage is contained in the "four stakes that bind the life force," an instruction that works like a set of stakes in binding our body, speech, mind, and actions to the enlightened body, speech, mind, and activity of the bliss-gone ones.

The Stake of Absorption

In the stake of absorption you begin by focusing one-pointedly on the appearance of the deity, for example a drawing inside a skull, as a support. By training like this, you can progress through all of the five meditation experiences, manifest the three types of objects, and let the intense clinging you have to your ordinary body be perfected into the form of the deity.

Of the five meditation experiences, the first is the experience of the *movement* of thoughts, which is to recognize thinking. It is like a waterfall cascading over a steep cliff. The next is the experience of the *attainment* of a slight easing of thoughts, like water rushing down a narrow ravine. Third is the experience of *familiarity* with the tiring out of thinking, like the movements of an old man. Fourth is the experience of *stability*, with only a slight formation of thoughts, like a pond undulating in the breeze. Last is the experience of *perfection* of unwavering self-control, like an ocean free of waves.

By training in this manner you can manifest the three types of objects in the following way. First, the maṇḍalas of support and supported appear vividly clear to the mind. This is called "appearing as an object of imagination." Second, by the power of training in meditation the deity's form appears as an object of your senses, which is known as "appearing as an object of perception." Finally, when the energetic mind is matured into the form of the deity, others will, on occasion, directly perceive your body as the form of the deity you are visualizing. This stage is called "appearing as a tangible physical object." I have heard firsthand the vajra holder Khyentse Wangpo say that this last stage is when you truly attain the level of a matured knowledge holder.

The way that the three principles of purification, perfection, and maturation apply to this has already been explained above, so it is unnecessary to repeat it again. Nonetheless, to serve as a convenient reminder in the present context, I will quote the words of the Omniscient Śrī Nirmāṇakāya in this age of strife:

> In terms of saṃsāra, this process will *purify* and refine away the habitual patterns related to the body, as they relate to the four types of birth. In terms of buddhahood, the fruition will be *perfected* within the ground. Here the fruition is the inconceivable secret of enlightened body, which is beyond having a face, hands, or marks, yet can appear in any form whatsoever, in whatever way is needed to guide beings. In terms of the path, the web of pure channels will be refined into the deity. This, in turn, will *mature* one for the practices of the completion stage, in which the vital points of the vajra body are penetrated.

The Stake of the Essence Mantra

The stake of the essence mantra will be explained later. Briefly, it means to chant with your attention one-pointedly focused on the essence mantra that revolves around the awakened life force (the seed syllable) within the three-layered beings. You carry out the recitation of a certain number, such as one hundred thousand for each syllable of the mantra, or else for a certain time span of months or years, or until a sign appears, such as having a vision of the deity. In particular, you should practice the vajra recitation assiduously, with the knowledge that the exhalation, inhalation, and resting of the breath are mantra.

From a saṃsāric perspective, this process will *purify* the nature of the sounds we use to communicate, the habitual patterns related to the ordinary speech of beings. In the pure context of buddhahood, the fruition will be *perfected* in the ground. Here the fruition refers to the inconceivable secret of enlightened speech, which transcends sounds, words, and expressions, yet appears in a whole range of forms, such as the infinite number of teaching vehicles. In the interim, in terms of practice, this process will purify the nature of ordinary speech and the subtle energies into the essence mantra. This, in turn, will *mature* one to carry out the completion stage practices in which one relies on the energies, as taught in the father tantras.

The Stake of Unchanging Realization

Third is the stake of unchanging realization. Whether you practice a peaceful or wrathful yidam deity, such the Great Glorious One, a hybrid deity, or an oath-bound protector appearing in the form of a mundane or wisdom deity, you must realize that it is none other than your own mind. This realization will mature you into its very essence: the great equality of the deity and reality. Moreover, everything external and internal, the universe and inhabitants that you visualize as the maṇḍala of support and supported, is simply a mental manifestation and possesses no other reality.

The nature of mind is primordially the identity of the three bodies of enlightenment. Its essence is empty, the dharma body. Its nature is lucid, the enjoyment body. Freed upon arising, with no clinging, it is the emanation body. Manifesting as its expression are the male aspect of relative appearance, method, and the female aspect of ultimate emptiness, knowledge. The circle of the Magical Web is the unity of these, a wisdom manifestation of indivisible appearance and emptiness.

In short, in the naturally present maṇḍala of appearance and existence as manifest ground, material appearances are enlightened body, sounds are enlightened speech, and thoughts are enlightened mind. Within this maṇḍala, the nature of all phenomena is primordially enlightened. This is the realization we should take up, the view of the natural state. In this way we can bind all concepts that fixate on a distinct duality—self and other, samaya and wisdom being, practice and goal, pure and impure—within the nondual expanse of equality. This is not only the life force of the development stage, but the completion stage as well. It is the sole crucial and indispensable key point throughout every aspect of the development, recitation, and completion stages. *The Advice of the Great Glorious One* pronounces:

> As the stake of unchanging realization, the Great Glorious One
> And the whole range of peaceful and wrathful deities
> Are none other than one's own mind.
> Even Rudra is the mind and is nowhere else.
> In being empty, mind itself is the dharma body.
> In being clear and distinct, it is the enjoyment body.
> And appearing naturally in a variety of ways, it is the emanation body.
> Appearances are the male consort and emptiness the female;
> The union of appearance and emptiness is wisdom's form.
> The limitless thoughts and memories as well
> Are completely perfect, the retinue of the Glorious One.
> They are inconceivable and enlightened right from the start,
> As they never move from this very nature.
> Without the stake of unchanging realization,
> Accomplishing the Great Glorious One

Will not bring supreme accomplishments,
Only the ordinary, and one will end up like Rudra.

Furthermore, *The Tantra of the Layered Lotus Stems* describes:

A practitioner who possesses this stake can practice
An evil demon in a charnel ground, and still,
Whichever results he seeks, supreme or mundane,
Will automatically, spontaneously emerge.
Without realizing this stake, he will mistake the deity as
concrete.
In that mindset he may practice a wisdom being,
And perhaps reach some temporary, trifling result,
But an authentic fruition will be nearly impossible.

This is the crucial key point, not which deity you practice nor whose mantra you chant, so you should take this alone as the life force of the path.

In terms of saṃsāra, this process will purify the negative mind and its habitual patterns that are present as self-aware, natural clarity. In the context of buddhahood, the fruition will be perfected in the ground, this fruition being the inconceivable secret of enlightened mind, reality free from the complexities of thought and perception, as well as all the various forms this inconceivable clairvoyance can take. In the interim, in the context of practice, by familiarizing yourself with the reality of nondual appearance-emptiness, you will be matured for the completion stage meditations on bliss, clarity, and nonthought, where one relies on the mind of awakening, in both its ultimate and relative forms.

The Activity Stake of Projection and Absorption

The activity stake of projection and absorption involves the creation of a miraculous display that brings the countless enlightened activities one desires under one's command. The basis for accomplishing this is the visualized deity and maṇḍala. Here you, as the deity, emit rays of light of the color that corresponds to a particular activity from the awakened life force of the seed syllable, the mantra chain, and your various body parts. In doing so, the two goals are fulfilled, and the universe and its inhabitants are united with the three maṇḍalas. The focus in the visualization of projection and absorption is redirected according to what you seek to accomplish. White light pacifies, yellow enriches, red magnetizes, green or black light creates wrathful activity, and blue or multicolored light rays bring about all activities, or else supreme spiritual accomplishment. A tantra explains:

> If the nail of the various projections and absorptions is lacking,
> You will not accomplish your goal just visualizing one thing.
> But if you know how to direct the projection and absorption,
> Then by practicing even the lowest *tedrang* spirit
> You will have unhindered activity and accomplish all deeds.

In a saṃsāric context this process will purify and refine away all ordinary forms of physical, verbal, and mental activity, such as defeating enemies, caring for loved ones, business, agriculture, and so on. In the pure context of buddhahood it will perfect the fruition in the ground, meaning all forms of inconceivable activity related to enlightened body, speech, and mind. In the interim, in the context of practicing on the path this will mature one for the completion stage, in which one trains on the path that purifies intentional efforts to accomplish the twofold benefit spontaneously. At this stage there is an ordinary path that entails a reference point and relies upon physical, verbal, and mental activities, as well as the practice of luminosity, which involves the direct realization of nonreferential wisdom. Through this all that appears and exists will be purified into bodies of light.

If you can penetrate the key points related to the instruction on the four stakes, you will come to see the deity's form firsthand and so capture the life force of enlightened body. You will also accomplish true speech, thus capturing the life force of enlightened speech. You will gain control of the natural state, thus capturing the life force of enlightened mind.

Your body, speech, and mind will merge in one taste with the enlightened body, speech, and mind of the bliss-gone ones, and so you will attain the life force of all saṃsāra and nirvāṇa. Finally, you will develop the power of wisdom and master the manifold enlightened activities.

Moreover, since the stake of unchanging realization is the view, it is also the ground. The stake of deity absorption is the meditation. The stake of the essence mantra is also an aspect of meditation, but implicitly the conduct as well; together these make up the path. The activity stake of projection and absorption constitutes the fruition since it brings about the supreme and common spiritual accomplishments and takes enlightened activity as the path in the present. Moreover, we should understand that they are all originally a unity, not different or separate from one another, nor are they alternating stages. In the words of Khepa Śrī Gyalpo:

> As the great purity and equality of reality itself, this unchanging realization is the enlightenment of space and wisdom. Its own display is the union of development and completion, which appears naturally as the relative maṇḍala of vajra space. Within this state one trains by transforming empty sounds, the natural sound of mantra, and by manifesting the enlightened activity of projection and absorption. Great wisdom, the enlightened body, speech, and mind of the buddhas, is free from deliberate effort and conceptual complexities. At the same time, it accomplishes the twofold benefit spontaneously. This fruition, which is here in this very moment, is what is known as the vajra vehicle of Secret Mantra, the vehicle of fruition.
>
> By realizing the view of the ground—that the circle of wisdom is the equality of saṃsāra and nirvāṇa—one gains mastery over the life force of both existence and peace. Through the path of meditation, the circle of deity and mantra, one masters the life force of both development and completion. Finally, by engaging in the spontaneous accomplishment of the twofold benefit mastery is gained over the life force of

the inconceivable, great skillful means. To give an example, when Rahula swallows the moon out of the sky, he naturally takes hold of all its reflections as well. In the same way, just by knowing these instructions on the four stakes that bind the life force, one will be able to practice all the inconceivable key points and intents of both sūtra and tantra simultaneously.

KEY POINTS FOR THE STAKE OF UNCHANGING REALIZATION

There are various key points that relate specifically to each of the four stakes. First are the eighteen key points that concern the stake of unchanging realization:

- Knowing the equality of saṃsāra and nirvāṇa is the key point that utterly purifies acceptance and rejection.
- Knowing the emptiness of one taste is the key point that destroys clinging to reality and attachment to true existence.
- Knowing appearance and emptiness to be a unity is the key point that perfects the two accumulations simultaneously.
- Embracing the view is the key point that prevents development and completion from parting.
- Not wavering from the state of realization is the key point of meditation arriving at the view.
- Being freed from clinging to the sublime deity is the key point that prevents errors in the development stage.
- Perfecting all that appears and exists as the manifest ground is the key point that eliminates dualistic fixation on self and other.
- Realizing that primordial liberation is perfected in the ground is the key point that eliminates the faults of the five poisons.
- Arriving at the realization of the dharma body is the key point that perfects the three bodies in one's own state of being.

- Knowing the ground and the fruition to be of one taste is the key point of not needing to practice or make a conscious effort on the paths and levels.
- Meditation arriving at the fruition is the key point of not searching for enlightenment elsewhere.
- Fruition arriving at the ground is the key point that liberates fixation and attachment to the idea that there is something to attain.
- Oneness in the expanse of reality is the key point that purifies clinging to the samaya being and wisdom being.
- Realizing the sovereign lord of the one hundred families is the key point of practicing one deity and accomplishing them all.
- Achieving the supreme accomplishment is the key point that spontaneously accomplishes the twofold benefit.
- Being beyond good and evil, and acceptance and rejection, is the key point of not depending on ritual purity or righteous conduct.
- Knowing nonaction to be primordially complete is the key point of not needing the gradual arrangement of ritual.
- Purifying attachment to philosophical systems is the key point of having reached the peak of all vehicles.

These are the eighteen major key points. As there are even more than this, however, these are the "life force of the life force." Since they bind even the life force of the other three life forces, they are utterly indispensable and, therefore, placed first.

KEY POINTS FOR THE STAKE OF ABSORPTION

There are six key points that relate to the stake of the development stage deity:

- Visualizing appearances as the deity is the key point that prevents one from straying into a one-sided emptiness.

- Taking the relative as the path is the key point that unites the two truths.
- Purifying the solidification of objects is the key point of abandoning clinging to things as being ordinary and truly existent.
- Perfecting the aspects of the ritual is the key point for perfecting the great accumulation of merit.
- Visualizing the features of the enlightened body is the key point that becomes the proximate cause of the form bodies.
- Being in harmony with the actual nature of the fruition is the key point that spontaneously accomplishes the three bodies.

KEY POINTS FOR THE STAKE OF THE ESSENCE MANTRA

Next are the ten key points that concern the stake of the essence mantra:

- Taking vajra speech as the path is the key point that purifies the obscurations of speech.
- Meditating on the series of three beings is the key point for simultaneously liberating body, speech, and mind.
- Focusing on the visualized mantra chain is the key point for abandoning ordinary thoughts.
- The recitation that is like a moon with a garland of stars is the key point for resting in the natural flow of meditative concentration.
- The recitation that is like a spinning firebrand is the key point for producing the wisdom of empty bliss.
- The recitation that is like a broken beehive is the key point for liberating voices and sounds as mantra.
- Counting the essential life force is the key point for receiving the blessings of the deity.
- Developing the strength of speech is the key point for assuring that all that one says benefits others.

- Accomplishing the true speech of knowledge mantras is the key point for accomplishing whatever aspirations one makes.
- Mastering the speech of the victorious ones is the key point for having gods and spirits, as well as all that appears and exists, follow one's command.

KEY POINTS FOR THE STAKE OF PROJECTION AND ABSORPTION

The last six key points concern enlightened activity, the stake of projection and absorption:

- Accomplishing the supreme spiritual accomplishment is the key point for the automatic occurrence of the mundane accomplishments.
- Being able to direct the visualization is the key point for not being dependent on other activity practices.
- Perfecting enlightened activity is the key point of effortlessly benefiting others.
- Spontaneously accomplishing the benefit of others is the key point for accomplishing the deeds of the buddhas.
- Being inspired by the impetus of engendering the awakened mind is the key point for not straying into the Lesser Vehicle.
- Ripening and liberating those in need of guidance is the key point for upholding the lineage.

As outlined here, these four fundamental practices contain forty key points, which subsume the entire range of key points that pertain to the path of the vajra vehicle of Secret Mantra. Without them, any path is sure to be nothing but a lifeless corpse.

The Stages of Visualization

The specific explanation of the visualizations has three parts: (1) developing confidence in the indivisibility of deity and mantra as a way to swiftly attain spiritual accomplishments; (2) a specific explanation of the recitation visualizations related to the four aspects of approach and accomplishment; and (3) an explanation of recitation technique, combined with the purpose and benefits of recitation.

Developing Confidence in the Indivisibility of Deity and Mantra

Generally speaking, recitation mantras essentially consist of vowels and consonants, the syllables of method and knowledge. Moreover, all of the vowels and consonants arise from, and have as their essence, the syllable A, the inexpressible source of all expression. The syllable A is unborn and, in the ultimate sense, primordially devoid of conceptual constructs such as birth, remaining, and cessation, reference point, or coming and going. For this reason, and because of being a natural equality, it is the dharma body, in the sense that all phenomena, as nothing but mere labels, are originally enlightened and possess no intrinsic nature. This is described in *The Tantra of the Secret Essence*:

> A is beyond reference points such as
> Empty, not empty, or their middle way.
> Everything is just labels, and all buddhas
> Abide in the garland of syllables itself.

This type of absorption is opened up by means of the inexpressible syllable A, so that the various vowels and consonants that are formed verbally appear. Since these expressions are unceasing and by nature originally enlightened, they are the enjoyment body. The same text declares:

> A itself appears in manifold forms,
> As KA and the rest of the forty-two letters.

The names of these sounds are all-inclusive
And are themselves surely the perfect complete king.

In this way, the unborn and unceasing basic space gives rise to collections of syllables of great skillful means that take on amazing and incredible appearances through various emanations. These, in turn, form the basis of all the purely relative and conventional names, words, and expressions. Moreover, they constitute the great miraculous display that reveals the countless ways of Dharma, in every way necessary, for those in need of guidance. These syllables are the sublime speech of the enlightened emanation body. The same text also mentions:

Incredible! This amazing and wondrous
Miraculous display of the forty-five syllables,
The basis for apprehension of every name and word,
Expressing and revealing all types of great meaning!

Ultimately, syllables have no substantial existence but are mental manifestations that, from the very moment they arise, have no inherent existence. The nature of mind is primordially empty and devoid of identity, never wavering from great equality free of constructs. Syllables are, therefore, also beyond the scope of dualistic mind, and remain as the wisdom mind of the enlightened emanation body. As it says in the same text:

The nature of unreal syllables is mind,
Beyond extremes, with no identity or reference point.

The syllables never waver from this state, yet their unobstructed display of interdependent appearances emerges as the various shapes and forms of symbolic letters that produce words and names. These magical syllable clouds produce a compassionate display that emanates in every possible way, such as seed syllables for developing deities and physical representations of scripture. This is how syllables manifest as the enlightened emanation body, performing an infinite activity to benefit beings. The tantra continues:

> Yet with names and words of color and shape
> They create and manifest a manifold display.

Finally it explains:

> The body, speech, and mind of the wisdom beings,
> Who appear throughout the four times and ten directions,
> Are complete within the forty-fivefold maṇḍala
> Of syllables culminating in KṢA.

In other words, the nature of enlightened body, speech, and mind of all buddhas is vajra wisdom.

More specifically, the mantras that we recite are effective because they are blessed with four types of establishment. First, they are established by the essence of reality itself since all syllables are primordially established as the essence of equality and great emptiness. Second, they are established by their nature since the nature of each is unfailingly established to appear in its own unique way. Third, they are established through blessings since the buddhas, who have mastery over all phenomena, have blessed certain mantras—from one syllable to many—by revealing in them the magical displays of wisdom itself. Finally, they are established with potency, similar to medicine or wish-fulfilling jewels, since mantras have an unfailing and unimpeded power to bring about spiritual accomplishment. For these reasons there is no short-term or ultimate goal unattainable through the power of mantra.

It is crucial then to take this confidence in the indivisibility of deity and mantra into the recitation and carry it out with one-pointed devotion. A tantra highlights this:

> The mantra is the form of the yoginī;
> The yoginī is the form of the mantra.
> Whoever strives for the sublime state,
> Do not divide them in two!

It also mentions:

If you practice with solid trust,
The sky may disappear, but it is impossible
To fail in the accomplishment of the mantra.
If the knowledge mantras pronounced
By deities and sages are infallible,
How could one fail in practicing
The secret mantras, pronounced free of desire?
They have never failed, and they never will.

In short, the wisdom of enlightenment can manifest in any possible way to the minds of beings in need of guidance. Whether a buddha appears in actuality to guide beings as such, or whether he appears as something ordinary to guide them in a mundane way, there is no qualitative difference since they are both the wisdom display of a single buddha. In the present context we are discussing how the buddha can manifest in the form of a mantra in the perception of ordinary beings. Furthermore, when the deity appears directly through accomplishment of the mantra, it is simply the case that the deity had previously manifested as the mantra. Then, through the process of practicing, the mantra remanifests as the deity to bestow spiritual accomplishments to the disciple. So it is of utmost importance that we develop confidence in the indivisibility of deity, mantra, and our minds.

The Four Aspects of Approach and Accomplishment

The second part covers two topics: (1) setting a foundation for the recitation and (2) the particular visualizations of projection and absorption.

Setting a Foundation for the Recitation

Continue to visualize yourself as the samaya being of any particular yidam deity, applying the three principles of vivid appearance, recollection of purity, and stable pride. At your heart visualize the precious domelike *citta* made of light. This may be a translucent, maroon-colored octagon, the shape of two cymbals pressed together, or else an orb of five-colored light. In its center is the wisdom being, sitting on a throne made of the sun and the moon. The wisdom being may be a likeness of yourself as the deity, or else bereft of ornaments and implements. In some cases this is framed in terms of an emanation and the source of the emanation, for instance Amitābha in the heart center of Avalokiteśvara, or Vārāhī in the center of Yeshe Tsogyal. You should visualize all of this according to your text.

In the wisdom being's heart center visualize a vajra, or the appropriate symbolic implement of the buddha family, resting upright. In the center of this implement may be a stacked sun and moon, or else only a moon in the case of peaceful deities, or a sun in the case of wrathful ones; it is about the size of a split pea. On this seat is the absorption being, the core awakened life force of the main deity. It is in the form of a seed syllable, such as HRĪḤ or HŪṂ, depending on the yidam. The syllable is the same color as the deity, shines brightly like a candle flame, and stands upright, facing the same direction as the deity. The mantra garland is arranged around this syllable.

In some practice manuals you visualize yourself as the samaya being with the seed syllable and mantra garland in your heart center. However, there are also manuals without a wisdom being or symbolic implement. So you should always follow your particular text.

The syllable we visualize can be in the Tibetan script, since the Tibetan language subsists primordially as the essence of vajra speech. The profound mystery of the buddhas' wisdom and miraculous display, moreover, connects to all beings in need of guidance in an equal manner. The difference between Sanskrit and Tibetan lies only in the shapes of the letters. Otherwise, there is no discernible difference, like one language being holier than the other. Therefore, simply use whichever script most easily comes to mind; there is no need to convert it to something else.

The mantra garland should be arranged so that it begins in front of the seed syllable, the core awakened life force. The letters of the recitation mantra should be miniscule, as if drawn with a single fine hair, and shine brightly as they rotate around the seed syllable. The other details should be sought in your specific text. Mantra garlands that spin clockwise should be facing outwards, so that they are readable from the outside, with the syllables upright and arranged in a counterclockwise sequence. As the mantra spins in a chain, the leading syllable, such as OṂ, will therefore be next to the final syllable, for instance HŪṂ or HRĪḤ. Long mantras should begin with the first syllable in front and facing inward, and then coil two or three times around like a snake, so that the final syllable is at the outside, directly in front of the first. When reciting with this type of visualization, it should rotate clockwise so it is readable from left to right.

Mantra garlands that spin counterclockwise should also stand upright and start in front of the awakened life force, but run clockwise and face inward, and thus be readable from the inside. If a mantra is long, it should coil from the inside out as described just above. These mantras should then spin counterclockwise during the recitation. Generally speaking, for male deities the mantra garland spins clockwise, while for female deities it spins counterclockwise, but this distinction cannot be made categorically; you must look to your own text.

For mantra garlands that do not actually spin, but project and absorb light while they remain stationary, the direction the letters face is the opposite of above. For these, the central factor is whether they are arranged with the letters running clockwise or counterclockwise. This should be taken case by case.

The Visualizations of Projection and Absorption

Approach

The first style of visualization is the arranged recitation, which is the aspect of approach, and is likened to a moon with a garland of stars. In this style you repeatedly bring your attention back to the seed syllable, the mantra garland, and the projection and absorption of light. Eventually all of the deities begin to let the mantra resound in their voices, and the syllables of the mantra, each making its own particular sound, rise slightly above the disc. At first it is merely the light from the syllables that is revolving. Then the mantra garland itself begins to revolve increasingly faster, and eventually projects light. As this light saturates your body, think that it clears away all illness, demonic influence, negativity, and obscurations, including even their latent tendencies.

Close Approach

The second style is the palanquin recitation, the aspect of close approach, which is likened to a spinning firebrand. In this style a second mantra garland emanates out of the mantra in the heart center. One syllable follows the previous without touching it in an uninterrupted chain, resounding with the mantra's sound. Like a spinning firebrand, the mantra chain emerges from the mouth of the wisdom being and then the samaya being before entering the mouth of the female consort. Stimulating her wisdom mind, it courses through her body and emerges from her lotus, from which it enters the male consort followed by the wisdom being through their vajras. Traveling upward, it produces an exhilarating rapture, the great bliss of the mind of awakening. Finally, imagine that it dissolves back into the seed syllable in the heart center, at which point you attain supreme spiritual accomplishment. This process stabilizes the subtle essences, creates an experience of clarity, and makes the downward-clearing energy pass into the central channel.

If done for too long, however, it can create an obstacle by transferring energy to the upper part of the body. To prevent this from happening, visualize the mantra garland traveling the other way from the male consort's vajra into the female's lotus, then out of the female's mouth and into the male's, before it dissolves into the seed syllable in his heart center. Just as before, visualize the mantra garland then reemerging and proceeding to revolve uninterruptedly. This is called the "palanquin," or "sedan," recitation. It creates an experience of nonthought, leads the life energy into the central channel, and prevents any obstacles deriving from energy moving into the upper body. If performed for too long, there is a risk that the subtle essence might weaken and the clarity of the visualization might fade. So it is ideal to practice these two in alternation, visualizing the mantra as it revolves toward you in the morning and dusk sessions, and away from you in the midday and afternoon sessions. Both of these are called the "spinning style" recitation.

This style can also be applied when there is a frontal visualization as well. Simply project and absorb the mantra garland back and forth between you and the frontal visualization.

Accomplishment

Third is the recitation of projection and absorption, the aspect of accomplishment, which is likened to a king's emissaries. By reciting the mantra, light rays of the five colors stream out of the awakened life force and mantra garland, filling all of space. Innumerable goddesses bearing offerings then emanate from the tips of the light rays, making countless gifts to delight the victorious ones throughout space, along with their offspring. The deities are overjoyed and in a state of stainless bliss; all of the spiritual accomplishments and the blessings of enlightened body, speech, and mind shower down like rain. These take the form of white, red, and blue light, or else bodily forms for enlightened body, seed syllables for enlightened speech, and symbolic implements for enlightened mind, which dissolve into your body, speech, and mind. As they do so, think that the two obscurations, as well as their habits, are purified; the two accumulations in their entirety are completed; and the four empowerments are attained all at once. This is the visualization of gathering the blessings for one's own benefit.

Then light rays stream out again, striking the sentient beings of the six classes and three realms, and instantly purifying them of all their karma, negativity, disturbing emotions, and their particular forms of suffering. Imagine as well that the listeners, self-realized buddhas, and bodhisattvas are freed from their cognitive obscurations, and that all beings' body, speech, and mind are transformed into the three vajras. This is the recitation of enlightened activity for the benefit of others. In this context you should also know how to perform the visualizations for any of the four activities that you wish to carry out.

Great Accomplishment

The aspect of great accomplishment is likened to a beehive that has burst open. In this style imagine that light rays project from the deity and the mantra, transforming the universe into a celestial palace, its inhabitants into the circle of deities, all sounds into the nature of mantra, and all thoughts into the play of wisdom. This is the recitation of the nonduality of self and other, which should be carried out in a state of nonfixation.

There are different ways to apply these four styles of recitation, such as in sequence or by focusing on one of them in particular, so it is important to see how they are presented in your particular text.

The Tradition of Oral Instruction

The fifth style is according to the special tradition of oral instructions, which is sufficient, in itself, for both approach and accomplishment. In this style, as you visualize yourself as the yidam deity before you begin the recitation, imagine that above you sits Guru Padmasambhava wearing the attire of Vajradhara, surrounded by multitudes of masters of the instruction lineage. Imagine that your sincere devotion rouses his wisdom mind, so that white, red, and blue light emerges from the three places of his body, forming a nectar that flows into you through the crown of your head. As it then saturates your body and purifies your obscurations, think that all the blessings of his wisdom mind penetrate you, so that you attain the spiritual power to swiftly accomplish every deity and mantra. With this in mind, chant one hundred or so of the VAJRA GURU mantra, and then dissolve the guru into yourself. Afterwards, carry out the consecrations of speech and of the rosary, etc.

Once this is done, continue to visualize yourself as the deity and imagine that a recitation mansion, complete in both supporting and supported aspects, emerges from your heart center into the space in front of you. The seed syllable and mantra garland in your heart center then emit light rays and mantra garlands that revolve between you like a spinning firebrand. Now the tip of your tongue projects a great mass of light that gathers in the sky, presenting sublime Samantabhadra offering clouds of great bliss to the conquerors and bodhisattvas throughout space, who appear to be pleased and satisfied. This causes them to manifest out of the dharma body and become active, throughout space, as form bodies appearing like the maṇḍala of deities you are practicing. They then enter the deities in the recitation mansion like a mass of falling sesame seeds and merge inseparably with them. The deities then emit light rays of enlightened body, speech, and mind that dissolve into you.

Next, the mantra syllables in the sky before you emanate innumerable light rays. The light pleases the multitudes of root and lineage knowledge holder masters, arouses the bodhisattvas out of their equanimity to benefit beings, and inspires courage in the mother ḍākinīs. It also incites the oath-bound Dharma protectors into action, rouses the listeners and self-realized buddhas from their state of cessation, subdues the haughty mundane spirits, and menaces the demonic and extremist adversaries. It overpowers the misconceptions of all beings in the three realms and annihilates malicious enemies and obstructors. Finally, the light dispels the obscurations of all beings, in every time and place, completely fulfilling their temporary and ultimate wishes, and establishing them all at the level of the yidam deity.

Then, one last time, light streams out, transforming the outer universe, all at once, into a celestial palace, the inhabitants within it into male and female deities, and perfecting it all—the entirety of appearance and existence—into the maṇḍala of the deity you are practicing. The natural sound of the secret mantra you are chanting then resounds in the voices of all the deities, and from spinning mantra garlands everywhere throughout space. The sound, which resounds throughout the universe, is as loud as a thousand lightning bolts thundering at once, a hundred thousand giant mountains collapsing, or a meteor strike.

The light that radiates and swells from the mantras corresponds in color to that of the main deity. Alternatively, the light may be of multiple colors, in which case it is dark blue in the center, maroon in the east, deep yellow in the south, dark red in the west, and dark green in the north. With all this in mind, carry out the recitation in a state of one-pointed concentration.

This description applies when the central deity is wrathful. For peaceful deities the basic framework is the same, while the light should be soft, and there should be an arousal of bliss. Moreover, you should chant the mantra with a melodious tune, as beautiful as the voice of Brahmā. Throughout all of the above recitation visualizations you should understand how they unfold within the single taste of great wisdom and bring all of appearance and existence under the sway of natural awareness. Doing so, you can use them as a way to attain all the blessings and spiritual accomplishments one can wish for.

When breaking from a session, imagine that the seed syllables and light rays in the sky—along with all of appearance and existence manifested as the divine maṇḍala—dissolve into the recitation mansion. The deities in the recitation mansion then dissolve into you, so that your physical radiance and splendor increase exponentially, and your body becomes entirely filled with miniature forms of the deity you are practicing. This can be applied to the recitations of each of the principal and retinue deities. As per usual, to make up for mistakes in the mantra recitation and to stabilize its effectiveness, at the end of the session chant the vowels and consonants, the "Essence of Dependent Origination," and the hundred syllables three times each.

This condensation of the oral instructions of the knowledge holders in the lineage of the Early Translations is the heart-extract of the omniscient Jampel Gyepa. There are many other common and unique details, including the general and specific points for practicing the three roots, as well as the visualizations for pacifying, increasing, magnetizing, wrathful activity, protection, exorcism, and slaying. You should learn these from the primary recitation manuals and receive thorough instruction on them from your teacher. If you then practice them in secrecy, you will reach the pinnacle of the two spiritual accomplishments.

The Technique, Purpose, and Benefits of Mantra Recitation

Recitation Technique

Generally speaking, there are many different ways to recite mantras. You can do vocal recitation and chant loudly and clearly, or chant softly, using the lips, tip of the tongue, and vocal cords only slightly. There is silent recitation, in which you hold your breath while focusing your attention on the form and sound of the mantra. Then there is also a technique called mental recitation, in which you do not hold your breath, but simply keep in mind the form or the sound of the mantra. There is also another style called vajra recitation. In vajra recitation you make the sound HŪṂ as you breathe out from the nāda of the seed syllable, while projecting light rays or bodily forms to accomplish the twofold benefit. You reabsorb these as you breathe in while making the sound OṂ, and dissolve them into the nāda as you make the sound AḤ while holding the breath. Here, however, we will only concern ourselves with vocal recitation.

You should learn about the requirements for a qualified rosary for counting, the way to consecrate it, and the manner of counting with the rosary for different activities from other general manuals. I will not go into them here for fear of being long-winded. In terms of the main points of recitation technique, the Great Master of Uḍḍiyāna has said,

> Recite with undistracted concentration.
> Should you become distracted elsewhere,
> Even reciting for an eon will bring no result.

In other words, if you recite while distracted, no matter how much you chant, it will not lead to any great spiritual accomplishments but merely lessen your verbal obscurations a bit. It is therefore vital to chant in one-pointed concentration with your attention focused on the vivid appearance of the deity and the projection and absorption of light rays from the mantra garland, without straying onto other things.

If you know such details, you should also be sure to utter the sounds from the correct place of articulation, with proper aspiration and pronunciation. Moreover, you should avoid certain faults, such as chanting the individual syllables too fast or overly slow. You should not shorten the long syllables or elongate the short ones, and be sure not to add excess syllables or leave any of the actual syllables out. Also, do not recite too loudly or quietly. When you are in session you should not interrupt the recitation by yawning, spitting, or engaging in excess conversation. *The Awesome Flash of Lightning* mentions these things:

> Not too loud and not too quiet,
> Not too fast and not too slow,
> Not too rough and not too weak,
> Enunciate the syllables in their entirety.
> There should be no distraction or idle talk,
> Nor interruptions by yawning and the like.

In addition, if you know the meaning connected to the mantra, you can accomplish the dhāraṇī of meaning and other such aims. This is described in a tantra:

For the expert with no doubt of the meaning
The spiritual accomplishments are near.

Nonetheless, even without knowing the associated meaning, you can recite with one-pointed faith and sincerity, and still the great spiritual accomplishments will emerge just as they ought to. It continues:

But the accomplishments linked to that meaning
Are still close to the fool who has faith.

This point can be seen in the old story about the adepts Darchar and Sakya Paṇḍita converting Harinanda.

There is a reason why mantras in Sanskrit are not translated into Tibetan, those in Tibetan mixed with Sanskrit are not translated completely into Sanskrit, and those in the symbolic language of the ḍākinīs or other foreign languages are not recreated or translated for the sake of communication. The rationale is that, in leaving them as they are, we do not alter the actualization of the true speech uttered by the ones who first articulated them. In fact, it is said that analyzing the practices of Secret Mantra only distances you from spiritual accomplishment. As it is explained:

Spiritual accomplishment is extremely far
From the intellectual with his logic and scrutiny.

Furthermore,

No accomplishment will occur if you scrutinize
The applications of sacred substance and mantra.
Though accomplishment may be otherwise near,
When you entertain reservations,
Waver in resolve, or slip in your faith,
You will undoubtedly regress.

Therefore, it is crucial to recite with one-pointed faith and sincerity.

Most mantras we recite involve an invocation of the deity through utterance of its name. For instance, if we translate the six-syllable mantra, we are calling out to Avalokiteśvara by name: "O Jewel Lotus!" Or in the SIDDHI mantra we are invoking Guru Rinpoche's heart commitment: "Vajra Master Padma, please confer spiritual accomplishment!" In truth, distinctions like invoking or not invoking, hearing or not hearing, and near and far do not apply to wisdom deities. Nonetheless, by reciting wisdom-knowledge mantras—which are the enlightened speech of all buddhas, and the nature of the dharma body—we gradually deplete our obscurations and come ever closer to realizing the deity of the fruition. In doing so, we naturally suffuse ourselves with the wisdom deity's blessings.

Gauging the Recitation

As briefly mentioned above, the best gauge of recitation is achievement of the signs of accomplishing the deity, whether in actuality, in a vision, or in a dream. This is called *indicative recitation*. Second best is *temporal recitation*, where you recite for the length of time recommended in your particular text, for instance half a year. Otherwise, the third option is *numeric recitation*, in which you chant the mantra of the primary deity in the maṇḍala one hundred thousand times for each of its syllables. Then you would chant the mantras of the other maṇḍala deities each a tenth of the number of the main mantra. On top of this, you chant an amending number of ten percent of each mantra, meaning for each hundred thousand mantras you chant, you add 11,111. In certain other explanations, you chant one hundred thousand per syllable if the mantra is fifteen syllables or less, and ten thousand per syllable if it is thirty syllables or more.

The main presentation above is the way of counting in the age of perfection. It is sometimes taught that this should be doubled in the age of three-quarters perfection, tripled in the age of half perfection, and quadrupled in the age of strife. Essentially though, the important thing is that we practice in accord with our personal levels of insight and concentration.

When doing recitation practice, moreover, it is said that you should insert the "one thousand verse," an offering and praise made after each thousand mantras. Nonetheless, if you fail to do that, you can instead make the offering and praise after you complete the recitation. At that point you would also chant the vowels and consonants, the hundred-syllable mantra, and the "Essence of Dependent Origination" in order to mend any broken commitments of body, speech, and mind. This also amends for recitation mistakes, such as mantras chanted in excess or left out, and stabilizes the effectiveness of your practice. You should also receive the spiritual accomplishments and so on as laid out in your text. Beyond this, you should become familiar with all the activities during session breaks, including proper retreat behavior, from the writings of the great saints of the past where they are described in detail. In particular, you should study the lord guru's *Great General Guide to Recitation* and other similar texts. It is important that we put these details into practice.

There is immeasurable value and benefit to focusing in practice on one-pointed visualization of the deity and correctly carrying out the recitation—whether numeric, temporal, or indicative. In this life alone you will pacify obstacles and obstructions, acquire powerful verbal abilities, please the deity and receive its blessing in your mind-stream, complete the two accumulations and thereby have your wishes fulfilled, create an extraordinary link between ground, path, and fruition, and mature your stream of being. In every lifetime hereafter you will be under the care of the sublime deity. Ultimately, you will become fully enlightened within the expanse of the lord of the family's wisdom mind. In the short-term, moreover, you will gain mastery over measureless and remarkable activity and spiritual accomplishment, and master the maṇḍala activities in the role of vajra master.

Subsequent Rituals

The additional explanation regarding the concluding activities covers four topics: (1) the gathering offering, (2) sustaining the torma, (3) receiving the spiritual accomplishments, and (4) apologizing for mistakes.

The Gathering Offering

The "gathering circle" refers to indivisible method and knowledge, and takes the form of a special ceremony. The term derives from *gaṇacakra*, literally meaning a *circle* composed of offerings that form a *gathering* of great bliss used to cut through the web of disturbing emotions. It consists of several different types. There is the gathering of worthy people, which is to say, the gathering of method and knowledge in union. Then there is the gathering of plentiful things, which means bringing all the sacred substances of inner Secret Mantra together. Third, there is the gathering of delighted deities, referring to the visualization and invitation of the maṇḍala deities. Finally, when we bring these three gatherings together and revel in them, we attain the gathering of merit and wisdom.

Performing a Gathering Offering

In this day and age people who can practice the gathering circle in its true and literal sense are quite rare. So we will instead look at how to bring together a sincerely emulated gathering based on a wisdom consort, the way tantric devotees commonly practice these days.

The first step is to prepare the arrangement of articles. Place whatever offering items you have in front of the maṇḍala. This should be according to common procedure and include the outer, inner, and secret feast offerings as well as food and drinks that are suitable as samaya substances. Next, they should be consecrated. For that, sprinkle nectar on the articles and then give rise to the pride of being the primary deity. With this confidence, imagine that the syllables RAṂ, YAṂ, and KHAṂ project from your heart center. They transform respectively into wisdom fire, wind, and water, which burn, scatter, and wash away all clinging to impure reality. In this way everything is purified into emptiness. Now imagine that a syllable BHRŪṂ manifests from the state of emptiness and becomes a radiant feast bowl, made either out of jewels or a naturally manifest skull cup. Inside the feast bowl the contents, such as the three syllables, all melt into light to form an elixir. This elixir is the essence of awakened mind and the nature of the five meats, five nectars, and five wisdoms. It manifests, however, as anything that could possibly be desired. Imagining that, increase it to the reaches of space.

Next comes the gathering and invitation. Visualize yourself as the central deity with consort and imagine that your heart center—or else your place of union—projects countless light rays to the Unexcelled Realm and the infinite natural emanation body realms. The light makes these realms burst open like sesame pods as the multitudes of masters and maṇḍalas of the three root deities awaken and manifest in actuality, spreading through and filling up the entire expanse of space.

Then, for the actual gathering offering, there are three parts; the first involves the offering substances. In this, you take the prime, first portion of the feast. Imagine that it is essentially the nectar of stainless wisdom yet appears in the form of goddesses of the six sense pleasures along with an inexhaustible quantity of every possible delightful thing. Make the offering as you imagine this filling all of space.

Second is the offering of apology. For this you take the second, middle, portion of the feast and visualize it as the five nectars. As you offer it, think that the deities are pleased and your bond with them is mended. It also causes you to be purified of concepts, obscurations, damaged and broken vows, and blessed by great wisdom. At this point, you should also chant the hundred-syllable mantra and so on.

The third and final part is the offering of liberation. For this you should set aside an effigy, if you have one, or a triangle, before consecrating the offerings. Now place it in front of the offerings and imagine that the goddesses of the sense pleasures are reabsorbed back into you in the form of the syllable HŪṂ. Use the effigy as a support for your visualization. Then visualize yourself as the deity and imagine that innumerable light rays and magical emissaries stream out of your heart center. They summon the objects to be liberated, those who meet the ten conditions. These ten conditions are described in the tantras:

> Those who destroy the Buddha's teachings,
> Bring down the prestige of the Three Jewels,
> Prevent the saṅgha from assembling,
> Denigrate the Great Vehicle teachings,
> Inflict physical harm on the teacher,
> Sow discord among the vajra relatives,
> Create obstacles for spiritual practice,
> Those who transgress their commitments,

Who are compassionless monsters,
Who lead people to wrong, extremist beliefs,
And who inflict harm on practitioners:
These are the "ten objects of liberation."

A Clarification of Commitments presents in this way:

Enemies of the Three Jewels, opponents of the master,
Violators, breakers, and transgressors of commitments,
Those who arrive at the assembly, who are harmful to all,
Those hostile to the commitments, wicked beings,
And those in the three lower realms:
These ten the practitioner should take on.

These are all summoned helplessly before you. You seize them by the heart with a hook, pull them by the neck with a lasso, bind their limbs with a chain, stun them with a bell, and then dissolve them into the physical support. Imagine that they remain there incapacitated and without any divine savior.

Then unify boundless great compassion—which is the ultimate state of mind, emptiness suffused with compassion—and magical illusory concentration. As you do so, let your empty mind manifest in the form of vajra wrath whereby you are the Great Glorious One. The dagger in your hand is the Supreme Son Kīlaya, and the effigy is the embodiment of everything harmful. With these three in mind, stab the dagger to the heart of the effigy. In doing this, you gather all its life, wealth, glory, brilliance, and splendor into a syllable A. Imagine that this syllable dissolves into you, where it becomes the mind of awakening, inseparable from your own vajra life force. This constitutes the transmission of life.

Next, visualize the effigy's all-ground consciousness in the form of NRI and lift it with the tip of your dagger, where you visualize a HŪṂ. It courses through the dagger's interior before you propel it with PHAṬ. This purifies the consciousness of its temporary stains, so that it turns into a subtle sphere that travels to the Unexcelled Realm. There it finally dissolves into the heart center of the Great Glorious One, or whichever is the central deity, thereby being empowered as its son. This constitutes the transmission of purification.

In this way you can employ the transmissions of life, purification, and elevation to liberate the supported consciousness into basic space.

Next you grab the support composed of the habitual aggregates—by the right leg if it is male, or by the left leg if female—and proceed to chop it up. As you work on this, consider the effigy to be, in essence, the three poisons, appearing as a mass of flesh, blood, and bones. Then offer it up as a meal to the primary deity, along with its attendants and emanations. Think that your offering empties the three realms of cyclic existence.

In this way the triple satisfaction is fulfilled. You benefit, as you are satisfied with the nourishment of the enemy's life-span and merit, which have become your own. The enemy benefits, as he is satisfied in becoming the son of the Great Glorious One and his continuous stream of bad actions and their ripened effects have been cut. Also, the deities benefit, as the large retinue of attendants and guardians is satisfied in partaking of the flesh and blood of the corpse. Please look to other texts, such as my commentaries on Vajrakīlaya and on Viśuddha and Kīlaya combined, for the extensive version of this.

After this it is time to enjoy the gathering offering. First, the vajra helper should make prostrations to the chief of the gathering and offer him the symbolic offering of the substances of method and knowledge. The master then symbolically accepts these. Next, the vajra helper distributes the feast to the other participants, in order of seniority. Avoid quarreling, chattering, and clinging to ordinary reality within the gathering. Instead, feel satisfied and delighted, yet remain without conceptual grasping as you enjoy the feast.

Imagine that the feast is an offering of nectar that is refined into a pure essential extract by the fire of inner heat at your navel, and then offered to the maṇḍala of deities within your body. In this way enjoy the feast as a type of "inner burning and pouring." In addition, make the secret gathering offering based solely on the wisdom consort. Finally, bring to mind the offering of suchness, great bliss free of concepts of the three spheres, in which subject and object are unified as natural awareness, while emptiness and saṃsāra and nirvāṇa are primordially present as the maṇḍala.

With the permission of the vajra master or vajra helper you may also perform vajra song and dance while inspired by your practice.

Afterward, collect the residuals without saving or hoarding anything. This constitutes the "impure torma," to which you add the "morsel offering," and top off with part of the three prime portions. Next, the vajra helper makes an invocation and the vajra master subsequently spits wine onto the offerings while saying mantras and making gestures. During this ritual the vajra master's tongue is visualized as Hayagrīva, sporting with his consort, until a stream of the nectar of awakened mind pours down. This transforms the offerings into nectar and increases them. The offerings are then placed either to the northeast or the southeast of the shrine, on a human hide or something of the sort. You then summon the "residual guests" with mantras and gestures, and offer them things like flowers. In accord with the oath they took in the past in the presence of the Great Glorious One, command them to partake of the great, stainless, delightful, and sacred substance that is the residual torma and to carry out the activities that practitioners enjoin them to. Next, carry the residuals to a spot that is seventy paces away from the practice place, which is called the "feeding path of demons." Finally, make aspirations and do whatever other rituals your text lays out.

Sustaining the Torma

The second of the subsequent rituals is the sustaining of the torma. For this, first invoke the assembly of maṇḍala deities to manifest out of basic space by reminding them of their sacred commitment. Then remove the protector torma from the row of tormas and sprinkle it with medicine and rakta. Next, consider the essence of the torma to be the flesh, blood, and bones of the enemies and obstructors. Transform it mentally into the form of stainless wisdom nectar and increase it. Now imagine that nonarising basic space gives rise to self-manifest oath-bound protectors of the three tantras who appear with their entourage of numerous haughty spirits. Remind them of their strict past oath and then offer the torma to them. You should do so outside while commanding them to carry out the four types of enlightened activity unimpededly. At this time, if you wish to throw a curse, you should visualize the torma as being made of disease, weapons, and poison, and imagine it being projected in the direction of the hateful, destructive enemies, who are annihilated beyond a trace.

Subsequently, sprinkle the torma for the earth goddesses with the select medicine used to rinse the torma vessel, and consecrate it with the three seed syllables. This torma is offered to the twelve primary protectresses of Tibet and Kham. On an inner level, they are the very embodiments of the twelve links of dependent origination being naturally purified, while externally they have a steadfast presence. Offer the torma to them along with their hundred-thousandfold entourage of *menmo* goddesses, and enjoin them to carry out the activity that ensures the welfare of the Snowy Land, from its interior to its borders.

After this, perform the horse dance. Suppress the object of your focus below the torma vessel, which you turn upside down and visualize as the central mountain. Seal it with the vajra, and then carry out the dance activity. While imagining that the entire universe with its inhabitants consists of multitudes of male and female wrathful deities corresponding to the particular activity, for instance Noble Supreme Steed Heruka, perform the dance in the nonduality of method and knowledge. Imagine that through this the particular activity—whether pacifying, increasing, magnetizing, or wrathful—is accomplished in the short term, and that ultimately all concepts dissolve into basic space beyond reference point, where they manifest as enlightened bodies and wisdoms and the music of great bliss.

Receiving the Accomplishments

Next among the subsequent rituals is receiving the spiritual accomplishments, which is usually done after one has completed the practice of approach and accomplishment. I hesitate to say much here about the extensive way to receive the accomplishments, which is better learned from the specific recitation manual of the maṇḍala you are practicing. So here I will just give a rough overview of what happens at the very end of your activity text.

When you reach the conclusion, visualize the accomplishment torma as the deity, and then supplicate it with devotion and invoke its resolve. As you do so, the main places of the principal deities send out blessings of enlightened body, speech, and mind, as well as all spiritual accomplishments, which take the form of the three syllables and light rays. Imagine that these dissolve into your three places, purifying your obscurations of body, speech, and mind, and granting you every blessing and spiritual accomplishment. Then touch the accomplishment torma to your three places, or else taste the inner offering of nectar and place a drop of it on each of your three places. Afterward, rest evenly in innate equal taste.

Apologizing for Mistakes

Next you should make the offering and praise of thanksgiving. When completing them, you should address the maṇḍala deities in the following way, with heartfelt earnestness:

> I am completely deficient as a practitioner, lacking any insight and concentration, and therefore have not gained confidence in your oceanlike realization and conduct. I have fallen prey to dullness and agitation. My concentration has been hazy, my recitation sloppy, and I have left out elements of the ritual. I have not assembled all the sacred articles and substances, and I let those I have assembled become polluted. In these and many other ways I have transgressed many general and specific root and subsidiary commitments. In the presence of all of you, oceanlike gathering of gurus, hosts of maṇḍala deities, and my spiritual brothers and sisters, I admit and confess to any and all faults I have committed. Please cleanse and purify them so they do not turn into temporary or lasting obscurations.

With this in mind, chant a specific apology or else the generic hundred-syllable mantra of Vajrasattva. Afterward, either dissolve the wisdom being or request it to depart, whichever is appropriate, and then dissolve the samaya being. Alternatively, according to the unique and special approach of unexcelled mantra, you do not request the wisdom being to depart but rather dissolve the samaya and wisdom beings indivisibly.

Enlightened Mind

The practice of enlightened mind corresponds to its object of purification, which is the process in which a child, after growing old, dies and then reemerges. You now dissolve the world and its beings into the protection circle and then gradually into the tip of the seed syllable, which symbolizes the outer and inner stages of dissolution that occur at the moment of death, as well as the luminosity of the dharma body in the death state. Afterward, in the breaks between sessions, you arise from this state as the deity, which parallels the existence of the intermediate state.

The steps in the process of purification are as follows. First, train as much as possible in the practices of deity and mantra as explained above. Then, when you are no longer able to continue the practice, perform the dissolution stage. It is said that if you did not cling to thoughts of a sublime deity during the preceding development stage, you can perform the dissolution stage all at once: simply let the entire maṇḍala of support and supported vanish instantaneously like a rainbow fading into the sky. Then rest evenly within the great and supreme dharma body of the indivisible two truths, holding nothing in mind.

If the case is otherwise, however, you will have to subsequently dismantle the maṇḍala. In that case, first imagine that light from your heart center causes the entire pure external universe and its inhabitants to dissolve into light, which merges with the protection circle. Next, the inner layered elements gradually dissolve into the protection circle, which in turn dissolves into the charnel grounds. These dissolve into the celestial palace, the palace into the retinue, and the retinue into the primary male and female consorts, who dissolve into the wisdom being in the center of the heart. The wisdom being dissolves into the absorption being, the seed syllable of the awakened life force, which itself dissolves gradually upward until reaching the tip of the syllable. After that fades away, rest evenly in the expanse of original purity, free of constructs, thoughts, and reference points. This eliminates the extreme of eternalism.

Afterward, utter the mantra by which you reappear in the form of the main deity, like a fish leaping out of the water. Bless the three places of your body, don "the armor for physical protection" and so on, and proceed to bring all experiences and activities onto the path as the play of the enlightened bodies and wisdoms. This eliminates the extreme of nihilism. Strive then to make your daily activities a continuous stream of practice.

Here the result of purification is the manifestation of the form bodies of buddhahood, which constitutes the enlightened activity of the dharma body. Since the wisdom of the dharma body is also the essence of basic space, the form bodies dissolve back into it. Generally speaking, the wisdom of the dharma body is characterized by unconditioned simplicity, so, of course, it is essentially beyond any notion of something to dissolve or a process of dissolution. Still, the term "dissolve" is applied because of something seemingly disappearing in the perception of others, those in need of guidance. The reemergence illustrates the continuous reappearance of the form bodies in accord with the particular propensities of the beings in need of guidance. In addition, this matures you for the higher path, as it creates a foundation for the ability to reemerge in the unified illusory body after having established the universe and its inhabitants in luminosity during the practice of the fourth empowerment.

Though the explanations up to this point have clearly emphasized the development stage, in fact they have been suffused with the genuine oral instructions of the precious Early Translation lineage. In this way they present a path of unified development and completion, as I have pointed out above. The crux of the matter is that all conceptual phenomena that appear internally or externally, including the aggregates, elements, and sense sources, are primordially the great divine circle of all-encompassing purity, the three seats of completeness. It is not that they become this way, or are newly crafted as such through the path of purifying obstacles and discards. *The Tantra of the All-Creating King* proclaims:

> Hark!
> This manifestation of the all-creating king, guide
> among guides—
> The essential maṇḍala of enlightened forms—
> Is the manifestation of all things as they appear and exist
> Within nonarising true reality.
> Everything, however it may exist or be called,
> Manifesting in language within nonarising basic space,

> Consists of essential, inexpressible speech,
> Which itself is manifested by the all-creating king.

There is also a song that says:

> There are no buddhas or sentient beings
> Outside of the jewel of this mind.

In this way, all conceptual phenomena are pure as the deities, whose bodies are forms of the wisdom of equality. Here "wisdom" means the naturally present wisdom of the nature of mind, which does not divide into concepts of subject and object and is originally and utterly pure as the essence of the vajra mind of all buddhas. Once we resolve our view in a way that is in tune with the true state of things, we can meditate and gain experience. In this way, the illusory nonexistent appearances of saṃsāric phenomena, on one hand, as well as our clinging to them, on the other hand, are all naturally purified. Thereafter, all appearances become a manifestation of great wisdom with a nature of bliss, clarity, and emptiness. At that point we can resolve that all outer and inner conceptual phenomena are an expression of our own minds, while the nature of mind is primordially the form of the deity. When that happens, there is no deity apart from our own mind, no mind apart from the deity, as mind and the deity's form are a unity. All experiences and activities are sealed by illusory empty lucidness free of fixation.

Everything that appears physically is the illusory form of the deity, appearing while lacking true existence, lucid while free of thought, blissful while free of clinging, the embodiment of the indivisible essence of dharma body, appearance of enjoyment body, and activity of emanation body. As we then train in this type of pure perception and take it as our path, all appearances become natural appearance, and all of emptiness, natural emptiness, while the union of appearance and emptiness manifests in divine forms as the circle of all-encompassing purity.

Similarly, all internal and external sounds—whether pleasant or unpleasant, made by animate or inanimate things, including verbal expression and breathing—are primordially nonarising empty sounds, the invincible enlightened speech of the conquerors, the great melodious resounding. There is no sound, speech, or utterance apart from mantra, no mantra other than sound, speech, and utterance. When we seal all sound, speech, and utterance in the animate and inanimate world with the vajra recitation of nonarising empty sound, breath and mantra indivisibly united, they become unbound as the inconceivable mystery of enlightened speech: echolike, invincible, empty resounding.

Moreover, when we release all the good and bad thoughts that occur to our minds into innate naturalness, they remain as the primordial essence of the vajra mind of the conquerors. Therefore, in the expanse of mind nature's nondual equality, great bliss free of constructs, discard and remedy are of a single taste. This is the basic state of things as it is. This state naturally expresses itself through an unceasing display of diverse manifestations: such is the way things appear in their extent. The way things are and the way they appear are essentially a unity. They are an inseparable equality as the identity of inexpressible and innate wisdom. This is also the nonconceptual wisdom mind of the buddhas. Thus, there is no buddha mind apart from this naturally lucid nature of mind, and no mind of innate lucidness other than the buddha mind.

In the expanse of the great perfection free of concepts—the equal taste of mind and appearances—saṃsāra and nirvāṇa are of equal taste, and the phrase "ground of delusion" has never even been heard of. When we cross decisively into this great primordial purity, all thoughts and appearances manifest as great wisdom. Therefore, this, in fact, subsumes all the key points of the completion stage of vajra mind, and is itself the crucial point of the special path of the great perfection.

At the outset we must distinguish conceptual mind from awareness. First, recognize the nature of mind directly. This means to realize that your present awareness itself—free of thought and concept, uncontrived, and unspoiled—is naturally present wakefulness, the wisdom mind of the primordially pure dharma body. Then decide on one thing, which means to sustain the continuity of your present fresh awareness—the fourth part without the three—in which thoughts of the past and future are absent. Finally, gain confidence in liberation, in which thoughts are naturally and tracelessly freed as soon as they arise—like waves dissolving back into the ocean—and sensations subside into the basic ground. All of these profound points about the view, meditation, conduct, and fruition need to be learned, in detail, from a teacher.

While training in this way, it is vital that we practice, throughout all sessions and breaks, by means of the tenfold understanding of mantra, and supported by the six commitments. The knowledge holder Jigme Lingpa has outlined the tenfold understanding as follows:

> (1) All sādhanas are like an illusion; (2) all names and words have no substance, like a mirage that deceives a wild animal; (3) all activities are like a dream; (4) all things lack any true nature, like the reflection in a mirror; (5) all lands and places are like a city of spirits; (6) all sounds are like an echo; (7) all divine forms are like the reflection of the moon in water—they appear but have no true existence; (8) the various meditative absorptions are like bubbles surfacing on a lake; (9) the entire range of projections and absorptions is manifold, like optical illusions; and (10) all miraculous displays appear in various ways but have no characteristics of their own, like magical emanations.

Secondly, the lord guru has said that we should keep the support of the following five commitments:

(1) Have the unceasing, earnest devotion to see the master who teaches you the pith instruction as a buddha in person. (2) Create favorable circumstances that aid you in meditation practice. (3) Give up any unfavorable, adverse circumstances. (4) Never let your meditative concentration fade throughout any activity, including when you walk, move around, sit, or lie down. (5) Never abandon the yidam deity you are practicing, and carry through with its practice and meditation until the end.

This fifth point means that you should not accept and reject when it comes to the yidam deity, but realize instead that no matter which deity you practice, the wisdom mind of all buddhas is the same. By simply meditating on one, you are meditating on every buddha. There are no buddhas to meditate on other than realizing your mind. Since the yidam deity is also a projection of your mind, there is nothing separate to meditate on or accomplish. In short, all buddhas are embodied in the yidam deity. Whether you meditate on many different yidam deities or on one alone, they are all projections of your mind.

(6) Maintain confidentiality about the deity you are practicing, its essence mantra, and the nature of your practice and conduct. Keep them utterly secret from those who are unsuitable to hear about them.

CONCLUDING ACTIVITIES

The third main topic is about the concluding activities, which consist of the three aspects of dedication, aspiration, and making auspicious prayers.

Dedication

Here what we are dedicating is everything positive in the past, present, and future, represented by the training in the development and completion stages that we have now carried out correctly in all its preparatory, primary, and concluding parts. The goal to which we dedicate this is the state of Vajradhara, the sovereign buddha of the sixth family, the embodiment of the five wisdoms and the four bodies of enlightenment, which is to say, complete and perfect enlightenment that does not dwell in either of the two extremes. We dedicate this goodness to all sentient beings throughout the reaches of space so that they may attain the result of unexcelled wisdom. It is dedicated in a nonconceptual manner devoid of subject or object of dedication, considering that in ultimate truth the nature of everything is nonduality. At the same time, on a purely relative and conventional level, there is a dreamlike illusory experience of someone doing something, an object of that action, and a virtue being carried out, though in truth there is no reality to them.

In harmony with this, chant the verse of dedication while thinking sincerely and one-pointedly: "Just as the conquerors who appear in the past, present, and future, as well as their spiritual heirs, dedicate, I too dedicate this virtue completely to unexcelled enlightenment." The value and benefit of dedicating in this way is such that your accomplishments become inexhaustible. This is described in *The Sūtra Requested by Sāgaramati*:

> When a drop of water falls into a great ocean,
> It will remain until the ocean itself dries up.
> Just so, when dedicated to complete enlightenment,
> Virtue will remain until enlightenment is attained.

Aspiration

Next, while suffused with the attitude of the mind of awakening, make pure aspirations for the vast benefit of everyone. Recite the aspiration verse from your specific text and make the ten great aspirations: to worship the buddhas, to uphold the sacred teachings, to always display form bodies, to enter into every realm, to complete the perfections, to bring sentient beings to maturity, to purify realms, to act out the activity of the bodhisattvas, to only behave in a meaningful way, and to attain great enlightenment. Make these prayers and countless others. Then chant "The Aspiration of Excellent Conduct" spoken by noble Samantabhadra and any other suitable aspiration, for example, that the teachings may flourish.

Auspicious Prayers

Finally, imagine that the maṇḍala deities, along with all buddhas and their spiritual heirs throughout every time and place, proclaim the true words of auspicious prayer, sing melodious vajra songs, and rain down a great cascade of heavenly flowers. With this in mind, join in their auspicious prayer, sing, play music, scatter flowers, and so on. In this way, no matter what situation we encounter in the four times and ten directions, may even the word "adversity" never be heard, and may excellent prosperity and auspicious signs proliferate as our hopes and aims are fulfilled according to our wishes.

* * *

This description has purely followed the style of practice called "devoted training." The part up to and including the three samādhis constitutes "approach." The visualization of oneself as the main deity constitutes "close approach." The visualization of the female consort, including the consecration of the secret space, along with the complete visualization of all the retinue deities, constitutes "accomplishment." Finally, the empowerment, sealing, invitation, and so on up to the recitation, offering, and praise constitute "great accomplishment." This is described in *The Tantra of the Great Practice of Kīlaya*:

> To define Secret Mantra in general,
> Developing the three samādhis is "approach,"
> Visualizing yourself as the deity, "close approach,"
> The female consort is known as "accomplishment,"
> While the other parts are "great accomplishment."

It is said that just carrying out the practice correctly in this manner during one single session—complete in all its preparatory, primary, and concluding parts—garners an eon's worth of the accumulations, which is evidence of the incredible richness of skillful means present in Secret Mantra. The fact that a sharp-minded person of superior intelligence and diligence can gather three incalculable eons' worth of the accumulations in one lifetime comes down to the same key point. Therefore, it is crucial that we strive solely in this approach. The other fine details of how to engage in the four aspects of approach and accomplishment and their proper practice can only be understood from the writings of past masters and especially from the instructions of the lord guru.

AFTERWORD

People like me may not be very fortunate,
Yet under the care of numerous teachers who are genuine buddhas
I have imbibed much of the nectar of ripening and liberation.
So perhaps I'm still fortunate at the end of the dark age.

Though I have surely spent most of my life lost in distraction,
I've posed in recitation retreat now for more than a decade.
Though I've not gained stability in the path of definite perfection,
I've gained a bit of acquaintance with devoted training.

What is the use of long explanations and verbosity—
Does that style even impress modern-day people?
Instead, I've combined my own limited experience
With a few quotations of the great saints of the past.

With the intention of aiding beginners, my Dharma friends,
Both those living today and those yet to come,
I focused on the ease of understanding as I wrote this.
I apologize to the protectors for any errors and mistakes.

Before, profound instructions were paid for in gold, and practiced.
These days people consider just reading books a hardship.
So what more can I hope for than to lend a small hand
To uneducated beginners like myself?

When life is so short, and sudden mishaps abound,
We can't expect to stay long in this degenerate time.
So take the essential, core meaning to heart,
And do not squander your lives, my friends.

Since no one can cover the vast span of all there is to know,
Why not apply whatever you have learned?

Thus, for this dark age with our minds rife with disturbance,
The vajra holders taught this supremely effective method.

It is said, not just once, but in many secret tantras,
That those who meet this teaching have reached the end
of existence.
So now that you have acquired the freedom to choose,
Strive as much as you can on the path of the two stages.

The three vajras of innate luminosity are the basis of
purification,
The three fleeting experiences and the veil of transference
are the object of purification,
Through the process of purification, the practice of the three
vajras,
May the result of purification auspiciously manifest in
this life.

In order to assist people who are as dull-witted as me I made the aspiration to compose a text that would serve as a supplement to *The Great General Guide to Recitation*. That text is authored by the lord guru and great vajra holder Lodro Thaye, the emanation body whom the Buddha himself prophesied to be a regent of the Sage in the northern land. He was an assembler of the scriptures on the definitive secret and none other than the lord of secrets, Vajradharma, in person.

Moreover, the supreme emanation body Kunzang Lodro Shenpen Thaye and, more recently, the diligent practitioner Jamyang Losel also both encouraged me with persistent and sincere requests. Finally, my younger brother, Tubten Geleg Gyamtso, and the eminent Lama Shingkyong advised that it would be good to compose it soon.

Even though the elements in my body were disturbed and ravaged me with the force of an ocean, I could not ignore these requests. So I brought the moonlike compassion of the Three Jewels to mind and decided to write.

Thus I, Gyurme Pema Namgyal from Shechen Monastery, authored this text at the Demchog Tashi Gepel Hermitage. May it bring all beings to the level of the all-pervading Lord Vajrasattva in a festival of supreme spiritual attainment, and may this cause the precious, essential teachings of the definitive secret to remain long and flourish.

Bibliography

Dilgo Khyentse. *Pure Appearance*. Halifax: Nalanda Translation Committee, 2002.

Doctor, Andreas. *Tibetan Treasure Literature*. Ithaca, N.Y.: Snow Lion Publications, 2005.

Dudjom Rinpoche. *The Nyingma School of Tibetan Buddhism: Its Fundamentals and History*. 2 vols. Translated by Gyurme Dorje and Matthew Kapstein. Boston: Wisdom Publications, 1991.

Jamgön Kongtrul Lodrö Thaye. *Creation and Completion: Essential Points of Tantric Meditation*. Translated by Sarah Harding. Boston: Wisdom Publications, 2002.

Jamgön Mipham. *Luminous Essence: A Guide to the Guhyagarbha Tantra*. Translated by the Dharmachakra Translation Committee. Ithaca, N.Y.: Snow Lion Publications, 2009.

Jigme Lingpa, Patrul Rinpoche, and Getse Mahāpaṇḍita. *Deity, Mantra, and Wisdom: Development Stage Meditation in Tibetan Buddhist Tantra*. Translated by the Dharmachakra Translation Committee. Ithaca, N.Y.: Snow Lion Publications, 2006.

Khenpo Namdrol. *The Practice of Vajrakilaya*. Ithaca, N.Y.: Snow Lion Publications, 1999.

Köppl, Heidi. *Establishing Appearance as Divine*. Ithaca, N.Y.: Snow Lion Publications, 2008.

Shechen Gyaltsap IV and Rinchen Dargye. *A Practice of Padmasambhava: Essential Instructions on the Path to Awakening*. Translated by the Dharmachakra Translation Committee. Ithaca, N.Y.: Snow Lion Publications, 2011.

Kunsang, Erik Pema. *Blooming Intelligence: The Practice of Guru Mawey Senge, The Lion of Speech, according to the Tukdrup Barchey Künsel.* Kathmandu, Nepal: Rangjung Yeshe Publications, 1995.

Kunsang, Erik Pema, and Marcia Binder Schmidt. *Blazing Splendor: The Memoirs of Tulku Urgyen Rinpoche.* Hong Kong: Rangjung Yeshe Publications, 2005.

Padmasambhava. *Advice from the Lotus-Born: A Collection of Padmasambhava's Advice to the Dakini Yeshe Tsogyal and Other Close Disciples.* Translated by Erik Hein Schmidt. Kathmandu, Nepal: Rangjung Yeshe Publications, 1996.

———. *Dakini Teachings.* Translated by Erik Hein Schmidt. Kathmandu, Nepal: Rangjung Yeshe Publications, 1999.

Padmasambhava and Jamgön Kongtrül the Great. *The Light of Wisdom.* Vol. 2. Translated by Erik Hein Schmidt. Kathmandu, Nepal: Rangjung Yeshe Publications, 1986.

Thondup, Tulku. *Hidden Teachings of Tibet: An Explanation of the Terma Tradition of the Nyingma School of Buddhism.* Boston: Wisdom Publications, 1994.

"Whether you're running a business, entering an endurance sport, or simply looking to navigate a career, *Built to Finish* provides a manual for success. Full of meaningful details, it provides a very honest and practical guide on how to prepare, compete, and ultimately achieve your ambitions. Steven's account of his highs, lows, and ultimate success as an entrepreneur, a mountaineer, and a triathlete is a fascinating and enjoyable read with life-affirming lessons for everyone."

—**NICK WILKINSON,** advisor, board member, and CEO of Wilkinson Advisory Services, director and screenwriter

"I appreciate a great story about adversity and transformation. Steven's journey from couch potato and college dropout to uber successful entrepreneur and IRONMAN World Championship competitor is very inspiring. His lessons learned and key takeaways should be heeded by anyone aspiring to mount a similar journey. This is a fast-paced, inspirational, and educational read. I highly recommend it."

—**JOANNA LOHMAN,** keynote speaker, former professional soccer player and member of the United States Women's National Team, and author of *Raising Tomorrow's Champions*

"*Built to Finish* is for the hero in all of us. If you're set on big goals in life, this book shows you the way forward. With Steven as your guide, this book is a compass for those seeking fulfillment on their own path to success."

—**JON GIGANTI,** vice president of CCC Intelligent Solutions and *USA Today* best-selling author of *With Intention*

"Any entrepreneur would benefit from running their business with an endurance mindset. This book will show them how. Steven's analogies from his racing and mountain adventures to the way he built and later sold his business really hit home. His self-deprecating humor allowed me to connect with him personally and feel the pain of his pitfalls and the highs of his summits. A really good read."

—**SCOTT WHITE,** chairman of the board and CEO of Invesque, best-selling author of *The Life is Too Short Guy*

PRAISE FOR *BUILT TO FINISH*

"A lot of business books teach the *why* of improvement, but few get into the *how*. Anyone who knows about elite athletes knows they must be focused on the *how*, and that's what *Built To Finish* delivers. Steven walks entrepreneurs and business owners through his own journey of scaling the heights of business and elite fitness to show us how we can be our own version of 'elite' in our lives and businesses. Highly recommended."

—**SHAWN RHODES**, chief sales sergeant of Bulletproof Selling, keynote speaker, and author of *Bulletproof Selling*

"Pay attention to the lessons and stories beautifully weaved throughout this book. You will feel inspired and motivated to be more and do more in the world. Whether you are an entrepreneur or corporate leader, you will find ideas you can apply personally and professionally."

—**NEEN JAMES**, keynote speaker, leadership strategist, and author of *Folding Time* and *Attention Pays*

"Steven has written an inspiring book about his family, life, relationships, athletics, and business journey. He has successfully extracted core lessons from those experiences in an engaging and delightful read. It's well worth the time to devour it."

—**JIM SCHLECKSER**, CEO of The CEO Project and two-time best-selling author of *Great CEOs Are Lazy* and *Professional Drinking*

"Business is tough; IRONMAN is tough! Through his experience of navigating the business world and over twenty triathlons, Steven gives us valuable lessons in achieving success. Every one of the key takeaways included in each chapter are lessons we must practice on a daily basis. *Built to Finish* is a must-read for anyone who needs guidance in building their path to the finish line."

—**MIKE REILLY**, voice of IRONMAN triathlon, author of *Mike Reilly Finding My Voice*